SHADOWS
ACROSS THE
MOON

*For Kris, my soul mate, and for the real Ibiza, which will always, always be there.*

# SHADOWS ACROSS THE MOON

OUTLAWS, FREAKS, SHAMANS
AND THE MAKING OF IBIZA CLUBLAND
**HELEN DONLON**

First published in German, 2015 by
Hannibal Verlag, an imprint of
Koch International GmbH, A-6604 Höfen
**www.hannibal-verlag.de**

This edition published in 2017 by
Jawbone Press
3.1D Union Court
20–22 Union Road
London SW4 6JP
England
**www.jawbonepress.com**

ISBN 978-1-911036-18-0

**EDITOR** Tom Seabrook
**JACKET IMAGE** bürosüd°, Munich
**PICTURE RESEARCH** Helen Donlon

Printed in China

1 2 3 4 5 21 20 19 18 17

# CONTENTS

# FOREWORD
## BY RICHIE HAWTIN

Two movies that were really inspiring during the original planning phase of my ENTER.Ibiza event were Gaspar Noé's *Enter The Void* and Stanley Kubrick's *Eyes Wide Shut*, with their overall feelings of escapism and voyeurism. Both also dealt with the contrasting feelings of isolation and acceptance within groups of friends and acquaintances which reminded me of many experiences I'd had within the party culture on Ibiza. Ibiza is a place far away from most people's 'real' day-to-day life, a place inviting people to escape, to isolate themselves from their own reality and to step into an alternate universe of make-believe experiences. A place far away from the norms of society where a type of freedom is suggested, if not fully guaranteed. All of these themes create the foundation of what ENTER. is. As you step off the plane on the island, you are leaving your reality behind and taking a step towards the fantasy that the island represents. Standing on that edge of what's real and what's not is where Ibiza lies. A black hole in the middle of the world where anything is possible …

**RICHIE HAWTIN, FEBRUARY 2015**

## INTRO
## BY HELEN DONLON

Pirates is an anagram of parties. Nowhere is this connection more evident than in Ibiza. On an island where there have been pirates, outlaws and freewheeling individuals destroying or laying down procedures for living and partying for centuries, not much has ever really changed behind the scenes, even if party operators now live more or less within some kind of 'civilised' island society.

Ibiza parties are just different from parties elsewhere, as anyone who actually knows the island will attest. Centuries of outside influence, including Roman decadence and Moorish drum rituals, and later, religious Hindu and Buddhist iconography, have all played a part, when combined with the freebooting spirit of piracy, in creating the fundamental tenets for an Ibiza party or after-party. From trance parties in the forests, drummers bringing down the sunset on the beach, or freaks gathering outdoors with guitars and tape machines blasting jazz and rock'n'roll for two or three days on end, what happened on the island before the clubs is also the reason the clubs became necessary in the first place.

The first nightclubs on the island were created by hippies, and brought together rich and poor, international and local, gay and straight on dance floors infused with elements imported by well-travelled freaks who'd done the 'hippie trail' and come back with their brains front-loaded with esoteric and colourful ideals, and psychedelic drugs. Cushions were spread around, and open-air dance terraces were created under the stars, under the sunrise. As they evolved, the clubs grew to become the world famous establishments they are today, but behind the scenes Ibiza clubland has featured shadowy mafia connections, crooked politicians, backstabbing, outmanoeuvring skulduggery, specious drug busts, assassinations, suicides and huge fines.

It has also included tales of quixotic originality and futuristic vision, widely talented impresarios and impulsive brilliance, idealistic utopian contexts and new definitions of how to integrate time, space and human bodies. But the most important aspect remains the ambience: Ibiza is the world's capital of chill-out culture, and when this goes hand in hand with the island's inimitable club nights, the whole experience of the party makes perfect, euphoric sense.

I wrote this book because, after spending many a season end-to-end on the island myself (where, among other things, I worked as a clubland correspondent and party promoter) for nearly a decade, I felt it was time to bring together a detailed original narrative to tell the whole story. I wanted to make *Shadows Across The Moon* a tale which would, for the very first time, combine the story of the island's clubs and their often chequered rise to glory, first-hand interviews conducted with some of the biggest DJs and other key players, and a contextual backdrop of centuries of history, including the vital sparks created by the twentieth century's dropout and freak communities which foreshadowed Ibiza clubland as we know it today.

•●•

It was mid-July 2013, and the loudest sound on the island was the rasp of the cicadas. We were driving through the baked red earth terraces of

Ibiza's dry countryside in my rental car. Miquel Costa and I had just been to a remote *finca* to visit a pair of graphic artists who had covered the floors of the house with colourful mocked-up layouts and poster prints, ready for the opening of Sant Antoni's radical new arts festival, Bloop, then in its first year. In the still of the afternoon, the pair, who had evidently been up all night, were showing Miquel options for a poster design for the opening party; all around them lay papers, spray paints and a lot of artists' methodical mess. There they were, as busy as hive workers in the heat, while in the gleam of the countryside the Ibicencans had taken to their traditional post-lunch siestas.

Bloop described itself as an 'international proactive arts festival' and was an urban stab at transforming the usual expectations of the island—which, largely supported by tabloid newspaper stories, was that of a nocturnal clubbers' elysium—and was focusing instead on the creation of open air galleries and installations, graffiti, workshops and photography. As it was Bloop's first year, no one yet knew how it was going to go down, and Miquel was overseeing the project, on behalf of the *Ajuntament*, the local council. Similar events had been springing up on the island in recent years, with things like Urban in Ibiza, a convoy of internationally famous graffiti artists who'd work on huge canvases and other objects, such as cars, in the wide open countryside of the Atzaró *agroturismo* complex in Sant Llorenç.

July is the busiest month in Ibiza for many islanders. The clubs are in full force and for most of the tourists arriving on the island during this period Ibiza could seem like one big nightclub. The Walsall-born graffiti artist Chu had even explained one of his giant graffiti canvases to me at one year's Urban in Ibiza event as 'a sound system. I've basically turned the island into a sound system. I get the feeling the island is just one big sound system anyway, and if it isn't it should be.' It certainly could feel that way. And now, in 2013, and with all else that was going on in Sant Antoni in midsummer—the overseeing of the activities of the super-clubs under its remit, the handling of peak tourist season, traffic wrangling, gorged hotels and crammed hospitals, the continuing threat of droughts and keeping an eye on the ever corroding coastline of some of the more beautiful parts of the region, the *Ajuntament* staff had their work cut out for them taking on the Bloop arts festival too. And then there was our Nico event.

After dropping Miquel back at the *Ajuntament* building by the sea in Sant Antoni, where he picked up his motorbike and headed off on to his next meeting, I stopped back in at the hotel round the bay where our guests were staying. The hotel, a quiet Ibicencan-run 1970s style establishment, with a lobby full of potted plants and a traditional dining room offering views of the legendary sunset that could also be seen from Café del Mar around the bay, was almost next door to Sa Punta des Molí, the old mill, now a heritage site, where Walter Benjamin had spent a few months in the 1930s. It was July 17th, 2013, and the next day Miquel and I, along with our colleagues would be holding a very special event at the small farmhouse style building that was used as a cultural centre, beside the old mill. Nico, the doleful singer with The Velvet Underground and friend of Andy Warhol, had died on the island at the age of forty-nine, some twenty-five years earlier, after falling off her bicycle in the afternoon heat, and sustaining eventually fatal head injuries. To mark the twenty-fifth anniversary of her premature departure we had put together a multimedia exhibition, and a specially commissioned recital and concert devoted to her memory.

Of all the rock musicians who had an association with an island so bound up in the aura of electronic dance music, Nico was possibly the most well known. She had been coming to Ibiza since she'd been a young girl, and all throughout the years of her spectacular rise and fall. Starting as a model in Paris for the big fashion magazines, she'd come to the attention of Fellini, who cast her as a glamorous socialite in *La Dolce Vita*, and she was soon to appear on the cover of Bill Evans's album *Moon Beams*. In 1962 she gave birth to Ari, her son by leading French actor Alain Delon, and started a career as a pop singer, before being introduced to Andy Warhol and his Factory scene, and becoming the icy blonde icon and lead singer for the band he sponsored, The Velvet Underground. Dubbed 'Pop girl of 1966' she then went on to create several staggeringly innovative solo albums, some produced by Welsh singer/songwriter and Velvet Underground exploratory musician John Cale.

In 1969, Nico met Philippe Garrel, the French underground filmmaker and lived with him for a few years in Paris, the two of them by then having fallen under the spell of heroin addiction, playing out their days in a darkened apartment with scant candle lighting and hours of 'artistic silences', as several of their friends reported. By now her blonde hair was dark auburn and she seemed to work hard to shrug off her image as a golden pop goddess, preferring to see herself as a dedicated writer, a true European artist. She continued to tour with her own band, playing to crowds of former Velvets fans and prurient young ex-celeb spotters, her creaking harmonium her constant friend. But Ibiza had been a refuge through all these various stages of her career, the place she kept on returning to. The place she felt free.

In the refreshing shade of the hotel lobby I checked my emails using their free wifi service and ran into Rafa Cervera, the resourceful Valencian rock journalist who was one of our team, and who'd interviewed us for a huge beautifully illustrated feature celebrating Nico's life and career for that month's Spanish edition of *Rolling Stone*. Rafa had just flown in to the island not only himself, but his priceless collection of recherché mint Nico and Velvet Underground vinyl and memorabilia, which were to take their place in the square glass exhibition cases that we were setting up in the Sa Molí cultural centre. The next evening at our event, he'd be giving a talk about Nico in Spanish, a history of her prismatic existence and the long-standing connections to the island that she had so loved.

Around the hotel's lobby tourists of all ages were coming and going at the leisurely pace of those exhausted from their daily lives back home and looking to disengage from what they perceived as their realities. This wasn't a clubbing crowd, but it was eclectic. Lots of Spanish and Italian faces blended in with the pale Brits and bronzed Germans, and on the whole it was a quieter and more charming set than the tourist crowds at the so called higher end establishments that were opening up in Platja d'en Bossa, the east coast resort which Miquel said was beginning to turn Sant Antoni into a dormitory town. But here at the hotel, at least on this side of Sant Antoni's crescent moon shaped bay, you could almost be back in the late 1970s or early 80s, shortly after Franco's tourism initiative had first transformed the island into a popular destination for European package tour operators.

The afternoon siesta-friendly heat had now all but cleared the tiled blue, relaxed swimming pool that glimmered at the outside of the hotel lobby, and only a few people were still braving its warm bath. I played with the idea of taking a dip—in July I always wore a bikini under my dress, but it was nearly time to get to the airport and pick up James Young. Back in the hire car I switched the air conditioning on to full. As I drove out of Sant Antoni and on to the *carretera*, one of the few dual carriageways on the island, this one connecting the town of Sant Antoni with Ibiza Town, I rummaged through my CDs and found *Bitches Brew*, which I let blast all the way to the ramparts of the medieval old town, subliminally casting aside Paul van Dyk, Sven Väth and Erick Morillo's faces as they gazed down from the giant billboards that flanked the sides of the motorway, inflated heads promoting their own super-club parties.

There was just a bit of time for me to stop for a café americano and a game of chess with a friend at Café Madagascar on Plaça del Parc in Ibiza Town, after I'd bought a bag of syrupy Ibiza oranges from the cheap mini supermarket on the corner. Plaça del Parc was relaxed, despite it being the height of the tourist season. It was mid-afternoon, and the lazy café terraces were populated by locals or seasonal regulars, people in their forties, fifties and sixties with that durable look of travel and adventure about them. They constituted the more interesting edge of the visitors who flock to the island every summer.

Back in July 1988, Nico was last seen, by Peter Hook of New Order, crossing this very square on her bicycle. Less than a minute later, she had fallen off the bike and was lying by the road, until a kindly taxi driver picked her up and took her to hospital, where she died because she wasn't treated quickly enough, having probably already suffered a heat-induced brain haemorrhage. It is said that she had popped into town to score some hash, leaving her son Ari behind at the house of Russian George, a friend they were staying with close to the nearby Sant Josep road. Ironically, having successfully quit the heroin habit that had plagued her for years, she had been surviving on methadone and marijuana on the island and gradually getting her health back, and the future had been beginning to look rosy again for her, after a few years of dark shadows.

As I left Plaça del Parc and drove on to the airport in the increasing afternoon heat, I tried to imagine what Nico would have made of the island of today. It was certainly a far cry from the freewheeling jazz age of her youth; the days when, as a young woman, she had discovered the island's sybaritic and untainted spirit.

When the Council of Sant Antoni had invited me to be a curator for the tribute event, I'd sought out, along with Miquel Costa in his capacity as a cultural director at the council, the evanescent phantoms of Nico's Ibiza past. These included the charismatic Irishman Clive

Crocker, a famous bar owner and one-time Ibiza playboy who had been a dear friend of the singer's, and who was a great help, providing us with carefully selected memories and anecdotes one spring afternoon at the Hotel Montesol. And we'd contacted two of Nico's most important collaborators, interviewed them and asked them if they'd fly in at our expense and prepare and perform a specially commissioned evening of song, recitals and music. The German musician Lutz Ulbrich (aka Lüül, guitarist with Ash Ra Tempel and 17 Hippies) had been Nico's lover in the 1970s, and had produced her live album *Fata Morgana*, a recording of her final gig. Then there was the pianist James Young, who had gone on the road with Nico during her later solo years and been involved in her later recordings, including *Fata Morgana*, as well as writing about those years on the road together in a wonderfully funny and bittersweet memoir of great repute called *Songs They Never Play On The Radio*.

At the airport the flights coming in were mainly delivering regular visitors to the island, many travelling solo, in from European cities. It was that time of day. From the evening onwards the package flights would be coming in, and by midnight the place would be a circus. But there was still a veil of siesta over the island at this moment and the airport was cool and hushed inside. It was James Young's first time here. After so many years, here he was visiting the place that had meant so much to his collaborator Nico, from way back in the days when he was just a young college graduate with a flair for the keyboard, and she was an unconventional artist struggling to maintain her singularly insubmissive modus vivendi against the levee of music industry preconceptions that characterised the 1980s. *Songs They Never Play On The Radio* is still held up as the paragon of books that tell the unusually realistic story of the crucible of life on the road for the vast majority of non-stadium level bands. Equally hilarious and tragic, it portrays a lifestyle far removed from Nico's halcyon Velvet Underground days or her years as a young model in Europe.

'She talked a little of Ibiza when we were in Manchester in the early 80s,' James had told me, 'and how she had rented a nice cottage there in the late 50s, and her mother came, but that it was too much the two of them together as they had opposing ideas … about the entire universe. So she ended up renting a separate place for her mother, which meant she had to return to Paris to model to earn the rent. In the end she found a bigger place for them both where they could be quasi independent but I'm not sure how successful that was. Nico liked the marijuana and jazz people of Ibiza … the beatniks. Her mother didn't get along with all that and wanted her to find a rich jet-set type and get married.'

Clive Crocker almost certainly fit that bill. In the 60s the urbane yet enigmatic young adventurer had established a name for himself as co-owner of the popular Domino bar, a beatnik and jazz lovers HQ set in the transient ambience of the port of Ibiza Town. The Domino had, amongst many other claims to fame, been the first place in the Balearics to preview John Coltrane's era-defining *A Love Supreme*, after a copy of the album was brought back from London by Irish writer Damien Enright, himself a resident of Formentera during the period. The owners of the Domino had a prodigious collection of vinyl that was said to include the works of Miles Davis, Billie Holliday, Chet Baker and all the other jazz greats, and many of the island's more colourful characters would populate its interiors every night until it closed at 2am, drawn by the lure of the trumpet or the tempo. Fired by amphetamines, some of the regular patrons would then wander round town and wait to greet the sunrise, or meet the arriving morning boats in the port. Nico met Clive at the Domino one night, and they began an intense relationship which lasted for many years, and which included trips abroad together and a long-lasting mutual trust and fondness that far outlived so many of Nico's famously transitory friendships.

After dropping James at the hotel in Sant Antoni, I headed back to my own temporary home. My friend Anja's old *finca*, Can Felix, is perched up in the hills set back above the golden strand of Platja d'en Bossa. No one was home when I got there. There was a method of booting the back door of the *finca* in with one swift kick that did it no damage, and which, at the height of summer, was a lot more effective than trying to negotiate the old rusty lock. Once inside, I stepped through the long cool hallway and into the generous living room, which was designed on two levels and had walls plastered with art that had been collected across the years.

Now in her eighties, Anja had moved to the island several decades earlier from her native Finland, and had married Harold Liebow, the American writer, photographer and author. When I'd first moved to the island in 2003, I had by chance come across Harold's enchanting columns, 'I Remember Ibiza', online, and they had completely mesmerised me. I still find them my favourite day to day tales of Ibiza ever written, albeit that they tell of an idealistic and somewhat utopian former version of the island as it was in the 1960s, and, sprinkled with characters called 'Dundee Doreen', 'Chinese Rita' and 'Big Mimi', they told of a simple life of tranquil and basic amenities, sewn together by anecdotes revolving around charmingly picaresque human interactions with locals and internationals all going about their daily existence whilst looking for a way to hospitably accommodate each other.

There was a time when dinner parties at the Liebows' *finca* were part of the legend of Ibiza, and I'd certainly witnessed a few myself in the later years of Harold's life, including his unforgettable ninetieth birthday party. He'd given a long and unprepared speech, standing bolt upright in the vast living room which was filled on both levels with friends of all ages, and during which, quite unaided by human or microphone, his voice had carried as clear as a bell throughout the *finca*.

Harold passed away a few years ago, leaving Anja to her wonderful memories, a collection of friends that included Ursula Schroeder (mother of the filmmaker Barbet Schroeder) and the peace of Can Felix, up there in the hills. Anja still swam frequently in the sea, and loved to socialise. She couldn't wait for our concert. Now, with an empty house, I got changed and headed off towards Sant Llorenç, further north on the island, and had dinner with my friend Kerry, a wedding planner from South Africa with more energy than a hill of ants, and a heart whose beauty is reflected in her gorgeous face.

We sat outside Juanito's old farmhouse restaurant eating classic Ibiza food; *pollo pagès*—a local dish made with organic chicken steeped in herbs and served with rice—and drank *hierbas*, the Ibicenco digestif made with anise, rosemary, thyme and fennel—all typical Ibicenco plants. Although it was midseason, and we were seated alone outside on the terrace in the warm late evening breeze at the side of the one road that connects Ibiza Town with the small but popular town of Sant Joan to the north, the night was dark and almost completely silent but for the sound of cicadas and farm dogs in the distance, and the smell of rosemary and sage growing around us, which made us feel like we were far from civilisation. Wherever you go in Ibiza, you are never more than a short drive away from this kind of peace.

Halfway back to Can Felix in the car after dinner, I realised I'd somehow managed to break one of the straps on my new sandals. I'd bought them especially for the following evening's event, but I immediately decided, based on vast experience, to place my faith in Ibiza. For some reason, when you do that there, things often have a habit of just working out. Everything would be ok. I parked my car outside Can Felix and quickly discovered that Anja was asleep when I tried the front door, so walking barefoot around to the back of the house, past the cosy outdoor pool under the stars and above the Mediterranean, I gave the back terrace door a swift kick and snuck off to bed in a quiet room at the back of the *finca*.

I crept out again early the next morning, before Anja was up. I had of course warned her that for the week of the Nico event, during which she had kindly let me stay at Can Felix, coming and going as I pleased at all hours of day and night, we'd only be able to spend some quality time together once the inaugural concert and exhibition opening was over. She was accommodating to a fault and would prepare coffee for us on the terrace on the mornings when she was up before me. I'd had to get up before her this particular morning, as it was going to be a long day. Slipping out through the front door, and past the giant aloe vera plants that grew wild in the driveway, I climbed into the car and put on my shoes. Damn. I'd forgotten I'd broken that strap the night before. I'd have to manage somehow for now, at least until it was time for some miracle to occur, as I still believed it would.

I drove down the hill, with the smell of the morning mists on jasmine drifting in through the open windows, and the bright early morning sunshine dazzling me through the windscreen, vibrating enticingly from the glistening surface of the Mediterranean below. I'd heard the bass pulse sounds of a party rushing upwards towards Can Felix from the iconic nightclub Space at 2am before going to bed as I'd crept in past the pool the night before. Now d'en Bossa was quiet, but it still sizzled in the heat like the last cinders of a good time at the end of a bonfire. At the bottom of the hill down I hit the main road into Ibiza Town and headed for the port to get a coffee and an almond croissant, and to watch the early ferries depart for Formentera and Barcelona—something a lot of people still like to do in the mornings in town.

After breakfast I called Miquel at the *Ajuntament* and told him I'd be picking up James and taking him round the old town, to give him a taste of the Ibiza that Nico had known and loved. Miquel was already busy and just heading off to the cultural centre at Sa Molí, to finish up the arrangement in the display cases which were now bursting with Rafa Cervera's Nico and Velvet Underground memorabilia, and he had to try to get the video displays he'd installed earlier to work. I promised to join him and help out once I'd despatched James back to the hotel for his pre-concert siesta. Picking up a couple of copies of that day's *Diario de Ibiza*, the island's daily paper, I stopped en route by the Multicine cinema complex, where on so many a Thursday over the years I'd gone with friends to see a film in their art house/foreign-with-subtitles programme, *Anem al cine*. I parked the car in the giant car park so that I could take a minute to scan the *Diario* to see what kind of coverage we had for the event.

Our TV press conference of two days earlier had made it in there with a picture of us all. The press conference had been held at the *Ajuntament* building in Sant Antoni, and the multilingual group of us representing the event had stumbled along in Spanish (or in my case a kind of Catalan/Italian confection). To my relief, they'd quoted some of the things I'd said about Nico, so I got a chance to see what I had actually managed to get across, since I couldn't really recall anything except how odd my version of Spanish was, even after all these years. Throwing the newspapers onto the passenger seat of the car, I made a quick stop at the nearby petrol station. I knew there was plenty more driving to do in the coming days and wanted to get that task out of the way.

James was awake and waiting for me in the hotel lobby, eager to explore a bit. So far, his only impression of Nico's island had been the road from the airport and the Sant Antoni hotel. We set off in the by now blazing static heat back towards Ibiza Town, specifically to the medieval walls of the old town, Dalt Vila, to walk where she had walked so many times over the years. Finding a parking spot right by the main wall at the back of Plaça del Parc, James thought I was joking when I said we were in luck having to only pay for a couple of hours parking as the meters would hit siesta time after that, but it's true, the parking meters in Ibiza take siestas too.

Entering Dalt Vila, we soon had to hide from the heat in one of dark and damp ancient tunnels, and in which we found some kind of medieval prison/torture chamber, but eventually we drifted down towards the port where back in the carefree days of her youth Nico had first found what she described as the freedom to be herself. Now that James was experiencing firsthand the island that had so mesmerised her, he claimed he could feel her presence along the old town walls and told me that he finally recognised how the kaleidoscope of atmospheres and architecture, colours and character combined would have made her so happy there.

We walked on through the old market place and bought a small bag of fresh and locally grown figs, which we took with us to the port to have with a cold drink. In front of us two enormous boats were moored. They belonged to the now annual caravan of Mediterranean and Arab playboys who frequented the island at the height of club season, and whose owners would float like social butterflies from one VIP table to the next in the clubs and more expensive beach restaurants. They brought in a lot of money for the clubs and restaurants, but their presence was typically greeted with bemused indifference by locals.

As we headed along the port we passed the site of the former Domino bar, and the pre-clubbing bar the Rock, which had once been Clive Crocker's bar too (it still says 'Clive's' on the door today) and I asked James if Nico had ever mentioned Clive to him. He had no memory of that, but he was beginning to understand that there was so much of her he never knew about. Her Mediterranean alter ego had been there underneath the grime of touring all along.

The last time James saw Nico was on the night of the final gig they played together, at the Berlin Planetarium in 1988 (the one that became *Fata Morgana*). Although she had by then dealt with her heroin habit, she was still struggling with daily existence in other ways and had even told a few friends that she was thinking of coming to Ibiza to die. 'I think Ibiza meant for Nico a refuge, a place of re-evaluation where she could live a less chaotic existence for a while,' James had told me. 'But it might also be that she was re-imagining and wishing to re-enter the ethos of an era that was now gone. For European intelligentsia as well as bohemia, the Mediterranean, during the immediate post War period, represented something life-affirming after all that horror and destruction: the sun, the sea, fertility, Picasso, Matisse, Robert Graves, Lawrence Durrell, Bardot, Loren …'

Of course, it was now thirty years later: 1988, and the beginning of Ibiza as European party capital. 'Nico was definitely not a party animal, ' James continued. 'I don't think she would have liked the Ibiza of today, the industrial sized clubs, the package holidays, the Ecstasy, the sexual exhibitionism, the hedonism. Nico was a bohemian, yes; a junkie, sure … but also a puritan.'

It was an interesting perspective on a woman whose peripatetic existence had meant that she was parted from her one child, her son Ari, for very long periods of time, and frequently, as she moved from one New York abode to another, or California, or Paris where she lived in near obscurity for years with her lover, the filmmaker Philippe Garrel. Ari had grown up partly on the island too, staying for long periods with his grandmother in her house there.

'Last year I was talking to Ari,' Young continued, 'and he thinks she knew she was dying. So now, ultimately, I guess there was another agenda. She went to Ibiza to die. She didn't want to die in Manchester, or Berlin or Paris or New York. She wanted to die in a cradle of life. As a girl she saw Berlin on fire, watched the death trains to the camps roll by, lived her dream life literally in a graveyard. The Mediterranean would bathe her body clean, bleach her bones, return her to the source. I am touched by this idea of an Ibiza tribute to Nico. I think, for Nico, Ibiza represented freedom: freedom from the world and, ultimately, freedom from herself. It was a place she chose to live, to re-invent herself ... and to die, a free woman.'

We stopped for a quick sandwich near the Hotel Montesol, the old yellow and white 1933 building on Vara de Rey—the charming avenue that runs from the top of the port into the main drag of Ibiza Town. The Montesol had been a meeting place for travellers since Walter Benjamin and his ilk first came through in the 1930s, and by the 60s it was beatnik central. These days it was still a favourite meeting place for locals, and served, alongside its regular lunch and dinner menus, the most incredible hot chocolate and *churros* on winter nights.

As we walked on past the giant elevated clock that also serves as a barometer at the top of Vara de Rey, we turned uphill into Via Punica and stopped at the exact spot where Nico had fallen off her bicycle. We took photos in the shadows; in the urine-scented alleyway just off the main drag of Avenida Espanya, where the blazing summer sun had by now turned the afternoon into an eternal siesta. The alleyway contained a dowdy and old-looking flower shop and no other signs of life. James pointed out the sad irony of the florists being probably the last thing she saw before she fell off her bike: apparently she had been considering retiring from the world of touring and opening a flower shop herself.

We headed back to Sant Antoni and decided to take a quick swim in the hotel pool. As tempting as it was to fall asleep afterwards in the shade, I had to head over to Sa Molí and find Miquel. Leaving James to his pre-concert siesta, I swung the car round to the old mill next door and soon spotted the busy figure of Miquel who was still bringing things together in the heat of the late afternoon. The graphic artists from Bloop, who I'd met the day before, had just arrived to help out. They'd made us some Warhol pictures and were busy hanging things. I helped Ubi, a local artist who was part of our team, to put together fifty fabric roses with welcome messages that she had made specially to commemorate the occasion, and that we'd be giving out to the exhibition visitors later on.

Slowly the last elements of the show were all coming together. Until, a couple of hours of putting out chairs and testing electronics later, we realised at almost the very last minute that we didn't have a suitably sized chair for James to use when he sat at his keyboard, so various frantic phone calls were made, during which time microphones and stands were arriving and being tested, a chilled out Chilean artist friend of Anja's bashed some staples into my broken sandal to make it work again (a makeshift fix that would last me another three summers), people started slowly arriving in clouds of perfume and long gowns, and the mayor was pulling up in her car. She'd come to open the event, and pretty soon we were all lined up beside her in front of the seated outdoor audience.

The moment had arrived, and on that evening of the concert at Sa Punta des Molí on July 18th, 2013, the warm evening winds blew around Sant Antoni bay as ghosts of Nico's past (Clive Crocker and others who dutifully turned up and shared stories) mingled with fans and, according to James Young, with her spirit: Chelsea Girl, muse, poet (Jim Morrison had given her the necessary encouragement to start writing songs in earnest), the enigma, the lost soul. Anja told me later she'd found the whole evening incredibly moving. People like island historian and publisher Martin Davies had turned up, too, as well as other faces, such as the Swiss novelist and painter Jean Willi. During the course of the evening, Lutz Ulbrich told us more about the circumstances of what had happened after learning that Nico had died, with a talk he gave in German (following Rafa's in Spanish) in which he described the days following her untimely death.

After Lutz's talk, which covered ground similar to the interview he had given me, James Young performed some songs that he'd written especially for the event, and you could have heard a pin drop, despite the fact we were in the middle of Sant Antoni at the peak of the summer season. The event had been packed, and Anja was right: it was very moving. Afterwards, at midnight, and after a quick photo session and a cooling off beer, we all headed down to the beach for an outdoor dinner at a nearby chiringuito, where we sat at a wooden table with paper tablecloths and our feet in the sand as we drank celebratory toasts in Nico's honour, and dined on the plates of fresh fish that the owner prepared specially for us from his catch of the day.

Lutz and James are almost eternally young men, in the sense that they were both very young when they knew Nico, and being part of this event had brought them back face to face with the innocence they knew back when she was such a major part of their lives. They'd both been such willing and devoted participants in the event from the moment we'd first asked them if they were interested in joining us, and this was despite the fact Lutz had another concert the following night in Germany, and was going to be leaving the island at daybreak.

• ● •

After saying our thanks and goodbyes to Lutz back at the hotel, we all scattered to our various parts for the night, which for me meant going back to Can Felix, where I found Anja already deeply engrossed in my copy of James's book. She was very animated after the evening's doings, and we sat up talking for a long time. I'd first met Anja through a mutual friend, Martin Davies. Martin is probably the most authoritative figure on matters of Ibiza history—be it art, politics, the various periods of settlement from the Phoenicians and Moors to the Catalans and Castilians. He also publishes, as Barbary Press, some beautiful books about the island, including two renowned black-and-white coffee table books that feature many historical photographs of Ibiza and its people.

Martin knows most of the writers on the island, and he had known Harold and Anja for quite some time when he first took me to meet them about ten years ago. I hadn't realised until I was at their front door that the man I was about to meet was the Harold who had written those columns at liveibiza.com that had so enchanted me. Like Harold, Martin also wrote columns about life and traditions. We all shared a great love of literature, from the Mediterranean, from anywhere.

Anja was already back to reading *Songs They Never Play On The Radio* when I woke up the next morning. By lunchtime, though, we'd hooked up with Martin and were sitting at a table in the sand at the Bar Flotante in Talamanca, just outside of Ibiza Town, past Pacha and the luxury yachts in Marina Botafoch, and we had a lunch of fresh fish and ice-cold local rosé.

It was the last day with James and Rafa, so along with the German artist Ubi, who lived on the island, Miquel and I took them off that evening to experience Pike's, the quiet hacienda style rural hotel set up in the 1980s by the famous Anthony Pike, friend to Freddie Mercury and Julio Iglesias, ex-boyfriend of Grace Jones, and all-round Ibiza celebrity. He had recently passed on the hotel to the ex-Manumission couple Dawn Hindle and Andy Mackay, who had turned it into an extension of their Ibiza Rocks empire—an empire which revolved around the promotion of live rock music as a counterpoint to the ubiquity of electronic music on the island.

Liam Gallagher's group Beady Eye were due to play a gig at Ibiza Rocks that night, and now, in the early evening, Liam had taken refuge at Pike's, at a table next to ours. He looked worried, which was almost certainly down to his making headlines that week back in the UK for having been caught out cheating on his long-term partner, Nicole Appleton. But apart from the subdued Beady Eye group, Pike's was empty, and we were given a table above the famous 'Club Tropicana' bar and pool where Wham! had filmed the video for their single of the same name, and in which Pike himself features, sporting pyjamas and an exaggerated moustache.

After a few drinks I took James and Rafa by car to Santa Gertrudis, a small but lively village in the centre of the island, for dinner. Santa Gertrudis has one main plaza, which for a very long time only featured an antiques auction and clearing house, a couple of humble but lovely cafés, an Ibicenco-run tobacconists and general store and, perhaps most famously, Bar Costa. Miquel Costa was actually born above Bar Costa, and the establishment has been in his family for years. When I first moved to the island, in 2003, I used to drive up there every other morning from my house in nearby Sant Llorenc for breakfast, and I loved how they played blues music, or David Bowie's *Station To Station*, there in the calm middle of a Mediterranean island. Locals came there for Bar Costa's famous boccadillo sandwiches—toasted and tomato-spread baguettes filled with manchego cheese or serrano ham, and above the bar whole legs of ham were hung up to mature before being taken down and sliced up. Inside, the white walls of Bar Costa are covered in a selection of highly eclectic paintings, relics from the days when the village was a centre for poor artists who'd pay off their ever-rising bar credit in art. Santa Gertrudis had changed a bit in recent years, and the village had expanded to include several new rows of houses, the island's favourite bookshop, Libro Azul, the local vets and a few *chichi* restaurants. I took

James and Rafa to one of those. If we'd had more time together, I'd have loved them to experience one of Bar Costa's traditional breakfasts.

After a hearty outdoor dinner surrounded by locals who had a bit of money, I decided to drive James and Rafa back to their hotel in Sant Antoni not by the main road, via Ibiza Town, but through the quiet and magical country roads that took in the valley of Santa Agnès—where in early February the vast corona of almond trees in full bloom is arguably the most sensational sight (and scent) in the Mediterranean. Even now, in mid-July, the lingering scent of mead coming in through the car windows was a rare but comforting pleasure.

Despite any changes to the size of Santa Gertrudis, and despite the fact that James and Rafa would be flying off to their real lives in the morning, the charm of driving through that beautiful timeless valley of Santa Agnes, with not a soul in sight anywhere, reminded us that our short lives were so insignificant compared to this virtually unchanging, centuries-old landscape.

# CHAPTER ONE
# THE MYTHS OF ES VEDRÀ • AN ISLAND INHABITED BY BATS • THE PHOENICIANS
TANIT AND BES • AN ISLAND OF BARBARIANS •
THE ROMANS • THE MOORS • MOORISH MUSIC •
THE CATALANS • BUBONIC PLAGUE • CORSAIRS
AND PRIVATEERS • THE CASTILIANS • THE CIVIL
WAR • COURTING RITUALS • THE PORT BARS •
AN ARTISTS COLONY • THE JAZZ AGE • THE ART OF
HIPGNOSIS • FREAKS AND PELUTS

*'You will experience every jolt ... every jar of a Psychedelic
Circus ... the Beatniks ... Sickniks ... and Acid-Heads
... and you will witness their ecstasies, their agonies
and their bizarre sensualities ... You will be hurled into
their debauched dreams and frenzied fantasies!'*

This was the gauntlet thrown down on the poster for *Hallucination Generation*, a lurid drugsploitation film shot in Ibiza in 1966, mostly in black-and-white, except for the loaded sepia tones of the trip scenes. In the film, the island is depicted as a crossroads for freewheeling beatniks and potheads, their days spent lingering in old *fincas* (countryside white farmhouses) or edging around the bars of the port area in black shades and jerseys, with a moribund Ibiza the backdrop to their proudly sybaritic lifestyles. A mostly forgotten and often absurd LSD-geared version of the 1936 film *Reefer Madness*, *Hallucination Generation* is nonetheless manna to local historians, an early glimpse into the unique international bohemian port scene that augured the imminent hippie invasion.

The beatniks were the first real 'freaks' to arrive as individuals in any number, and while their coterie was relatively small, everyone in it knew each other. It was during this halcyon period that the famous bars around the ancient port of Ibiza Town staked out their reputation as a garrison for pathfinders and outlaws, characters for whom the release of a new jazz album was often a major event on the social calendar. The beatniks' more colourful understudies, the hippies would be dropping anchor within a few years, and would harmonise with all the natural beauty the island had to offer.

The locals (Ibicencos) called the hippies *peluts* (Catalan for 'hairies') and generally maintained a serene if beguiled entente cordiale with them. After all, the *peluts*, like the beatniks, would just be the latest in a long line of aliens to alight on the island, in varying degrees of welcomeness. Tourism itself, the brainchild of Generalissimo Franco, was still a long way off its peak in Ibiza, although building work had started in Mallorca, another of the Balearic cluster of islands. As is ever the case, when tourism did finally arrive, it splattered its cheap and cheerful identity across several parts of the island at some velocity.

Today, Ibiza tourism's chief protagonist is its extraordinary and notorious clubland cosmos. For most observers, this scene is the island's fatted calf: a savage circus of music, dance, stimulants, overpaid DJs, superclubs gorged with tourists, and prodigious merchandising spinoff opportunities. Few outside of the party scene are even aware that Ibiza, as close to Algiers as it is to Barcelona, is in fact the bantam of the Mediterranean, at less than 45km long and 25km wide, or that the club season is just that: a summer-only period lasting a mere few months, its peak coinciding with Sirius's 'dog days' of early July to mid-August. Or that, even at this busiest point, the loudest continual sound on the island is the sizzling chorus of cicadas.

In recent years, the most eulogised Ibiza clubs have been Pacha, Privilege (originally Ku, it is the biggest nightclub in the world, according to the Guinness Book of Records), Amnesia, Space, DC10, Eden (now Gatecrasher) and Es Paradis. Others come and go, and there is a hallowed pre-party scene at beach bars that sees local and international DJs warm up for the evening's festivities, usually accompanied by a set carefully programmed to synchronise with the sunset. For those whose partying culture also (or only) involves locations where the streets have no name, there are the often intriguingly off-piste after-parties, held in private villas or on sequestered beaches, and a colourful culture (less prevalent now, but still in existence) of trance parties held far from the superclubs, in the more sylvan corners of the island, especially in the north.

In order to fathom what ultimately defines this fecund party scene, which at its best and more than any other clubbing epicentre in the world remains equally scandalous and magnetic to this day, it's crucial to look behind the curtain in time as well as space, and understand how the thousands of years of this unique island's history have given a very particular background context to its clubland. Making ecstatic island whoopee did not set in only with the onset of mass tourism. There is something about this charismatic Mediterranean rock which has long ensnared a distinguishable type of character: receptive, curious, fiercely independent, hedonistic, tolerant and feminine are the descriptions you hear over and over in narratives of the island's past and present. Equally, it can often feel like a place with no centre, and its foreign residents can and do attract adjectives such as vain, aimless, violent, greedy, shallow, charlatan.

Feelings towards the island by foreigners who have lived there can swing to great extremes, but one thing everybody agrees on is that beneath the human element the island itself has a unique energy. *Vibe*, if you prefer. Visitors with their antennae primed can sense it very quickly under the touristic veneer that foreign tabloid newspapers have never quite been tempted to pierce. Ibiza has been 'ruled' many times throughout its checkered history, but the essence of the island's resilient and alluring character has always remained.

Some historians claim that reports of this unique 'energy' stretch as far back as Homer. Many people still believe that it was the mysterious and commanding rock of Es Vedrà, which lies off the south coast at Cala d'Hort opposite the enigmatic Atlantis Beach that was being described by Ulysses in *The Odyssey* when he reported:

> I had hardly finished telling everything to the men before we reached the island of the two Sirens, for the wind had been very favourable. Then all of a sudden it fell dead calm; there was not a breath of wind nor a ripple upon the water, so the men furled the sails and stowed them; then taking to their oars they whitened the water with the foam they raised in rowing. Meanwhile I took a large wheel of wax and cut it up small with my sword. Then I kneaded the wax in my strong hands till it became soft, which it soon did between the kneading and the rays of the sun-god son of Hyperion. Then I stopped the ears of all my men, and they bound me hands and feet to the mast as I stood upright on the cross piece; but they went on rowing themselves. When we had got within earshot of the land, and the ship was going at a good rate, the Sirens saw that we were getting close in shore and began with their singing.

Woven endlessly into repeated stories of the island's power, the Es Vedrà connection here is a stunning and fabulous myth. In both senses apparently, since according to local historian Martin Davies, it is just that—a myth. 'We don't really know a lot about the Sirens, but that rock was probably in the straits of Messina,' he says. 'That's one of the points in the Ulysses story which most experts agree about. It would be between Sicily and the toe of Italy, so in fact Es Vedrà has nothing to do with the *Odyssey*!'

In any case, the myth has always been a popular one. One night during London's Swinging 60s, the guitarist Eric Clapton (who would play at the Plaza de Toros in Ibiza Town in 1977) ran into underground artist, filmmaker and illustrator Martin Sharp at London's Speakeasy club. Just back himself from a trip to Ibiza, Sharp had written a poem that was inspired by both Leonard Cohen's 'Suzanne' and the Es Vedrà legend of the Homer sirens, and he gave it to Clapton to turn into a song. 'Tales Of Brave Ulysses' was to appear on Cream's album *Disraeli Gears*, for which Sharp also designed the psychedelic cover image.

Es Vedrà has basically always remained free of human habitation, with the notable exception of the Catalan friar Francisco Palau. '*Ibiza, that beautiful, rich and fertile possession of Spain*,' he wrote in the 1860s, after having been arrested and exiled to the island by a group of mercurial Spanish Carmelites. Palau then spent six years in deep and gratifying solitude and prayer, living the life of a hermit on the imposing rock that would later appear on the cover of British musician Mike Oldfield's 1996 album *Voyager*. Other than Palau, though, Es Vedrà's only long-term inhabitants have been the wild goats, and a colony of the endangered Eleanora's falcons.

Many musicians and artists have been drawn to return again and again to an island whose golden light is also continually remarked upon. Ibiza's light is noticeably different from that further across the sea in Sicily, for example. Ibiza is affected by more shadows, as a result of the many low hills that are spread around the landscape. Clean winds blow away most traces of pollution, and the rich sunset is enhanced by its advantageous position in the Mediterranean.

The remarkable artists Hipgnosis (who designed dozens of commanding album sleeves for Pink Floyd, Led Zeppelin, AC/DC, and others) started to bring this light into their work a long time ago. Aubrey Powell, one of the founding partners of Hipgnosis, has had a house in Formentera, Ibiza's small neighbouring island, for many years. He told me:

> The light here in Formentera was very influential for me in terms of what we did with Hipgnosis. It was something I saw very early on; the particular vistas and landscapes that you get here which are very Dalíesque. You could see why Dalí painted in Cadaqués because it has the same kind of vibe, and that incredible light that you get is very like what you see in Hipgnosis works, those particular types of landscape. Take *Elegy* for The Nice, with the desert and the beautiful sky, or the diver on the back of the Pink Floyd album cover *Wish You Were Here*, the still water with this incredible blue sky. Hipgnosis were very into landscapes, it would give the impression of an atmosphere as it happened. For me, as the main photographer for Hipgnosis, I was definitely influenced by what I saw here.

Once upon a time, archaeologists and historians claim, Ibiza was inhabited only by bats. In 1994, the bones of sheep and goats, dug up at Es Pouàs near Santa Agnès, revealed that the island would later have been inhabited by a Neolithic group who had made their way across the sea from the Spanish mainland. Further remains of horseshoe-shaped houses were also found at Cap de Barbaria over in Formentera.

The Greeks passed through and took note of Ibiza in the ninth century BC, but it was the Phoenicians of the Levant, the masters and commanders of the Mediterranean sea, who are traditionally recognised as the first settlers to establish a culture on the island. These maritime sovereigns (who were originally based on the coast of today's Lebanon and Syria and became known as the Carthaginians after the founding of Carthage) were drawn to the Balearic Islands, and perhaps especially the tiny Ibiza, as it provided for them a very handy recess between the active port of Sardinia and the Spanish mainland. They arrived on the island around 650 BC and brought the first alphabet that was used in Ibiza with them.

The first Phoenician settlement has long been believed to be at Sa Caleta, on the south coast. The site is still marked there today. However, local historian Martin Davies points out that this is now up for debate, as archaeologists have recently claimed that it wouldn't have made sense to have ignored such a beautiful and strategic bay as the main one in Ibiza Town in favour of Sa Caleta. 'All these things depend on what they find, a ceramic fragment or whatever,' he says, 'and one newly found object can change the whole picture. The archaeology of the island is a constantly updated field.'

Nonetheless, several hundred Phoenicians congregated at Sa Caleta, and they are believed to have survived thanks to their advanced hunting and fishing methods. They had brought with them their hunting dogs, whose probable descendant is the *Ca Eivissenc* (the native Ibiza Hound) or *Podenco*. To this day, *Podencos* are the most noble and independent-minded of any dog you can see on the island. They can easily roam for over twenty miles in one stretch, and are often spotted in the countryside at night, fearlessly roaming for hours in search of prey as they trot like confident racehorses down the middle of the country roads, unperturbed by traffic.

The Phoenicians named this tiny island Ybšm, and the generally received wisdom is that the name comes from Bes, the Egyptian god of home protection, music, dance and sexual pleasure; although a few linguists argue that their word for balsam, perhaps referring to the scent of the pines, is the true source. After all the Greeks named Ibiza and Formentera the 'Pityûssae', islands of the pines. Phoenician coins did feature an image of Bes though: a bearded elfin god with a huge phallus. Ybšm was a great hideaway and warehouse even then. Sailors could store goods picked up on their travels on the island, where there was less chance of theft than there was on the Spanish mainland.

So it was that Ibiza developed its significant early role as a sanctuary, and by the time the Phoenicians had settled in, it became one of the major ports in the Western Mediterranean. This era saw the introduction of viniculture to the island; a pioneering Phoenician development that to some extent inspired both the Greeks and Romans in their winemaking techniques. Wine was transported and stored in the huge rounded earthenware amphoras that to this day are a celebrated artefact of the island. During the Phoenician era Ibiza's wondrous salt pans were also focused on, and they began to form a major part of the island's economy, as did the mining of silver and lead, and the growth of arable farming.

One of the most magnificently unspoilt areas on Ibiza's west coast is the now almost inaccessible crumbling promontory of Punta Galera, where at dusk the light causes the Cadaqués-like rock strata to resemble animals crouching towards the sea. It is easy to imagine that even in the time of the Phoenicians this stunning sunset would have been hard to miss. Franco-Swiss filmmaker Barbet Schroeder shot a good part of *More*, his dark 1969 film about listlessness and addiction, at his mother Ursula's house at Punta Galera. His cinematographer, Néstor Almendros, captured the unique golden evening light in the scenes where the protagonists, a young couple toying with love but possessed by impending heroin dependence, bask in a timeless halcyon tranquillity on the ancient rocks, against a soundtrack written especially for the film by Pink Floyd.

The pagan Phoenicians were sun and moon worshippers. Their goddess was Tanit (partner of Baal), and her energy is still said to guard but endlessly challenge the fiercely independent women who have always been drawn to live on the island. Tanit represents dance, fertility and death. Archaeological findings seem to suggest that both Bes and Tanit were being worshipped on the island by 700 BC. Their legacies certainly live on today, not just on the dance floors of the clubs but through the island's full moon and beach parties, and in places like Moon Beach in the north and the Sunset Ashram at Platges de Comte, or anywhere people stop to observe the sun come down on the horizon of the Mediterranean, a moment which in Ibiza heralds the coming excitements of the evening.

'An island of barbarians' is the now famous description of Ibiza cast circa 60 BC by Greek historian Diodorus Siculus. Some would say nothing has changed. He also described the men of the Balearic islands as, 'of all men the most fond of women, and value them so highly above everything else that, when any of their women are seized by visiting pirates and carried off, they will give as ransom for a single woman three and even four men'. Throughout Ibiza's eventful history, pirates and barbarians of various origins are a common thread in the narrative. But however violent the pillaging and destruction, either on land or sea, it has always come in human form, since another of the island's great charms is that, due to the specifics of the soil and an awful lot of good luck, there have never been any poisonous reptiles in Ibiza. Or at least not until recently … for since early 2003, snakes have been reported as creeping in at various countryside locations. This recent and quite anti-Ibicencan phenomenon is blamed on the importation of non-indigenous olive trees.

In *The Journal Of The Royal Geographical Society Of London 1830–31, Volume 1*, it was reported that 'the peculiar boast of the natives is, that no venomous reptile can live in Formentera, whether from the presence of the semper-virens, one of the snake-roots of antiquity, or that their earth has the quality of destroying serpents, as Pliny records that of Ebusus [Ibiza's Roman name] to have done'. Pliny the Elder had indeed earlier stated, 'There are various other kinds of earth, endowed with peculiar properties of their own. … The earth of the Balearic Islands and of Ebusus kills serpents.' This has led historians to all basically concur that the presence of snakes today is absolutely recent.

The licentious dwarf god Bes was claimed by believers to be the defender of the land against snakes. Just to the south of today's Ibiza Town there still lies the ancient Phoenician necropolis of Puig des Molins, which is said to have contained over 3,000 tombs. Some journalists have tried to assert that the Phoenicians would never have buried their dead in a place that had poisonous serpents, and that this is the reason for the existence of the renowned burial site, but the fact that millions of burials took place all over the Mediterranean—including Phoenicia itself—would disprove this. Some also claim that it was believed that burial in Ibiza's earth would speed the journey on to the afterlife, and that rich people often paid well in advance to ensure a place for themselves or their relatives in the necropolis.

In his fascinating countercultural memoir *Bore Hole*, the English author Joe Mellen recalls of his time on Ibiza in the 1960s that 'access to the tombs was only by one hole in the mountain where the caretaker sat in front of the gate. I went down once and remember the total darkness when the caretaker switched off the electric light, pitch-black darkness. With the lights on I could see a few skeletons in open tombs, carved like chests out of the rock, and a maze of passages that extended far beyond the light's penetration. It was an eerie experience.'

For anyone interested in taking a close look at some of the archaeological remains and other ancient heritage sites available to see in Ibiza, there are many well-preserved locations dotted all over the island, indicated by clearly marked pink signposts along the main roads. Apart from the fabulous museum up behind the medieval walls in Dalt Vila (the old 'high town', which in 1999 became a UNESCO protected site) and the necropolis of Puig des Molins in Ibiza Town, there are remains of the Phoenician settlements at Sa Caleta, sites at Ses Païsses near Cala d'Hort and Es Pouàs near Santa Agnès, the remains of Roman aqueducts at S'Argamassa on the east coast, and the goddess Tanit's sacred sanctuary at Cova des Culleram in the north of the island. High up on a steep and winding hill path a long drive from the village of Sant Vicent, Cova des Culleram is still treated as a shrine, and is adorned with all sorts of trinkets and hope-filled messages to the goddess.

The Roman general Scipio came by in 217 BC, and he looted the island for three days, before sailing off with the spoils. When Carthage fell in 146 BC, Ibiza had a period of independence, before falling under full Roman suzerainty, and for roughly the next two hundred years the island had a shared Roman/Carthaginian identity, which included a growing bilingualism. The island's currency now bore Roman figures on one side and Carthaginian gods Bes and Eshmum remained on the other side. The Romans, who introduced slave labour as well as setting up olive presses and fish farms, eventually came to accept the island's love of Bes, and talismans bearing his likeness were soon being created.

Gradually, though, all other traces of the Punic era were wiped out: Ybšm was renamed Ebusus, and Eshmun's temple in Dalt Vila was now to be dedicated to Mercury, the great god of commerce. It was Ibiza's first temple of Mammon. As if on cue, things now took a turn for the worse. The Romans distractedly slipped away to concentrate on developing North Africa, taking the slaves with them. For the next half millennium not much evolved on the island, although the disruptive Vandals arrived for an eighty-year stay in 455 AD. Then the Byzantines conquered Carthage in 533, before also taking control of the Balearics in 535.

Other tribes who have come, seen, conquered and danced include the Moors, the Catalans, and large gangs of North African pirates. The Moors resuscitated island life when they took calm control in the tenth century. Renaming Ebusus Yebisah, they brought in the

Arabic language, and Islam. It is probable that the greatest influences on traditional Ibicenco music come from the Moors. The vocal style is haunting and often melancholic. Despite centuries of Christianity and multiple outside influences, it is still possible to witness traditional performances out in the countryside on village fiesta days, sometimes with a female balladeer whose back will be turned to the audience as she incants some tragic tale. Men create and perform on wind and percussion instruments, including drums, flutes and castanets, and the traditional costumes usually worn are elaborate and beautifully crafted, a skill that is still lovingly passed down from one generation to the next.

And here Bes comes back into the picture again. Bes is strikingly similar to the Greek goat-god Pan or his North African equivalent, the Moroccan Bou Jeloud, and has even been linked by historians to the Christian Satan. It's worth taking a short diversion here, simply to illustrate some close similarities between traditional music rituals in North Africa and the latter day outdoor trance party scene in rural locations in Ibiza.

To this day, Sufi trance rites are still performed annually in the village of Joujouka in Morocco's Rif Mountains in a celebration that resembles the Roman Lupercalia or Pan Rites. For centuries, these traditions had disappeared into obscurity until interest in the rites was regenerated in the West by British artist, writer and sometime Moroccan resident Brion Gysin. In the Moroccan rites, villagers gather to put on elaborate trance rituals in an attempt to summon Bou Jeloud (the Pan/Bes figure), accompanied by the Master Musicians of Joujouka. This is a group of Berber Sufi trance musicians who, despite performing centuries-old traditional rhythms, have famously collaborated with latter-day western artists such as Brian Jones of The Rolling Stones, free jazz composer Ornette Coleman and singer Robert Plant.

According to legend, Bou Jeloud had made a Faustian pact with a young shepherd by the name of Attar. He would teach him the secrets of music if Attar promised he would keep the secrets safe. If he did, Bou Jeloud's own reward for this gift of music would be to take his choice of bride from the village. Attar failed to keep the secret, however, and as a consequence Bou Jeloud was offered Aïsha Kandisha—a goddess who resembled Astarte, and in some ways Tanit, who is claimed to have danced him to exhaustion, driving him insane and hence away from the village all alone, leaving the villagers to a bounteous harvest. This ritual event is still re-enacted annually in an ecstatic trance dance ritual that symbolises a blessing for the coming harvest, while the Joujouka musicians perform their accompanying soundtrack to the rites.

British artist and exile Genesis P-Orridge called the Joujouka music 'as profound and spiralling as DNA. This is the raw genetic material of all sacred music.' Timothy Leary said, 'Here is religious intoxication which pre-dates the Vedic soma-psychedelic scholars, ten thousand generations older than Buddha and Christ. Oldest blood-seed ritual. Fierce, unstoppable unity dance of life, ancient, pre-human mutational congregation, fertility worship, source of totem, shameful seed of evolution.' In the 1950s, The Master Musicians would perform to an international crowd in Brion Gysin's 1001 Nights café in the International Zone in Tangier, the area known as the Interzone in William Burroughs's work. 'We need more diabolic music everywhere' Burroughs himself declared after hearing them. Timothy Leary proclaimed the Master Musicians to be 'a 4,000-year-old rock'n'roll band'.

The intrinsic value of the Bou Jeloud rites is to create a healing trance setting. That healing element of trance rituals still continues on in Ibiza through a combined lineage descended partly from the Moors, and partly via the 'freaks' that started making their way from Europe and the US to Goa, the Portuguese fishing colony on the coast of India, back in the 1960s. By the 90s, that Goa freak community had expanded, taking in new generations who pioneered the modern electronic version of psychedelic trance party culture.

Today, there is a whole community who have grown up on the Goa-Ibiza trail. Their Ibiza rituals are less about pipes and flutes, as they were with the Moors, since the drum is now more usually the basic instrument for outdoor parties on the island. Tribal drumming at sunset can still be witnessed, for example, on Sundays at Benirràs (itself an Arabic name given by the Moors), a beach on Ibiza's northern coast, and is another example of this kind of outdoor ritual. The psychedelic trance parties in remoter parts of the island is yet another.

Drummers at Benirràs gather from all corners of Ibiza and perform together in a climax of rhythm as the sun sets. It's not unusual for small groups of drummers to appear in the island's bars and superclubs from time to time as well. However, in recent years, the presence of drumming communities has started to be less prevalent on the island, as times have changed and the hippie community which celebrated the ancient traditions has begun for the first time to go more underground, or even to move on.

The Moors famously boosted the agricultural economy of Ibiza with their superior irrigation systems. But they couldn't resist using the island as a renegade base from which to storm the Christians of Catalonia, Pisa and Tuscany, which *coups de main* saw Ibiza pillaged in 1114 by a Papal-sanctioned Catalan and Pisan naval incursion. Moorish domination nonetheless prevailed through several dynasties, during which time they laid the grounds for some incredible musical styles and traditions (especially when accompanied by natural mind-altering substances such as marijuana). The traditions were extensive and contemporary Ibiza clubbing practices are in many ways just a twenty-first-century translation embracing many of the ritual aspects of that culture.

These days, Ibiza is a part of the autonomous Balearic Islands community of Spain, and is officially called by its Catalan name, Eivissa. The Catalans (actually Catalan-Aragonese) first arrived in 1235 and ended the Moorish age of Yebisah, launching a beautiful period in the island's history which saw a new 'freedom charter' exempting its citizens from military service, granting free legal aid and a provision for islanders to retain all profits from the sales of salt. Agricultural workers from mainland Spain were encouraged over to help with farming, and in return they were offered a house and some land of their own. Now the official language was Catalan, and the official church Catholic.

Bubonic plague has swept the island twice. The first outbreak is thought to have occurred in 1348, the second in 1652. This latter extended assault on the island's health saw the port declared a contamination zone and marked as highly unsafe, which basically closed down maritime activity. The pall cast by this grimly dark and dispiriting epoch provoked a destructive famine that is alleged to have taken the lives of one in six of the islanders.

The one gung-ho archetype to have been a consistent presence throughout the island's history (and even unto this day) is that of the pirate or corsair. The Catalans even sportingly authorised local corsair activity, viewing it as a great way to make money. To a certain extent, this 'if you can't beat 'em, join 'em' approach was even a reasonable response to the permanent inevitability of piracy in the Western Mediterranean.

'Privateer' was the preferred nomenclature in this era of proactive island defence. Even in 1356, one Pere Bernat, a notorious Ibicenco corsair had been issued the state's full authority to defend the island from marauding Moorish ships. State-sanctioned Ibicenco privateers were furthermore eventually entitled to an excellent 80 percent of all booty captured, while the crown was only asking for their 20 percent commission. By the seventeenth century, the Ibicenco corsairs had become widely notorious and feared in the western Mediterranean, not just claiming vast quantities of stolen goods, but also gaining a heroic reputation for recapturing slaves that had been taken by the Moors. In 1806 Ibicenco privateer Antoni Riquer Arabí captured the *Felicity*, an English sailboat helmed by the infamous bloodthirsty privateer Michele Novelli, aka 'The Pope'. Arabí's boat *El Vives* and his fearless retinue are still celebrated in local lore.

The capital, Ibiza Town, had at one point in the sixteenth century been wasted by Turkish marauders, and conical watchtowers were later built along the coast and inland. Many of these still survive today. The Castilians came to claim the island in 1715, and quickly renamed it from Eivissa to Ibiza, imposing Castilian Spanish as the official language, and renaming the various island districts to Castilian versions of their names. They also started to set up local town halls, flogged off the salt pans, built more churches and installed the island's first Catholic bishop. On the whole, historians tend to agree that the island would now enter a long and maudlin period of cultural depression.

Ibiza only began to recover its colour towards the end of the nineteenth century, when the first settling travellers were to arrive by way of the new ferry services to and from the mainland. The initial bohemian travellers of the early 1930s, including characters such as the artist and Dadaist photographer Raoul Hausmann, were joined by other artists and writers escaping the spread of dark political clouds such as the nascent fascism movement that were spreading across Europe. These escapees represented in many ways Ibiza's first proto-hippies.

Not that this would lead to mass tourism just yet, since by 1936 the bloody Spanish Civil War had broken out, and the lives of Ibicenco families would be affected in ways which are still too painful for most locals to talk about today. A nightmare bloodbath ensued as the island saw itself align with forces on two opposing sides—Nationalist and Republican. Island cafés were marked as designated hotspots and news centres for one group or the other. Massive bloody barbarities were executed by both sides. The most brutal single act of horror was carried out by the Catalan Anarchists, who had briefly gained island control after hoisting the Francoist Nationalist forces. The Anarchists murdered more than a hundred Nationalist inmates who were locked inside a holding enclosure in the castle in Dalt Vila. When the Nationalists hit back, they scoured the countryside for Republicans and tortured, executed or imprisoned them (many subsequently died from starvation) in a specially constructed concentration camp at La Savina in Formentera. The smoke from the Civil War fires still leaves a subliminal trail around the island, and for several families many hatchets remain unburied to this day.

Christian holy days eventually replaced the traditional pagan festivals that had long been in place. The annual summer solstice Nit de Sant Joan in the north of the island is a great example of an old pagan festival that is now being held in the name of a Christian saint, while keeping the old customs and rites alive. The festival is open to people of all ages, and until recently still included a late night trance party which took place right outside the town hall in the centre of the village of Sant Joan. The highlight of the whole event though is jumping over the bonfires that are lit at midnight in a field close to the village. Locals leap over each of the fires in quick succession, avoiding the flames and supposedly burning off negative feelings and making wishes as the jumps are made. Another similar solstice tradition is to write down your hopes and dreams on small pieces of paper before ripping them up and burning them, one by one.

Much is made of courting rituals, traditional and modern, in Ibiza. Often described as an island that is good for flings but unsophisticated in the ways of love, clubland's generally short-term flirtations come from a long tradition that cherishes outlandish coquetry above subtle and steady entreaties. Gifted British linguist and translator John Ernest Crawford

Flitch grasped this when he witnessed some heated scenes in the church of Santa Eulària. In his 1911 book *Mediterranean Moods*, he reports, 'The fire was no mere *feu de joie* but a deadly encounter; not a smile that was merely flippant or trivial or coquettish, but regards that were grave, as all ardour is grave. Then I knew that Mass may have other uses than that of devotion. One breathed something more intoxicating than the smoke of incense. The air was also heavy with the smoke of passion … life burning at the fever-point. Certainly the chief business of Santa Eulalia is loving.' Later, after observing youths dancing and making music on their pipes at the sea's edge he observes that 'courtship in Ibiza is a delicate and dangerous negotiation. The girl is not hasty to attach herself to a single lover. Why should she be when she has the hearts of half a dozen suitors and more to play with? But the game is full of dangers and it requires a firm and adroit hand to play it without disaster.'

German philosopher (and translator of Proust and Baudelaire) Walter Benjamin spent many happy times in Ibiza in the early 1930s. He and his friend Jean Selz, who claimed to be the 'only Frenchman on the entire island', were just two of the visitors who came to Ibiza and reported in their writings what life was really like back then. This era in the island's history is often nostalgically evoked by older residents, as it represented an era of beautifully unpretentious and calm bucolic living in a tiny and still untrumpeted community. The few visitors that were on the island all seemed to recall spending their days swimming, hill walking, meditating and reading in blissful solitude, and all against a backdrop of great natural beauty.

Benjamin lived in an old house in Sant Antoni but would frequent the Migjorn bar, which, like the Hotel Montesol (originally the Gran Hotel) on the town's central avenue, Vara de Rey, first opened its doors in 1933 and soon became a social hub for the few foreigners in the community. As is so often the case, the freedom of spirit afforded by the unspoilt and calm natural beauty of the island's daily life would translate even back then into scenes of dissolution on the Mediterranean bar terraces. One night Benjamin, who was usually a picture of temperance (although he had famously smoked hashish in 1927 in Berlin), proceeded to get catastrophically drunk after knocking back some 148 percent proof gin in the Migjorn bar, whereupon he collapsed on the sidewalk before insisting on walking the fifteen kilometres back home to Sant Antoni. Benjamin and Selz also sat smoking opium one night above the port in Dalt Vila. A brilliant critic and noted philosopher, Walter Benjamin took his own life at Port Bou in 1940, rather than be held captive by Nazis.

When France's Socialist leader Jean Jaurès was assassinated by the outlaw Raoul Villain, and mobilisation for what became World War I was declared in France three days later, it was to Ibiza that the runaway executioner eventually fled. The curiously named Villain knew of the island's reputation as a safe place for a stowaway, and with the help of artist Paul Gauguin's grandson he built himself a house in the then remote Cala de Sant Vicent, in the far north. Hoping to spend the rest of his days in peaceful obscurity, Villain's luck changed rapidly when he was apprehended during the Civil War by Republican troops who found his behaviour odd and suspected he might be a Fascist. He was convinced the soldiers were looting his precious worldly goods and had tried to defend his home, rather than taking to hiding as his neighbours had strongly advised but his verbal protests backfired horribly, and Villain was shot dead on the beach. It took him two long painful days to die, mainly because the troops had issued a severe warning to the neighbours not to help him in any way, but once he was seen to be dead, the ever-hospitable Ibicencos buried him with a French flag.

• • •

Ibiza's evolution from a melancholic hinterland doused in the malingering murk spilled during the Civil War into a dazzling and seductive tourist zone took a matter of only a few years once building started. The bohemian travellers, most of them artists or outlaws (and often both) had started to congregate in the island bars and take up residence in apartments around Ibiza Town, Dalt Vila and Figueretes, or in countryside *fincas*. At the time these were all very cheap to rent by European standards, particularly once you factored in the gloriously warm, sunny, natural and stress-free environment that was a crucial part of the package. Aside from the Migjorn and the Montesol, other bars were opening around the port, including Clive's, run by the enigmatic charmer Clive Crocker, and the Domino bar, which had become a base for the beatniks, jazz lovers and black marketeers. Then there was the Bar Alhambra next to the Montesol on Ibiza Town's Vara de Rey, and behind the medieval walls in Ibiza's old town, stood the Hotel El Corsario ('the pirate').

El Corsario was opened by one Emil Schillinger. Already the proprietor of the well-known port side hostel El Delfín Verde, Schillinger was a former Nazi who had gained social respectability on the island after sheltering the Jewish refugee art dealer Ernesto Ehrenfeld. This is an example of the island's tacit code of immunity, which many similar stories would back up. As a further example, at the end of the Algerian war, the island took many exiles of the OAS, the country's dissident secret army, into its bosom without any fuss.

El Corsario soon became a lively meeting place and social club for the so-called Grupo Ibiza '59, a posse of artists including such luminaries as Erwin Bechtold and Egon Neubauer, as well as architects such as Josep Lluis Sert (who worked closely with Le Corbusier) and Erwin Broner. Errol Flynn would often stay at El Corsario, and across the early years of Ibiza's reign as a celebrity island, other paparazzi-friendly names—including Aristotle Onassis, Grace Kelly, Romy Schneider,

Dean Acheson, Maximilian Schell, Walter Gropius, Prince Rainier of Monaco, members of Pink Floyd and many more—would add colour to the hotel's lively and comfortable rooms. Then the proto-nightclub La Cueva de Alex Babá was opened in the mid-60s by Alejandro Vallejo-Nágera, a local man who was considered by many to be the first real Ibiza hippie. Cannabis and opium were now being consumed on the island, as was LSD. In fact, many of the very first reports of successful (and otherwise) LSD trip tales anywhere were reported as happening in Ibiza.

The Irish writer and broadcaster Damien Enright lived in Ibiza and Formentera in the early 60s, until his dreams of paradise were shattered when the woman he loved took off with someone else behind his back, and his once idyllic life came disastrously undone due to his being undermined by fair weather friends. He eventually got enthusiastically but naively embroiled in a high risk international drug running gamble which went chaotically wrong for him, and later wrote a memoir which captures both of the famous Ibiza extremes—the highest of the high and the lowest of the low. In his memoir, *Dope In The Age Of Innocence*, he lovingly describes the Ibiza Town portside bar scene, and the exuberance and near religious fervour of the jazz lovers of his circle. That circle included Bill Hesse, the American saxophonist who would stand by the sea at the edge of Formentera and blow his saxophone passionately into the night winds, completely naked, and who, according to Enright, 'had taken acid. As he put it, he had seen the man, he had seen the light. Bill lived for music. When I came back from London and told him I'd bought Coltrane's *A Love Supreme*, he got up next day at dawn and crossed on the boat to Ibiza to hear it at the Domino bar. He passed by our house that evening, to tell me about it. There were almost tears in his eyes.'

The Domino bar, whose owners had a vinyl collection that included the works of Billie Holliday, Miles Davis, Chet Baker and all the jazz greats, would close at 2am. Drunks would then roam meaninglessly around the port side, or sleep it off on the pavements outside the bar, or perhaps, fired by amphetamines, sit and talk till dawn as the fishing ships came in. These hours, roughly between 2am and 9am, are locally known as *la madrugada*—the morning hours that in fact comprise the late partying hours of the day before. The phrase is still used in Ibiza clubland today.

In 1963 there were still only about 37,000 inhabitants on the island, and it is estimated that even by 1965 there were only a hundred or so acknowledged foreign resident faces around town. Everyone knew each other, so they said, and certainly those hanging out around Dalt Vila and the port would have. On the other side of the island, meanwhile, the town of Sant Antoni was slowly evolving from a quiet fishing village into a tourist area with specially built hotels to cater for the new European tastes and expectations. Aided by its stunning sunset position and the remarkable beauty of the surrounding area, Sant Antoni's development was the result of Franco's main tourist drive in Ibiza, which also included the installation of a bullring (a concept totally alien to Catalan thinking)—and that bullring has in fact gone down in history as one of the first great rock'n'roll arenas on the island. Bob Marley played there, as did Thin Lizzy and Eric Clapton.

The French-Algerian writer and philosopher Albert Camus remarked on the scene in the harbour cafes in the mid-1930s, where he'd sit and write, or watch the world go by. 'Towards five in the evening the young people would stroll back and forth along the full length of the mole; this is where marriages and the whole of life are arranged. One cannot help thinking there is a certain grandeur in beginning one's life this way, with the whole world looking on.' The highly acclaimed British travel writer Norman Lewis spent time in Ibiza in the 1950s, and later wrote of how, 'according to local gossip, in which I was soon included, the peasant women (although not the fisherfolk, who were more honourable in such matters) disposed of unwanted husbands by poisoning or other methods. A local beauty who ran a bar a few miles away was said to have got rid of hers by throwing a stick of dynamite down the well in which the man was at work.'

With the island's very mixed-up international tribal history, the natives' tolerance of outsiders and visitors couldn't help but evolve rapidly and considerably over time. New groups of individual international settlers were accepted, and the *peluts* were eventually as integrated as the earlier beatnik, artist, traveller, dropout or experimental cosmonaut.

The British actor Terry Thomas, renowned for playing upper-class bounders in dozens of films and television programmes made between 1933 and the mid-70s, was coaxed into moving to Ibiza in 1967 by fellow thespian Denholm Elliott. Thomas built his own house high up in the hills above Sant Carles, on the east of the island; it is still run by his son and daughter-in-law and used for weddings and other gatherings. At one event held at this charming hilltop roost a few years back, I sat down with filmmaker Terry Gilliam who, despite coming up against endless Ibicencan bureaucratic hitches and obstacles, had thrown himself into the role of patron of the island's Film Festival.

'It seems to me there's no escape from Ibiza,' he sighed, with some resignation. 'I mean once you sort of show some interest you become like a prisoner of the island. It's like the siren song was sounded.'

# CHAPTER TWO
## THE LOTUS-EATERS AND DRAFT DODGERS • THE HIPPIE TRAIL • THE SMUGGLERS AND THE JET SET
DATURA AND LSD · TREPANATION · THE FIRST
BOUTIQUES · HIPPIE MARKETS · NICO · THE FAKERS:
ELMYR DE HORY, CLIFFORD IRVING AND ORSON
WELLES · BEACH AND VILLA PARTIES · BARBET
SCHROEDER'S MORE · JENNY FABIAN'S CHEMICAL
ROMANCE · YOHIMBINA · THE FIRST NIGHTCLUBS · A
LAND OF FIRST NAMES AND NICKNAMES

*'Consider Bes ... this naughty Egyptian Pan-like*
*figure with a huge cock. He's a curious one because he*
*was even on the island's Roman coins. Ibiza couldn't*
*ask for more.'* **PRODUCER AND DJ LENNY IBIZARRE**

The overnight ferry from Barcelona pulls into the port of Ibiza at sunrise, as it has done for decades, and the approaching horizon cries out centuries of adventure in misty waves. Within walking distance of the dock, itself lined with bars and cafés that evoke the confidently international feel of the island, it's all there, on the other side of the obelisk that greets arriving ships with its motto *Ibiza a sus corsarios* ('Ibiza to her pirates'): the ancient burial grounds, a fortress settlement, giant headless Roman statues, a working town and tell-tale signs of legendary parties past and present.

Though the roots of the Ibiza hippie scene can be traced back to the first wave of travellers in the early twentieth century, the international bohemian community really took root in the late 1950s, when young beatniks first reached Ibiza. The island became a lotus-eaters' paradise, drawing a community of European artists and members of the Spanish counterculture, with its cheap living costs and an accommodating and laid-back local population. As well as the action in the portside bars, a small but notable Dutch community grew in Figueretes, and was eventually joined by hippies, fugitives, escapees from one situation or another, and Vietnam draft-dodgers.

Bob Dylan was rumoured to have stayed in Formentera, and Joni Mitchell's track 'California' contained lyrics said to have been written in Ibiza. The new music and drugs had arrived with jazz and then The Beatles, and with them the next era of island hedonism, when the freaks, and later hippies established themselves as the new avant-garde. These *peluts* swiftly put Ibiza on the international freak map and the island was now being talked about thousands of miles beyond its tiny borders. All-night parties on the beach or at countryside *fincas* were so popular that they eventually paved the way for the first nightclubs. When Pacha, Ku (later to become Privilege) and Amnesia first opened, it was completely in the spirit of the hippie scenes being lived out at these island parties that the character of the clubs was formed.

Ibiza soon became an important stop-off point on 'the hippie trail' that stretched from London to Kathmandu, Goa and Bangkok, via Morocco, Istanbul, Tehran and Kabul. Hippies would travel overland either by bus or train, or hitchhike, and take ferries where necessary, all the while touching base with known freak-friendly café cultures and communities en route. The trail only fell apart in 1979, with the revolution in Iran and with the Soviet invasion of Afghanistan. Huge numbers of 'trailers' always dropped in on Ibiza to or from their travels east, and they brought with them all sorts of new music, instruments and dance rituals. And vast quantities of high-grade drugs.

Kitted up with the spoils of the hippie trail, beach parties on the island became more elaborate, and sitars or African drums became popular, as did Western sound systems, albeit fairly primitive ones at the time. The sunset was integrated as an important moment in the party, as the soft waves of the non-tidal Mediterranean slowly changed colour under the striped pastel layers in the twilight sky, adding to the atmosphere. With the effect of nature on the surrounding horizon during events the chill-out session was born.

Within a few years, word of this free-living and non-judgmental lifestyle had spread, and all sorts of outlaws and curious non-tabloid-friendly individuals had clocked in. Parties were not only held outdoors, however. The countryside *fincas*—to this day, the best after-parties are away from town and deep in the *campo*—would be filled with an often implausible and compelling mix of individuals all seeking freedom from the nursery-like patterns of standard Western daily living. They believed they'd finally found a place that not only represented this but which seemed to magically draw like-minded creatures from everywhere, all seeking the same freedoms of expression and desire to party. There's a great saying amongst Ibiza's now heavily decreased freak community that 'no one cares where you're from, it's where you're at that counts', and this was certainly true of the party crowds back then.

The hippies arrived on an Ibiza that already held a lively, if small international community of interesting artists. Architect Erwin Broner, who arrived in 1933 to escape the Nazis, had founded the avant-garde Ibiza '59. The group, which counted German artists Hans Laabs, Egon Neubauer and Erwin Bechtold among its members, lasted until 1964. Its members would gather at El Corsario and the newly opened Ivan Spence gallery up in Dalt Vila. Broner's distinctive houses fused the traditional Ibicencan *finca* style with the modern. His house in Sa Penya, an old cobbled area behind the port, is still there today.

The eccentric English writer and forger William Donaldson, aka Henry Root, came to Ibiza and promptly blew his inheritance on a glass-bottomed boat—one whose license had in fact already expired. The ex-GI 'Bad' Jack Hand (later busted for murder) set up a jazz-lovers community in Ibiza, importing friends and musicians who'd played at his club in Barcelona. In 1956, the New Zealander Janet Frame sailed to Europe after winning a literary scholarship. When she got to Ibiza she discovered sex, losing her virginity at the age of thirty-two to an American bohemian.

Thoughts of hedonism, music and tribal union also brought groups looking for areas to meditate, and others wanting to express their sexual preferences more openly, or just get involved in a thriving new European arts scene. When the port was cleaned up in 1973 for the arrival of Spanish prince Juan Carlos, he famously asked Ibiza's mayor, 'What have you done with my hippies?' For Aristotle Onassis, Prince Rainier and Princess Grace, sailing into Ibiza meant embarking on an island whose hippie community was at the leading edge of Mediterranean style. Later, Formula One driver Niki Lauda, actress Ursula Andress and director Roman Polanski came to build houses, inspired by the new scene.

But Ibiza had also become a central point for drug smuggling, and the darker side of the community housed shady and violent drug dealers and thieves, pimps and exploited sex workers. The other side of beatnik. From the regular tourist's point of view, Ibiza was still a bit run down in the 1960s and 70s, and in some ways, despite the charming hippie elements, it was seen as an '*isla non grata*' while neighbouring Mallorca was now being developed for tourism. In September 1963, Ibiza's daily newspaper, the *Diario*, described the community as 'this slovenly and amoral flock ... pure social trash, pure dregs and misfits ... dirty, dishonest, contemptible rabble'.

Monica Gerlach, a long-term Ibiza resident, is Dutch, although she grew up in Angola, 'in the sticks, totally wild and running around half-naked'. She married Richard Brooke-Edwards, a writer and the illegitimate son of English royalty, but like many other expats, when he got to Ibiza, he couldn't settle. 'They'd all be sitting in the bars all day drinking, telling stories, playing backgammon and chess. He became an alcoholic and died quite young.' But despite the drug experimentation that was starting to creep in at parties, Monica remembers the 60s and 70s as quite an innocent time. 'It was very natural. People danced and drank a bit, smoked a bit of pot but there weren't the hard drugs everywhere … yet.'

The bar Anfora had opened in Sa Penya. Now a world-famous gay club, it was then one of the first live music bars in town. 'We'd either go there, or to Lola's, another place that's now a gay bar,' Gerlach continues, 'and that's where we'd all meet after dinner, have a few drinks, smoke, fall in love. We were all in our twenties and from all over the world. And Ibiza in those days was a bit like the scene in Hemingway's *A Moveable Feast*. The town was full of foreign artists, all of them poor.'

By now the island had attracted many musicians from across Europe who had come there to live and compose, sucked in by the beauty, the free-spirited people and the hedonistic lifestyle. While peasant women walked around in traditional dress, covering themselves up, hippie musicians would play guitars on the beach and bathe naked at Figueretes beach (near Ibiza Town) whenever they could shy from the censorious eyes of the police. The two communities watched and over time grew to accept each other, slowly but surely. This coexistence has never really gone away.

Platja d'en Bossa, the long golden strand of beach on the east coast just along from Figueretes, was where the small Dutch community lived. Beat poet Simon Vinkenoog was the master of ceremonies at an experimental happening known as *The Big Kick*, which involved ingestion of psychedelic delirium-inducing Datura weed. Writer Cees Nooteboom lived in the community in the 50s, as did actress Ingrid

Valerius. Another of the Dutch crowd was the counterculture writer Jan Cremer, who would stomp around in his leather jacket and biker boots from bar to bar in the full sunshine. He lived in Ibiza from 1961 to 1963 and also managed to hook up with the Grupo '59, before writing his bestselling semi-fictional memoir, *I, Jan Cremer*, on the island.

Another curious Dutch couple were Bart and Barbara Huges. By the 1960s, Bart had discovered, through practising headstands with an Ibiza freak called Titi, that there was a link between the volume of blood in the brain and the ability to maintain a state of being high, which in turn led to him opening up his 'third eye' permanently by boring a hole in his head. This, he said, helped maintain a childlike level of unrestricted brain blood volume for the rest of your life, which in turn enhanced a wider consciousness. On learning of this, John Lennon considered trepanation himself for a while.

Amanda Feilding, the Countess of Wemyss and March, runs the drug policy organisation and charitable trust the Beckley Foundation from her ancestral home at Beckley Park in the UK. She self-trepanned after seeing the positive effects it had on both Bart Huges and her then partner Joe Mellen (author of *Bore Hole*, himself influenced by Bart in Ibiza to self-trepan). Feilding appeared as a guest speaker at Ibiza's groundbreaking 2014 World Ayahuasca Conference, and she is actively engaged in worldwide drug policy reform. According to Feilding, Shiva, the Hindu god of altered consciousness, was trepanned. (Evidence of trepanning was also found in one third of the 120 skulls that were excavated at a French burial site dated circa 6500 BC.)

Ibiza was now becoming the unofficially acknowledged Mediterranean centre for drug experimentation. Huges hid his newly bored 'third eye' under his hair. He was also one of the first people to reveal that the American CIA was using LSD in controlled brainwashing experiments. He brought acid from Amsterdam and advised those taking it to dip sugar lumps into lemons and eat those first. He was insistent that maintaining an intake of sugar at intervals throughout the trip would keep it from turning into a bad one.

According to Joe Mellen, in *Bore Hole*:

> It was obvious to anyone who met Bart that he was someone who knew what he was talking about. He came from a family of doctors and had a thorough knowledge of medical science. He never blustered or tried to blind one with scientific jargon. Ask him a question and he answered it in the simplest way he could. What more could one want from a teacher? … It is a fact that with low blood sugar a person is highly suggestible, so the words of the guru are lent added power in such a situation. Thereafter he will be revered by his sheep. With sugar-taking none of this is necessary.

'Domino's and Clive's opened, and there were three restaurants near the port that we'd all go to,' Monica Gerlach continues. 'One of the bars was owned by an Ibicenco who drove an American limo, which obviously caused quite a stir. We'd all hang out on the beautiful Platja d'en Bossa beach, and nearby was a whole colony of Dutch artists, and writers from everywhere. At that time we were only a hundred foreigners on the island, so when there was a party everybody was invited.'

In 1963, the American writer Irma Kurtz came for a week and stayed for a year, smitten with what she found. She fell in love within an hour of arriving.

The Domino bar was the heart of jazz lovers' Ibiza. Co-owned by the German Dieter Loerzer, the French-Canadian Alfons Bleau, and the Irish Clive Crocker, the bar kept an incredible collection of jazz records, and foreigners would make the most of the selection while either confronting or ignoring their own relationship infidelities, double-crossings and existential irresponsibility as they sat clustered around tables in the late hours. In *Dope In The Age Of Innocence*, Damien Enright remembers how on a 'typical deep winter night, island-itis rages. A kind of "stir-crazy" like inmates get in jail. Through the bar the punters come and go. Few are sober. Some are hyped on Benzedrine, as well. Many haven't been off the island for a year; they have unpaid bills and no money for a ticket. There have been few newcomers since summer. Most of the couples who arrived then have split up.' This description matches impressions of winter life amongst foreign residents even today. This could be 2016, but for the fact that, rather then the latest deep house tracks or old school disco, 'Mingus is on the stereo. *Ah-um.*'

It was around the period of the hippie trail that Ibiza's fashionable 'hippie chic' look first started. In the mid-70s, a fashion haven called Boutique Azibi was opened up at Cala d'Hort, the beautiful beach facing Es Vedrà, by two young Americans who made their dresses from silk saris. They also stocked handmade silver jewellery and bikinis, and Afghan rugs covered the floors. Boutique Azibi is in fact still there, and continues to operate during the summer season. A hippie commune had also been established at Atlantis beach close by. Similarly, the Paula and Mopitz landmark boutique in Calle de la Vírgen sold stunning dresses that today sell for small fortunes on eBay. Meanwhile, the Serbian 'Princess' Smilja Constantinovich, allegedly the lover of King Peter II of Yugoslavia, opened the Adlib fashion boutique in 1971. British *Vogue* came to the island to report on her refreshingly beautiful new line of clothes, which were all inspired by simple white fabrics and lace. The Adlib label remains a key Ibiza fashion statement even today.

According to some, though, it was the British violinist Malcolm Tillis who opened what was probably the first boutique in Ibiza Town, before he was forced to leave the island after writing an incendiary anti-Franco article. Fleeing with his wife to India to seek his own spiritual path, he later wrote a book of interviews with westerners about finding fulfilment in the east. 'He made kind of butterfly dresses with batik, and we all wore them,' Monica Gerlach remembers fondly. 'He was a real character.'

By 1970, the American-Armenian Nancy Mehagian had opened the Double Duck vegetarian restaurant. She was 'a real hippie', according to Gerlach: she 'took a bus with her man through Turkey, the Kurdish regions, Iraq, Iran, India' and ended up imprisoned on a drugs bust along the way. This is not an atypical story. Damien Enright's Balearic idyll also turned black when he escaped arrest in Barcelona and went underground in Ibiza. Everyone turned their backs on him and made him feel he was going mad, but for his one remaining friend, Chris, an artist, architect and flautist who helped get him off Ibiza when the entire island had apparently turned hostile to him.

In 1954, a little countryside bar had been opened up near the village of Sant Carles in the northeast of the island by farmer Joan Marí. It was to become the now world famous Las Dalias hippie market and restaurant. Marí's son Juanito started the market on Valentine's Day in 1985. It precedent was the very first hippie market, at Punta Arabí on the east coast, which had opened in the 1970s.

'My mother and I were selling stuff at Punta Arabí that we'd collected in Africa,' Gerlach continues. 'Eventually we all started to move over to Las Dalias, where people could also have a drink and eat, and then we'd go on to Bar Anita's in Sant Carles village, which was full of hippies. They still make this fantastic *hierbas* from anise and seven of the island's herbs. They'd cull the herbs from the countryside and bottle it and chill it for a few months which is what makes it turn yellow.' *Hierbas* is still the island's most famous liqueur. Along with absinthe and *frígola* (which is made with thyme), it can be found in most of the island's bars.

Sometime in 1960, Clive Crocker, who had arrived on the island one year earlier, met a young striking German woman, the daughter of a neighbour in Platja d'en Bossa. She was an actress (having just had a charmed role in Federico Fellini's era-defining *La Dolce Vita*), a model, and a future Warhol associate. Christa Päffgen, aka Nico, would also go on to be the world famous lead singer for The Velvet Underground, and an acclaimed solo artiste. The young Crocker was smitten. In a summer that was defined by nights of jazz, chess and foreign intellectuals and artists, Nico walked into the Domino bar, and the pair began an amorous friendship that lasted for years.

Nico was already taken with some of the jazz musicians who lived in and around the port and she fitted naturally into the Domino scene. Blues legend Victor Brox encouraged her to sing, while the photographer Herbert Tobias named her Nico after his great love (Parisian filmmaker Nico Papatakis) while he sat with her on holiday on the island. Nico's lifelong love affair with Ibiza had begun. The relationship with Clive Crocker was intense; she once bit him (he still bears the scar) and sent roses to the Domino bar the next day by way of an apology. She gave birth to a son, Ari, by French actor Alain Delon, although Ari's life was mainly spent either with his grandmother (Delon's mother) in France, or with Nico's mother at her Ibiza house in Figueretes.

Graduating downwards over her years of travel and adventure from marijuana to heroin dependency, Nico felt she could always be herself on Ibiza, and would escape back there whenever possible: in between Velvet Underground or solo recordings or tours; with lovers such as French filmmaker Philippe Garrel; with Ari; chasing the light in her Spanish leather boots and flowing dark cape; in the countryside and along the port.

Within a couple of years the Domino partnership had folded, no longer able to sustain itself due to the huge amount of unpaid bar bills its foreign patrons had incurred. Clive Crocker opened El Pórtico (now El Pirata) a few doors away, but once again the establishment ran up huge debts for non-payment of bills. Clive's next bar was simply called Clive's.

It went on to become the renowned pre-clubbing bar, the Rock, in the 1990s, although out of respect the name Clive's still appears on the door.

In the early 1960s, Crocker had moved to Dalt Vila and into one of the medieval streets where one of his neighbours was a curious Hungarian character called Elmyr de Hory. In 1961, Elmyr had arrived on the island and moved into La Falaise, a house built by Erwin Broner. De Hory went on to dark glory when Orson Welles made a film, *F For Fake*, about him. He was one of the most notorious art forgers in history. Despite an eventually tortured existence, thanks to the machinations of his erstwhile friend and partner-in-crime Fernand Legros, who broke into and squatted his house when he was away in Madrid (it was eventually decided that both had a right to live there), de Hory lived the high life for most of his time on Ibiza, and was at the centre of Ibiza Town society. He would hold court at bars such as La Tierra and the Alhambra, his monocle in place, his exotic Hungarian accent the centre of the crowd as he sipped on his Cinzano. He got away with painting forgeries for years. As Erwin Broner himself saw it, de Hory wasn't talented enough to have done the forgeries, and so for a long time his denials were plausibly accepted. De Hory eventually committed suicide on the island, after a spell in prison and fearing extradition, but his time on Ibiza also established him as a legendary party host, and attracted many socially adept characters to the house up on the cliff.

One of those was the American writer Clifford Irving, who not only wrote a book about de Hory (*Fake! The Story Of Elmyr de Hory, The Greatest Art Forger Of Our Time*) but also appeared in interview in the Orson Welles film *F For Fake*. His description of Ibiza in the 1960s in *Fake!* sums up the social landscape of the time:

> There were beatniks, potheads, artists, writers, actors on holiday, escapees
> from New York advertising agencies, a couple of Canadian ex-con men who

had sold shares in a non-existent asbestos factory and beat it from Montreal only one step ahead of the Mounties, longhaired wives with daddyless babies, German land speculators, a few rich men, many more poor ones, and even a reported Nazi war criminal whose bull neck, beady eyes and kindness to children made him a caricature of what he was supposed to be. Life was strictly on a first-name basis. In case of duplication, people received names like Wanted John and Spade John, Pretty Pat and Hairy Pat, Danish George and Fat George, Eduardo's Karen and Carl's Karen. Elmyr, of course, was original—'man, dig that cat!'

In a bizarre twist, Irving went on himself to concoct one of the biggest literary conspiracies of the twentieth century. He claimed, via a series of faked letters, that Howard Hughes had chosen him to write his official memoir, his highly constructed lies proving enough to convince a huge American publisher, McGraw-Hill, to pay him a vast advance. The scam later became a 2006 film, *The Hoax*, directed by Lasse Hällstrom and starring Richard Gere as Irving.

'Ibiza was home,' Irving writes in *The Hoax*, his own memoir. 'I had first come there in 1953, settling there to work for a season because it was cheap and old exotic and beautiful.' Orson Welles became interested in the sensational aspects of the de Hory/Irving stories and, using footage shot in Ibiza by cinematographer François Reichenbach, attempted in *F For Fake* to tell the story of the forger, the forger's biographer, and his subsequent fake biography of Howard Hughes. It was the last film Welles completed before he died. When de Hory later committed suicide, Irving even suggested that the act itself was possibly a fake.

Also appearing in Welles's film is Nina van Pallandt, one half of the famous singing duo Nina & Frederik. Despite being married to, and living on Ibiza with, her husband and collaborator, the Baron Frederik van Pallandt, Nina conducted a long love affair with Irving, whose artist wife Edith Sommer also lived on the island, just to complicate matters. Nina and Frederik held elaborate parties and invited *le tout Ibiza*. They also set up a benevolent foundation and sponsored Dutch designers Marijke Koger and Simon Posthuma, aka The Fool, who, with the money from the van Pallandts, went off to London and designed clothes for The Beatles and their Apple boutique. In Ibiza, Marijke and Simon had also come to the attention of British photographer Karl Ferris, whose work includes the psychedelic fisheye cover of the US edition of Jimi Hendrix's album *Are You Experienced?* (and who now lives in Ibiza).

'Nina and Frederik had a beautiful house and everybody would go there for parties,' says Monica Gerlach, who was in the centre of the island's party scene at the time.

> We'd all be smoking pot and there were always guitar players there. Not really hippies at first, we were all just bohemians. There were a lot of parties on the beaches that lasted for days, but Ibicencos strangely enough didn't care very much because we were foreigners. But we girls were told not to go topless. It was the time of the big bikini, you know? Topless was introduced later by the Germans. These parties were just so incredible. It was either Salines or Platja d'en Bossa. They were more like happenings and they just sort of developed. You'd stay as long as you wanted, or go home and come back again, or whatever. They just went on and on for days.

It was on a trip one day to the famous Cova des Culleram, shrine of the goddess Tanit, with Nina van Pallandt, whom he had just met, that Clifford Irving realised he and the glamorous singer had been struck by cupid's arrow. 'If the goddess had visited a curse on those who ravaged her resting place, we were its victims,' he later wrote.

'She's a bit tricky, Tanit,' Gerlach adds, 'so there's a kind of curse on Ibiza. They say that if you come to the island and you're a couple, and you manage to stay together and you're happy and in love—then it comes from the heart, it's a real love affair. But if it's some other kind of setup it won't take long before you part. It happened to me twice, so … '

While he continued his charade with his New York publishers, all the while hoping Howard Hughes would never emerge from seclusion to blow the whistle on his false claims of being his biographer, Clifford Irving had his wife Edith don a wig and a false passport and set off to open a bank account in Switzerland in which to deposit the vast publishing advance. It was sheer lunacy. The entire scam was constantly at risk of being bust open, as this passage from *The Hoax* makes clear:

> SCENE: The waiting room at Ibiza airport. Dick [Susskind, Irving's partner-in-crime] glances at his battered attaché case clamped between his feet. It contains our most precious possession: a thousand pages of transcript worth a minimum of half a million dollars. He peers under the table, says, 'Where's your basket?' I look around puzzled. 'I must have left it at the newspaper counter.' With a yelp of agony Dick leaps to his feet. He dashes out the door, and returns a moment later with the straw shopping basket. He is pale. His brown eyes blaze. 'You're out of your cotton-picking mind! You've got almost ten grand in cash in there, and the checkbook of HR Hughes at the Credit Suisse in Zurich.' 'I carry everything that might be incriminating. Suppose someone broke into the studio when I was away.'

Eventually, Hughes did of course blow the whistle, and Clifford, Edith and Dick all served prison sentences for their parts in the conspiracy. Later, Edith returned to Ibiza. Frederik van Pallandt became part of a major drugs syndicate and was shot dead in mysterious circumstances in the Philippines. Elmyr de Hory is immortalised in a line in the song 'No More Heroes' by the British band The Stranglers.

Historian Martin Davies met Irving, 'a couple of times. He was obviously a very good-looking guy in his day, a bit of a fox, and quite rangy! His book *Fake!* is one of the best ever books about the island. Nina van Pallandt I met a few times too. She was very distinguished-looking, like Clifford, and you could see why they got on. She was obviously smart and intelligent.'

In his seminal counterculture film *More*, Barbet Schroeder shows a side of the island that was beginning to become increasingly familiar: the grip of drug addiction set within a less glamorous scene full of unpleasant characters. According to Mimsy Farmer, who starred in the film, 'All I can remember is, at the time, Ibiza was a haven for ex-Nazis. Franco was still around.'

Pink Floyd, who recorded the soundtrack to *More*, already knew the island. Syd Barrett had been sent to Formentera (where he learned sitar, and wrote the lyrics to 'Wined And Dined') to chill out with keyboardist Rick Wright while Roger Waters stopped in Ibiza. Album cover designer Aubrey Powell first visited Formentera in 1968 with the band's Dave Gilmour, then returned later with Barrett. They'd always land in Ibiza before taking the ferry across to the smaller island, where they found a community similar to Ibiza's—a band of artists, writers, cosmic astronauts.

Producer and Killing Joke bassist Martin Glover, aka Youth, helped produce the 2014 Pink Floyd album *The Endless River*.

It's funny, because they're not psychedelic people, but the music is, and the band is totally associated with Ibiza and Formentera. Those late 1960s albums, *Ummagumma* and *More*, really did capture the essence of those times in Ibiza and Formentera, and they were the in-house band of that aesthetic. I think they still create the most sublime psychedelic music ever made, way more so than the Grateful Dead or any of those American bands who accuse Pink Floyd of being cold. I just think their music is absolutely sublime, and they seem just right there on that totally instinctual edge. They don't need to live that lifestyle in order to tap into what it is that makes everybody love it.

German musician Jaki Liebezeit had been a jazz drummer with Chet Baker in Barcelona before heading from there down to Ibiza. Experiencing a period of intense melancholia while on the island, he tried to end his life by jumping off the steep end of Tagomago, a small private island off the east coast. Later, his band, Can, created an album called *Tago Mago*.

British author Jenny Fabian's book *A Chemical Romance* includes long descriptions of the time she spent in the expat hippie community in Ibiza. She wrote it after the phenomenal success of her first book, *Groupie*, which became a bestseller in the UK and Germany. She told me she was 'looking for a change of scene, because the pressure of being the author of the scandalous *Groupie* was getting to me':

Fame and fortune don't necessarily bring health and happiness. The circuitous daily grind of waking up with either a druggy hangover or a random rock musician, sometimes both, was losing its appeal. The trek to the hairdresser's, the banal interviews, the listless afternoons spent getting spaced out on cushions listening to the latest formless riffs of spaced out musos, deliberating whether to drop acid to liven up the evening which usually ended up going down the Speakeasy … and so on. There must be more to life, thought I somewhere in the ultimate curlicues of my mind.

Looking around me there seemed to be movement away from the Big Smoke. As rock musicians became rich and starry, they bought places in the countryside. When I returned from a surreal book launch in Germany exhausted by bratwurst and coleslaw I found my flatmates had been casing the scene in Ibiza, and were extolling the advantages of sun, sea and the simple life. Goat bells tinkling on the hillsides, reclaimed shepherds' huts lit by candles, a kind of prelapsarian existence amongst others of a like persuasion (loads of dope, natch, to enhance the fantasy). Here I could escape the hassles of agents and publishers, the paranoia of walking down the London streets in clothes that said 'bust me'.

Fabian dedicated *A Chemical Romance* to her island lover Neal Phillips, 'a legendary traveller/doper/scribbler, who died of a drug overdose on a street in Bombay'. Phillips had contributed an article headlined 'Sex drug over the counter on hippie holiday island' to the underground magazine *Oz* in October 1970. While in Formentera he'd been researching the mysterious properties of yohimbina, an elixir extracted from the African yohimbe tree bark that had long been used in African folk medicine. Yohimbina was then available at local Ibiza and Formentera pharmacies, and a few drops a day were noted to gradually increase libido. 'Never felt anything so strong from a woman perhaps,' he wrote, 'and the thing between us is an electric creation which is certain to test all the fuses in our systems. Yohimbina, your name is Ecstasy. Let it happen.'

There are at least two interesting things to note here: that Phillips describing the drug as 'Ecstasy', and that a bit of research reveals that this yohimbina elixir was already being advertised in Spanish newspapers as far back as 1903.

Fabian continues:

So, inspired by Dr Sam Hutt [musician Hank Wangford] and Sarah Lee-Barber, who had gone on ahead to find a suitably remote hermitage on a hill, I took off, equipped with shades, a bikini and some Jesus sandals. I flew in, night flights, and Sam met me at the tiny little airport. My memory of the drive to the house is cloudy. Through the darkness I could have been going anywhere, and the shepherd's hut on the hill was a dark shape without, primitive within, earth floors, whitewashed mud walls, no doors, just low archways leading into different little corners. The next morning, although it remained shadowy inside the hut, outside the sun blazed on a hillside unspoiled and apparently deserted, although goat bells could be heard tinkling in the distance. Nothing like the green and pleasant land I'd left behind, far less lush, dry yet covered with a brittle kind of grass and lots of scrubby bushes. And so bright. It was like stepping into a Biblical landscape without the robed figures, we were the characters in the story now. A new, purer kind of civilisation, simpler values, so I thought. People who had stepped off the acquisitive roundabout with a common purpose, to live a less corrupt kind of life. And the locals, they seemed so friendly, always welcomed us at the bar, smiling benignly, and glad of the trade.

Sam and Sarah introduced me merely as Jenny, their friend. If it came out later, which it sometimes did, that I had written *Groupie*, it didn't necessarily carry the same cachet as someone who had just come back from Nepal having gone native with the nomads for several months. Girls with wild eyes who had passed through customs with prophylactics stuffed with nose-powder up their snatches were celebrities on this scene—guys who had suffered time inside for dope-related offences were the heroes. Drugs were of all-consuming importance to our group. Exploits of carrying dope from the Far East were like dispatches from the front line. The sense of danger gave an edge to the idyll. If on first impression Neal looked like a prophet from the mountains, and in one sense he was, he also carried the baggage of having been incarcerated in foreign prisons, the kind of places that leave scars on the body and the soul. And to trip inside one of these prisons hardly bore thinking about, but trip they did. It was what you took and how you handled it that counted in the Ibizan community of freaks, and to shake your reeling head at the smouldering cones being endlessly passed round classed you as an inferior head. Red Bart was one of Neal's favourite people, he flew in from time to time in his Learjet, never took to the sky without acid in his blood, always laying out lines of coke from his little Chinese box. Rock stars trying to recover from burnout like Syd Barrett, who had made the Ibizan pilgrimage, were regarded sympathetically, but without particular reverence.

By the end of the 1970s, a lot of darker elements had taken root in the foreign hippie community. Drug deaths had increased dramatically; communes were falling apart. 'There was always one who had to pay for everything,' Monica Gerlach adds. 'One woman always had to do the cleaning. Flower power is all very beautiful, but in the end it's about doing nothing.'

For the first time, the police had started to realise how much hard drugs trafficking was actually going on. Once they did, arrests became rife. The first person to ever get busted for opiate possession in Spain was the French actress Michèle Breton. She had starred with Mick Jagger and Anita Pallenberg in Donald Cammell's 1970 film portrayal of London's late 1960s underworld, *Performance,* and had had a small role in Godard's *Weekend* in 1967. A year after *Performance* was released, Breton was living in Formentera, in a house 'in complete disorder, and in a reprehensible physical and mental state', not to mention in possession of a vast quantity of heroin, according to Spanish newspaper *ABC*.

By the late 1960s, promoters were starting to arrive or simply evolve on the island, eventually creating one-off events or dedicated weekly parties. At Las Dalias hippie market (which is still there, and relatively unchanged), records and tapes were being exchanged, and regular parties were being held. The Namaste party, one of the longest-standing Eastern-inflected parties on the island (its name a Hindu greeting), was created by the well-travelled residents Merel, Alok and Jean-Michel. It still takes place at Las Dalias today and is a popular and beautifully organised party.

Gradually other small nightclubs started to appear. The Toro Mar at Salines, for example, was an illegal construction later used for after-parties by German techno event Cocoon, and the Ibiza Underground Resistance; the building has recently been bought by Pacha. Another venue, the Festival Club in Sant Josep, originally started life as an amphitheatre-style bullring, and was the venue for flamenco shows. Later, it was used to shoot a German porno film called *Gefangene Frauen* (1980). It has also been used as the site of illegal raves.

Meanwhile, over at the Can Bufí hippodrome on the Sant Antoni road, Glory's was one of the first of the disco-type clubs to open in the 1970s. Another small venue, Heaven (later Angel's, then Penelope, and most recently Booom!), opened in the area across from the port known as Marina Botafoch. 'The owner of that club when it was Angel's went to prison—there was some dirty business involved,' Monica Gerlach remembers. In 1963, the Playboy Club was opened in Sant Antoni by Pepe Roselló, later the much-loved founder of Ibiza superclub Space. Playboy eventually became a new club called Idea, but it didn't last long.

'Absolutely nobody gave a shit what anyone's second name was,' says Tina Cutler, daughter of flamboyant British politician Sir Horace Cutler. 'I wouldn't know what the hell anyone's surname was because nobody cared.' Cutler spent childhood summers on the island with her parents before moving there full-time and setting up several successful businesses. Today she works as a vibrational healer, having completed years of intensive training.

'There was one character at the clubs called Ziggy,' she continues. 'He used to be a dancer at Pacha, and then there was Manel, who now runs the Sunset Ashram—well, you always remembered him because of his beautiful blue eyes. Then there was Teresa and her husband who ran the shop Graffiti, and they were well-known party hippies, and my girlfriend Victoria who is still there and runs the Elefante shop. Her husband is a world expert on tetanus immunisation. There are all sorts of well-known characters who are still there, although a lot are dead now too.'

With the benefit of a lifetime of hindsight and experience of the island—she threw herself relentlessly into the Ibiza party scene for years—Cutler is still enamoured of the island in hugely enthusiastic ways, although she can just as quickly despair of it. This seems to be typical of any long-term resident. Cutler remembers the hippie good times from her childhood, when she was surrounded by all these island characters. But did it truly seem like such an innocent time, and was it really all flower power and sunshine? And who were these Ibiza hippies really?

'Trustafarians,' she assures me. 'They were hanging around Ibiza, and they never worked, and they were hippies only because they could be! Somehow or other they always had money and they always managed to do things. The fact is, Ibiza itself is the black sheep of society. It encourages people who don't fit in to anything else. But most "hippies" in fact came from very wealthy families.'

## CHAPTER THREE
# ENTRANCEMENT • THE PIED PIPER AND THE SHAMAN • UNDERGROUND DANCE PARTIES
CARL COX AND HIS CARIBBEAN MUSIC ROOTS ·
FROM THE MUSIC OF THE SPHERES TO DRONES,
KEYBOARDS AND AMBIENT PERFORMANCE ·
ELECTRONIC TRANCE MUSIC COMES OF AGE ·
NOMADS, SANNYASINS AND THE GOA/IBIZA PARTY
CROSSOVER · IBIZA TRANCE PARTIES · AYAHUASCA ·
LENNY IBIZARRE AND THE PSYCHOACTIVE TOAD ·
MIKE OLDFIELD'S IBIZA MELTDOWN

The hippie community created a bridge between celebrations often influenced by Eastern arts and religion and the firm establishment of Ibiza as a party island. The first big nightclubs were opened as hippie venues and featured rock music to dance to, while the outdoor parties that inspired them harked back to ancient traditions such as watching the sun rise or set, and involved gatherings set in beautiful natural landscapes with drums, guitars and sitars providing the soundtrack to what were, effectively, the first regular ambient or chill-out parties.

Masters of ancient wisdom assert that the entire mystery of the universe is contained in sound, and to many people who have flocked to Ibiza for parties over the decades this would still seem to be the case. 'In music alone we see God free from all forms and thoughts, in every other art there is idolatry,' Hazrat Inayat Khan proclaims in *The Mysticism Of Sound And Music*. Yet at various points throughout modern history, this purest and most abstract of arts has been masterfully wrangled by musicians and later, DJs, who definitely did begin to see themselves as mediums and shamans. In recent years, the Superstar DJ has become, like the rock star, as 'important' as the music they are playing or channelling. The skeleton archetype behind this is probably any ancient form of Pied Piper, leading the masses to where they believe they want to go. The key seems to be in our ever-prevalent desire for entrancement.

Of course, there is nothing new about using music as a basis for transcendence. It has long been a tool of religious ceremonies, and in many ways is a combination of prayer and music being used to shift consciousness 'upwards' to a state of ecstasy. Throughout history, shamans and other spiritual masters have appeared in order to act as conductors of this state. The primordial belief that music is an otherworldly form that carries an ability to transform the human spirit goes as far back as Pythagoras claiming that making music on instruments was a watered-down version of a pre-existing 'music of the spheres'—sounds that came from the planets in movement. NASA has even attempted to record these sounds, which are supposedly the root of all ambient and manufactured drone music, and Zoroastrians have claimed to be able to hear them.

Throughout history, losing yourself to music in order to achieve satisfaction at some higher level has been seen as an irresistible temptation, yet it has been seen by both church and state as an unleashing of a pleasure beast that could have serious (read 'dangerous') repercussions for the status quo, or daily control of the human spirit. Greece evolved the Bacchanalia, a dance ritual infused with the spirit of Pan and the cult of Dionysus, in which dancers headed towards orgasmic release via manic movement based on both panic (a condition actually named after the god) and desire. Together with the Apollonian tradition, a less frenzied form led by the lyre (and, much later, guitar), the roots of modern dance came to evolve.

At one point, however, Greek Christians forced dance performance underground, from where it became a renegade pagan form of celebration. The Vatican stepped in, too, banning the tritone and polyphonic sound, claiming it to be too dissonant to incorporate notions of godliness. When Gregorian chant was introduced, it was carefully constructed to be as unsensational and unstimulating as possible. In Spain, the *sarabande*, a fifteenth-century African dance ritual brought over by the Moors, was banned in the sixteenth century by the Vatican, which then later banned both the waltz and the tango. Movement of the hips was just too dangerous. 'Why adopt such ridiculous and barbaric contortions from Black and Indian people?' Pope Pius X allegedly declared of the tango.

'If music be the food of love, play on; Give me excess of it, that, surfeiting, The appetite may sicken, and so die,' William Shakespeare implored in *Twelfth Night*. Driven by that most human of drives—the desire to lose oneself—we have always found a way back to entrancement through music. In Goa, which features prominently in the creation of modern electronic dance-party culture, popular Hindu festivals were being outlawed as 'noisy barbarous amusement' by the Catholic Church as far back as 1777. Even in the twentieth century, drones and trance-inducing repetitions made their way into confrontational Western avant-rock music such as that produced by New York's Velvet Underground and Suicide, as well as through the work of composers La Monte Young and Philip Glass, and artists elsewhere such as Sun Ra, Can and Faust.

The first real discos came about in wartime France. Indeed a 'Discothèque', allegedly the first one, was established in the Mediterranean port of Marseilles and served as a library for the records left behind by sailors while they went away to sea, and to which they'd return and listen to them together. The Nazis vehemently opposed jazz, with its liberal musical freestyle, and it was subsequently banned from German radio. Jazz dancing was also prohibited, and became the mark of the Resistance, the music of Duke Ellington and Louis Prima forming the lively soundtrack to insurrection. Clandestine smoke-filled basements sprung up in Paris as the disco became synonymous with misdoing and subterfuge. The nightclub underground was born. In 1941, La Discothèque on the Rue de la Huchette in Paris opened its doors to a mixed race and gay and hetero crowd, which effectively made it an early European prototype of the US disco scene that sprung up in the 1970s. Eventually, this scene would arrive in Ibiza.

New Yorker David Mancuso created loft parties in Manhattan in 1970. Serving acid punch, food, conversation and eclectic music, Mancuso would play for rent money. 'It was the opposite in many ways of the disco scene,' Kris Needs, who worked as the assistant editor of Tommy Boy Records' in-house magazine, *Dance Music Report*, in 1989, tells me.

With early disco there'd be a lot of rich people swanning around and not dancing, whereas in the Loft you'd have Frankie Knuckles and Larry Levan dishing out the punch—that was their apprenticeship, watching Mancuso weaving a mood. He'd play stuff like Barrabas, who were very popular in New York, a tough percussive rock funk band. Stuff like 'I'm A Man' by Chicago, because of the percussion break, The Doors' 'Riders On The Storm', and 'Love Is The Message'—Tom Moulton's eleven-minute version is probably *the* track of the 1970s, it's the ultimate end-of-the-night song. The Loft was before Moroder, and before twelve-inches, so Mancuso would play albums. That went through till the Paradise Garage opened in 1977, and by that time Frankie Knuckles had gone to Chicago and Larry Levan had been offered Frankie's Warehouse [where the term 'house music' was born] gig in Chicago but had turned it down and opened the Paradise Garage instead.

The Paradise Garage was like walking into another world, a runway with lights on either side and free fruit and no booze, and the most incredible vibe of all time. It was a mixed crowd who were all there just to dance, which they did until 10am, and Larry would play right through. He'd play 'The Magnificent Seven' by The Clash next to 'Love Is The Message', but he was the cutting edge and it was all about his attention to detail. He even got a stepladder out during his set to polish a mirror ball, stuff like that. That all continued until New York politics and Larry's failing health closed it down. Then there was also the Danceteria, which was pivotal for bringing all the different dance music styles together with its different floors catering to different crowds. They had a video lounge, which was an innovation at the time, and you might hear Herbie Hancock's 'Rockit' there.

It was at the Danceteria that Madonna worked in the cloakroom, LL Cool J worked the elevator and Sade tended bar.

By the late 1970s, DJs had arrived in the mainstream, and clubs featuring the 45rpm classic disco tunes of the day felt the need for something longer. Producer Tom Moulton recognised the problem of not being able to match the beats every three minutes while being faced with a huge crowd of engaged dancers who needed a sound that would not interrupt the magic. He painstakingly compiled a forty-five-minute tape of edited disco tracks, effectively pioneering the dance mix. Moulton also devised the twelve-inch format of disco singles, and by seamlessly mixing Gloria Gaynor's first album *Never Can Say Goodbye* (1975) he was responsible for the birth of the continuous beat. After this, DJs started looking to bring in extra elements to add to these longer mixes, and plenty of influence came in from Caribbean and Latin cultures.

In Jamaican dancehall culture, the DJs operating the sound systems worked alongside 'selectors', who picked the discs. Dancehall culture rose from the ghettos of Kingston and focused on ska and reggae, and by the 1950s its sound-system parties were bigger than local live music events. With enormous speaker boxes known as 'houses of joy' and enhanced bass frequencies, the selector and the DJ would mesmerise the growing crowds. Dub plates (singles produced uniquely for their own sound systems) came into being, and eventually labels like Studio One were formed, laying down the origins of dub.

Influenced by all of the above, Carl Cox, one of Ibiza's most well loved and popular DJs, started off himself as a selector—in his case for his parents, while growing up in the UK in the 70s:

My father used to go out and buy music, and I'd be listening to it whether I liked it or not, but I enjoyed the fact that when my mum and dad were playing this music to their friends they'd all be dancing and enjoying the sound, and I got sucked into it by default. One day I was sitting on the bannisters by the stairs watching them all, my dad being the DJ and putting the records on. At the time the record player was a mono one with a turntable which had the ability to stack seven-inch singles, so you chose your ten records, put them on the spindle, and each record would drop one by one until the records ran out and my dad would have to go and re-stack them. So he said to me, 'Well, if you're not going to go to bed you might as well come downstairs and re-stack these records.' So I was like, oh, this sounds like a chore! All the time I was putting a record on and they were dancing to the music that they really liked I thought—this is actually *really cool*. So that was my intro to being a DJ, right there.

Today, Cox runs the hugely successful Music Is Revolution (previously Carl Cox & Friends) party at Ibiza's Space, where he has been in residence every year since 2004. It is a far cry from his humble beginnings, he recalls.

> My mum used to run a mail-order catalogue, and in there was this box with two turntables, a small mixer, some speakers and those traffic lights for DJs which were very cheesy! All in one for £587, and I had to pay it off at two pounds and twenty-seven pence a week. So I asked my mum if she'd order it for me, and I would make sure I did my paper round or my milk round, and it was really good standing for me because it was a commitment, you know? I had to make sure my mum got the money every week or she'd have taken it away from me and got the money back. Of course, when I got the unit, it sounded like crap. The turntables were rubbish and the traffic lights lasted about three weeks … but it got me to understand what it's like to be a mobile DJ. I used to have my house parties, literally parties in houses or flats, school discos and that sort of stuff, and then I started building up my sound system. I went to college for electrical engineering—to learn and understand about electronics. I started to build my own EQs, amplifiers and speaker boxes, so my little unit became a very big unit and I was known for having this great sound system, over and beyond me being a DJ. That's how it all started.

Cox's family originally came from Barbados to the UK, which meant he grew up with additional Caribbean and Latino influences.

> The music [in Barbados] is calypso and soca, which gives between 110bpm and 118bpm. Well, that energy is house music, I was already onto that 4/4 beat from since I was born! So when I heard a 4/4 beat in house music I could see something fresh was happening, and of course I came up through

the 1970s and disco music, so tracks like 'You Make Me Feel (Mighty Real)' by Sylvester, 'Do What You Wanna Do' by T-Connection—all those records for me seemed like home-grown new-school soca or calypso-based records. Even though I was into my downtempo soul and hip-hop—that was really cool for me at the time—as soon as I heard Sylvester, the energy and the sound in that record, it was all about what I really, really enjoyed, and what I wanted to progress to.

The 4/4 beat was also present when trance music became an integral part of the electronic dance music scene that captivated Ibiza, but it came in a form deliberately speeded up to an extent designed to induce hypnosis with a continued assault on the senses. In *Future Shock*, his 1970 book about the conflict between the advance of technology and the pace at which humans can keep up, Alvin Toffler foresaw 'a new kind of information system in society: a loop, rather than a ladder. Information must pulse through this loop at accelerating speeds, with the output of one group becoming the input for many others, so that no group, however politically potent it may seem, can independently set goals for the whole'.

In Toffler's view, history would soon gain momentum at such a pace that it would catch up and meet itself right here in the present—a phenomenon that seems to have become reality now, with old and new information existing equally, side by side in cyberspace. With the advent of digital music and the Internet, tools that the electronic music community has thoroughly embraced, the mixing in of ancient sounding drums and chants could now be recreated thanks also to the advent of samples and sequencers. Plenty of events known as 'trance' parties were then starting to happen in Goa, but were also springing up in European cities such as Berlin and Frankfurt.

'The first time I even heard the word trance was probably in relation to Psychick Warriors Ov Gaia, a European percussive commune who released several mysterious twelve-inches in the early 1990s,' recalls DJ and writer Kris Needs, whose own single, 'Sugar Daddy' (recorded under the name Secret Knowledge with vocalist Wonder), made number eleven in *DJ Magazine*'s 2014 list of the 'All-Time Great Trance Tracks'. 'That was trance in its original more percussive and ritual form. At the same time, the Frankfurt scene was starting to take off.'

Modern European electronic trance music was picked up and restyled by DJs in Frankfurt and Berlin during the 1990s, often using 4/4 time signatures, repetitions, minor keys, rapid arpeggios and tempos of around 150bpm. Klaus Schulze's 1981 album *Transfer*, Cosmic Baby's 'The Space Track' (1992), Hardfloor's 'Acperience 1' (1993), and The KLF's 'What Time Is Love (Pure Trance 1)' (1988) are often cited as among the first to present trance in electronic dance music form. Paul van Dyk and Cosmic Baby's 1992 album *The Visions Of Shiva* is also seen as one of the first trance projects of this new genre, but the slower ambient concepts of Jean-Michel Jarre are just as important (his 1976 track 'Oxygène' was number one in the *DJ Magazine* list).

Subgenres of trance include ambient trance, tech trance, euphoric trance, epic trance, Euro-trance, and 'all this stuff on Eye Q, Sven Väth's label', Needs continues:

Over in the UK we called this movement progressive house. They injected elements of progressive rock—some of it could be traced back to Tangerine Dream, big riffs with European classical influences in the string melodies— but mainly it was a cleaner version of the dirtier house music coming from Chicago with its organ riffs and acid squelching. This was a kind of clean German answer to Chicago's underground car park sound.

Sven Väth was probably the first great DJ shaman. And I saw Paul van Dyk at the E-Werk in the 1992 Berlin Love Parade—an event which definitely contributed to establishing the DJ as shaman—and that was the first big declaration of that new kind of music's existence. I was on the Belgian techno label R&S's float and witnessed the event bring the city to a standstill. Over the years the Love Parade just got bigger, with all these enormous floats all banging out techno, and in the evenings there'd be events at places like the Tresor, which was very hardcore. It was an old basement vault with one flashing red light.

DJ and producer Paul van Dyk is a long-time fixture on the Ibiza trance scene. Born Matthias Paul in East Berlin in the days when the records he wanted weren't available, he would tune in to the banned Western radio stations as a penniless teenager. He started using house sampler albums to teach himself how to mix on half-broken turntables. After a brief spell living in Hamburg, he moved back to Berlin at the start of 1991, and made his first ever DJ appearance in March during the opening month of the Tresor, the club that would go on to achieve legendary status as a techno command post. Releasing music on Mark Reeder's MFS label, van Dyk established himself as a pioneer in Berlin's trance scene. His 1991 remix of Humate's 'Love Stimulation' was perhaps the biggest track of the 1993 Love Parade.

Now one of the leading names at Cream, the weekly party in Ibiza's multi-award-winning club Amnesia, van Dyk remains a purist, and he can be quite disparaging about a lot of the DJs he perceives as having jumped onto the trance bandwagon in recent years. Another popular and credible act flying the trance flag at Cream in recent years is the English trio Above & Beyond, whose *Trance Around The World* radio show was being broadcasting to three million listeners in thirty-five countries by 2012. The solar eclipse used in their performance visuals at Cream effectively sums up Ibiza's chiaroscuro night-and-day/darkness-and-light personality.

Above & Beyond's recording label, Anjunabeats, is named after the famous Goan oceanfront site of full-moon 'psytrance' events that started in the 1960s and exploded in popularity in the 1980s, when global partygoers looked to the events for more than just a musical experience. This—and indeed the whole Goa trance scene—became quite influential on the developments in Ibiza. And the use of psychedelic drugs is of course an important element of this culture.

'Psychedelics have always been a very big part of the trance scene,' says Youth. 'It's always had that ecstatic, hypnotic element to its essence and it goes hand in hand with the music. And electronic psychedelic music does the same thing. It totally facilitates the psychedelic experience, which is why people take psychedelics with it. It's totally been distilled down to work in an environment where people are on psychoactive substances.'

From the 1960s onwards, many people based in Ibiza have continued to travel to Goa and Pune in India, and to Thailand, Bali and Japan. In fact, the original links between the Osho commune in Pune and past sannyasin settlements in the north of Ibiza can still be felt today. Ibiza has always been viewed as a relatively liberal place, but also one in which spirituality—Christian, sannyasin (religious ascetic), or otherwise—is accepted as normal within the community. Osho's sannyasins, who arrived in some number on the island in the 1980s, even earned the affectionate nickname *los butanos* from the Ibicencos, on account of the long orange robes they wore, which bear some resemblance to the rotund orange gas canisters used in dwellings all over the island.

According to Youth, the very first Goa trance parties held outside of Goa took place in Ibiza.

> Even when the rave thing was kicking off on the island, there was this counterultural movement that was, and is, I think, the heart and soul of

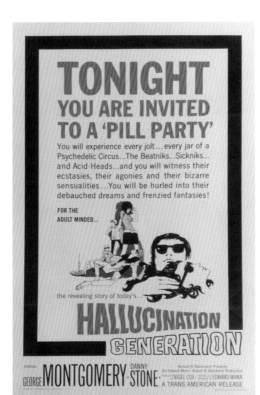

**LEFT** Poster for *Hallucination Generation*, 1967. (*Helen Donlon Archive*)
**BELOW LEFT** Statue of Tanit. (*Museu Arqueològic d'Eivissa i Formentera*)
**BELOW MIDDLE** Bes on a Roman coin. (*denarios.org*)
**BELOW RIGHT** Monument to the pirates, Ibiza port. (*Helen Donlon*)

Ooh, I feel love
Ibiza 2013

THE ONLY ONE

THE ORIGINAL

Produced by PiTi

**FLOWER POWER**

SINCE 1977

**TUESDAYS MARTES**

**PACHA**

came in a chain reaction I couldn't get enough!

When a women's fashion sap a triple is real in

rolling cherries fly rich tonight satisfaction

MADE IN ITALY IBIZA

It's only rock and roll but I'd like it!

**OPPOSITE, TOP** Paul van Dyk drives by the Ibiza Airport and sees his Cream poster by the roadside. (*Paul van Dyk GmbH*)
**OPPOSITE, MIDDLE** Pacha in the 1970s. (*Pacha*)
**OPPOSITE, BOTTOM** Ku when it was still an open-air venue. (*Ku/Privilege*)
**BELOW** Fous de la Mer, *left to right*: Jean-Charles Vandermynsbrugge, Sol Ruiz de Galarreta, Marko Bussian. (*Fous de la Mer*)

**ABOVE** Baby Marcelo performing at Cafe
Olé. (*Baby Marcelo/Cafe Olé*)
**OPPOSITE, TOP** Ushuaïa Tower, Platja d'en Bossa. (*Ushuaïa*)
**OPPOSITE, LEFT** Erick Morillo and Pete Tong at the
International Music Summit, 2010. (*Frank Fabian*)
**OPPOSITE, RIGHT** Martin Davies, reading from Homer at a
poetry and wine evening in Sant Antoni. (*Nora Albert*)

**FAR LEFT** La Vaca Asesina pre-party parade in Sa Penya, 1994. (*Baby Marcelo*)
**LEFT** La Troya pre-party parade, 2000. (*Baby Marcelo*)
**BELOW** Los Monstruos at Ku, photo. (*Baby Marcelo/Ku*)

Ibiza. That's because these people are twenty-four hour, seven days a week, 365 days of the year hippies. They're not part-timers. They're freaks all the time. And if they're not in Goa, they're in Ibiza, living outside of society, outside of the system, and finding their way through life, by DJ'ing the music, cultural exchanges of arts and crafts and so on. I first went to Goa in the 1989/1990 season, and there were a few people from Ibiza there then. I didn't really know anyone, and I didn't really plan to go to Goa, but once I found myself there it fulfilled the promise of Ibiza and Formentera and more, because you were really in this psychedelic society that was kind of an anarchist one too. There was no real governing body, except for a few police who irritated you, but the mayor and the local people were very tolerant and let people do what they did.

And also, the culture in India, the Hinduism, is that kind of acid, psychedelic culture, very Shiva. Very nature-oriented. Philosophically, the locals in Goa could understand and accept it all in a way that people couldn't in Europe, except for in Ibiza, of course. There's also this kind of pirate connection with Goa and Ibiza. Centuries ago, the pirates were in Ibiza for years, as they were in Goa, so they're both kind of 'pirate island' hideaways, where pirates could go and sort of rest up for winter. That still comes through in the local people, in both places. In Goa, you were well 'upriver', and there was really very little authority, so people could really get into doing social experimentation. You'd have a lot of international drug dealers, a lot of international models, escort girls from Japan, a load of rich kids from Europe, some Eurotrash types, middle-class Bombay kids with money. It all mashed up into the most fantastic recipe for a great party, and they were some of the best parties I've ever experienced. Then you also had the spiritual side, with all the sannyasins coming down from Pune, and people coming out of their yoga retreats, and they wouldn't be taking drugs but they would be dancing for eight hours and it created a very synergistic energy. That would go back to Ibiza and inform the scene there. But all throughout, that culture has had no press, no exploitation in the media, and that's probably why it's had such longevity, and why it still operates as a valid countercultural force.

Youth created the record label Dragonfly, one of the first Goa trance labels to exist anywhere in the world.

I'd originally set up a label in England with Alex Patterson of The Orb called WAU! Mr. Modo, which was a sort of British acid house label, and we were doing British dance music, and then acid house happened and a lot of the acid house DJs were playing our records. The Orb came out of that. But there were other tracks we'd put out that were a lot more industrial, and when I got to Goa, I was introduced to these DJs, and they had little books of their sets from all the best parties and it turned out that all these records that I made on WAU! Mr. Modo that had sold nothing in the UK were big anthems in Goa. Records I'd done in 1982 with Industrial bands like Portion Control, Executive Slacks, and Nitzer Ebb—the DJs in Goa had edited the tracks, and taken out all the vocals and turned them into these instrumental-acid sort of epics. So I was really warmly welcomed by the community immediately and I felt very at home there, and loved the synergy. All the different influences in the music and the different kinds of people, and I thought it was what I'd been waiting for all my life.

Inspired by this experience, Youth started Dragonfly to put out music specifically for those DJs, and for that vibe in Goa.

We had all the pioneers on that label, and very quickly it all exploded. By 1997 it was becoming another big kind of tourist destination for raving, as Ibiza had, and the individuality and the mix of people became a bit more uniform for a while, although people are still tapping into it even now. It's a very potent force, I think.

The core element to the Ibiza-Goa personality is more freak than hippie, because there's a very distinct individuality to their characters, these people living by their own rules, and getting away with it, in a very determined, tenacious fashion. All these freethinkers and outsider characters keep it going, and it's really inclusive and reflects all elements of society. They weren't, and aren't, just stoned hippies in their hammocks all day doing nothing. There have been some great photographers, filmmakers, artists, writers and other creatives in the scene, who just really enjoy the whole either hedonistic or shamanistic element of a twenty-hour party, outside, with a big sound system and electronic music. That's the glue that holds it all together. That said, these people were already there, and the music really came about as a kind of facilitation for what their needs were. The scene peaked in about 1997–98, since when it's just kept going.

Thanks to these outside influences, Ibiza has an illustrious heritage of secret raves held in natural settings, notice of which was traditionally spread by word of mouth. These, as well as events such as the *Namaste* parties at hippie market Las Dalias, were influenced by the much larger Goan outdoor party scene. Live music is also a smaller but significant part of the scene.

Israeli psytrance band Infected Mushroom started in the 1990s, combining synths, drum machines, vocal and guitars. They have a huge fan base all over the world, and their gigs are known to cause frenzies among their loyal audiences, especially in Ibiza. The audience they brought to a gig they played at Sant Antoni's Eden in 2008, for example, was hugely eclectic but included lots of the familiar local groups: some of the Benirràs drum crowd from the north of the island, the Sant Antoni live music lovers, and a veteran Goa crowd who packed the perimeters of the dance floor. Eden itself was decorated in neon mushroom props, and ultraviolet lights illuminated the stage for a metallic and highly focused maximum energy set, which resulted in the event being one of the most atmospheric evenings Eden had witnessed all summer.

According to Youth, the international trance scene has become fragmented in recent years and has very quickly overtaken many other scenes, or helped facilitate them, especially in America.

All the kids of the Grateful Deadheads were suddenly going electronic and psychedelic trance, where, prior to that, Deadheads would see electronic music as Satan's music, so that was a big shift. It also appropriated a lot of what was the New Age movement, whether it's yoga or an alternative lifestyle and energy thing. It started to be incorporated with that whole culture on an organic level, and with the more sannyasin/Eastern spiritual type cats. I think it's morphed in a way that it's no longer a niche cultural thing, and the scene's been really going for decades now with people who were into the free culture and hippie lifestyle. People from the scene have got more determined and maybe more politically aware or active in lots of arenas, and all this can be traced back to the 1960s hippies, and before them the beat scene of the 1950s, and even before that to Berlin and Paris of the 1920s. It's always been going on, this Dionysian cultural thing, as opposed to the Apollonian. With all those parties there's been a connection to ancient Dionysian rituals and ceremonies, parties that were done with exactly the same spirit. But they were always kind of outsider movements, and it's important for society to have those elements going on, because otherwise you'd just have a very sterile, logical, rational world.

'I used to absolutely love trance parties,' former Ibiza socialite Tina Cutler tells me. Her family had a house in the fishing hamlet of Port des Torrent, where one of her neighbours was Led Zeppelin frontman Robert Plant.

> They were always located in the dark and you had to find your way to them, usually someone's house in the middle of the woods somewhere. They were just brilliant. I remember how natural the parties were, very relaxed and you'd know everybody. It was all about just having a nice time and hanging out. Part of the fun was actually trying to find out where the hell they were. Amazing days, but this was the time before Ibiza got greedy and their nightclub association—the mafia basically—started filtering everyone into the clubs instead.

Inspired by the success of the early outdoor parties on the island, the first sizeable nightclubs gradually started opening. Ku (now known as Privilege) had opened in Sant Rafel, and Es Paradis in Sant Antoni. The scene in those days was 'very different', says Cutler.

> Pacha and Glory's existed, and Amnesia was basically just a bar. You'd start at Pacha and you'd work your way to Es Paradis, and you'd meet people along the circuit. You'd *never* stay in one place. That's only happened recently and the only reason that's happened—which is really only in the last sixteen years—is because of course they're making so much money now. Back then you knew everyone in the clubs and there was never more than about a hundred people anyway, and you went with your family most of the time. My club initiation happened when I was twelve. In those days you'd get asked to dance, and the music was completely different of course, rock music and so on. There weren't really any hard drugs, not that I saw anyway. No hard drinking either.

Up in the hills in the north of the island, a French party organiser called

Anand started organising outdoor trance parties with sound systems at his house, Can Punta. In 1993, a large-scale word-of-mouth outdoor party was held near the airport, with pre-sold clay medallions used as entrance tickets. Other large parties followed every couple of months, including a voluptuous Bedouin-style event that went on for seventy-two hours in the far north of the island near Sant Vicent. Another was the three-day event in 1999 at Ses Portes del Cel, a west coast cliff-top location with stunning views of the sunset. Equipment was dragged up on ropes and dozens of volunteers took part in the organisation and setting up. (Tragically, the next time a party took place there, in 2001, a diver plummeted to death after attempting the huge leap from the high cliff into the sea. The accident shook the trance community, which then took a respectful year's break before organising their next big party.)

Kumharas was a weekly event that ran in a disused former zoo, while the Tribe Of Frog parties that took place in the indoor room at Las Dalias came with all the hallmarks of a Goa trance party: the 150bpm tracks, ultraviolet lights, fractals and banners, and committed dancers seeking spiritual release in the confined space, all under the influence of hashish and incense (and often more). 'I went a couple of times to Tribe Of Frog,' Tina Cutler tells me. 'It was just brilliant. That's what the trance parties became known for—that abstract scene, and a lot of people on acid, with people like the producer Lenny Ibizarre, who was *so* much part of that whole movement here.'

'I was just around during that time,' Lenny tells me at his idyllic forest home near Benirràs in the north of the island, taking a humble view of his huge importance in this party community. 'I involved myself in those scenes, but I'd say I wasn't a fundamental piece of any of those scenes, mainly because, like Groucho Marx, I wouldn't be a member of any club that'd have me.' He is, of course, a legend in the Ibiza trance scene. Born Lennart Kisum Krarup, he runs the successful

Ibizarre Records from his house, which he recently converted into a world-class studio compound. Since 1997, when he produced his first album, *The Ambient Collection*, which was released by Warner Music, Lenny has become a multi-platinum artist. His famous remixes include a lounge version of The Doors' 'Riders On The Storm'. A co-founder of the prestigious DJ Awards, he is also a partner in the disco-house project *Aristofreeks,* and has recorded recently with Kathy Sledge of Sister Sledge.

> I was born in Denmark, grew up in Belgium, and was educated in England. And I've been living here in Ibiza for the last twenty years. I first came here to party and fell in love with just about everything about the island. I came here on holiday, then came back the next year and worked in Sant Antoni. It was a horrible job but you know what? I was happy as a pig in shit! Just to be here. The Ibizarre label was me wanting to do a lot of parties just to blow all the university stuff out of my head. I made tapes and sold them on the beach, and managed to make enough money to print the first CD. With the money I've managed to make, I bought this house, and since then I've just been crawling around, building stuff and experimenting.

While Lenny still enjoys the island, like many veteran party freaks he craves the winter months, when the clubs are closed. 'The island becomes itself in the winter. In the summer it's overrun by alien invaders, extra-terrestrials. It's an industrial exercise. I still play three or four parties a year, though. I give myself to it completely, and that's it.'

Unlike others, Lenny takes the long view that Ibiza hasn't actually changed intrinsically:

> It hasn't changed at all. Nothing does. It's like when you're fifteen, sixteen years old, I swear to God, Sant Antoni is the greatest place on earth. It's

just lots of similar-aged individuals who aren't into quality. Quality doesn't even matter. This is about finding the *absolute limit* of how much you can take, and Sant Antoni is the perfect fucking playground built for it! So anyone who says, 'Oh that's a terrible place', it's just because they're older. It's OK, though, because you don't want those kids at your party anyway, I guarantee you. It's the same with Pacha and Space now—they're all catering to the people who are going through that period in their life when that's exactly what they need.

Ibizarre is one of many on the island who have tales aplenty of long-term substance experimentation. As the drug scene has evolved down the decades along with the experimenters themselves, the last few years have seen a growing interest in ayahuasca, a psychedelic brew often combining a plant containing DMT and an enzyme that helps to ingest DMT in the stomach (where it would otherwise be broken down). Taken in ceremonial set and setting, often with a shaman, ayahuasca is said to cure depression and help treat long-term addictions.

At the World Ayahuasca Conference of 2014, which was held in Ibiza, the American researcher Dennis McKenna, famed for his discoveries of Amazonian ethnobotanical and shamanic resources, took part in a panel about sustainability in the face of a growing global demand for ayahuasca. Octavio Rettig, a Mexican physician whose main objective is to create a bank of ancient medicines to help resolve crystal meth and crack cocaine dependency, alcoholism, and other addictive behaviours, was also there, and presented McKenna with his book on the healing properties of a species of Sonoran Desert toad, *Bufo alvarius*. This toad is said to be the unique producer of a particular brain hormone that is believed to liberate and realign different 'spheres' of the body. Rettig has given more than five thousand sessions with the *bufo* medicine in the last ten years, to participants ranging in age from six to ninety-one. Rituals such as this, and others involving ayahuasca ceremonies, are now increasingly prevalent in Ibiza—if you know where to look. It's an area Lenny Ibizarre has been drawn to.

Basically people were concerned by my absolutely random consumption of substances, from morning to evening, and that was pretty much everything except for smack. And I'm very good at it, so I was feeling absolutely fine about it, but the rest of them were thinking I should share in their misery and stop enjoying myself so much! So after being pestered to do this thing, which I was told had the power to relieve people of their addictions, they were all very eager to put me into the machine. When I went to do it there were people who showed up just to see me do it, because they wanted to bear witness to two of the most unmoveable objects colliding at high speed. And that's exactly what happened.

I love my kicks, and this is exactly what I wanted—the ultimate kick. The all-out ultra-fucking-kick. It is so real, it is so strong, it just tore me apart. I have found a substance that is so infinitely potent it has just transcended everything. What's left is the ash of my former self. Since then, wow, if I put a spoonful of sugar in my cup of tea it would hit me like a whole bottle of whisky. I am tripping from morning till evening. Whenever I close my eyes *this* all disappears. I went through the toad process three times in a row, but that's all it takes. It has completely changed everything. I've woken up and seen infinity.

Lenny's experience influenced him to start setting down what he considers will be one of the most mind-blowing recordings ever heard— an attempt at painting infinity in music that echoes what Sun Ra was trying to do in the 1950s, using only brass and bowed strings:

The trip recording is one of the most incredible things I've ever made in my studio. It's a combination of working with the shaman, and with atonality and asynchronous rhythms. It's the sound of the infinite, or the sound of the reality behind reality. I've also used mantras, feelings not words. You're not supposed to understand what the lyrics are, you just feel it. This is a totally telepathic psycho-acoustic landscape.

I meditate all day and night now since having this experience. Sleep for me is to jump into a black hole. My experience has changed everything. I don't sleep any more the way most people sleep. They crawl down into a comfortable corner where they feel deep in a cave where no one will find them, then they roll the stone up in front of the door: that's what we normally call sleep. Last night I just lay down and spread-eagled, and surrendered everything, and died right there in front of everything and everyone. I'm still in a state of flux. I had to clean my body up even more to be present. I fasted for twelve days before I did this toad ritual, taking only lemon and cayenne, and lots of water so I was completely clean and clear.

Alone in his sylvan studio compound-retreat in the north of the island, the trailblazing DJ and producer spends much of his day in meditation and reflection, pouring out his thoughts and feelings with boundless creativity and no regard for the superstardom that would be his for the taking, were he to give a damn.

• ● •

In the heady centre of the island during the summer months, today's superstar DJ is the more commercial manifestation of the trance shaman. His ancestors are high priests, masters of ceremony, bandleaders and orchestral conductors. Funk music fans often cite past leaders of the dance such as James Brown and George Clinton, as figures plugged into a powerful connection between this world and the celestial plane. The global DJ is today's sorcerer of the dance scene.

When trance moved into the Ibiza superclubs, Paul van Dyk's enduring appeal paved the way for others such as the Dutch DJ Tiësto (born Tijs Michiel Verwest), who appeared in the mid-90s and became a resident at Privilege every Monday from 2008 until 2011, before moving on to Pacha for a summer season. After huge sell-out seasons catapulted him to the top of the commercial trance scene on the island, Tiësto came to believe that Ibiza has had its day. Claiming the island and its demanding summer seasons were simply taking too much out of him, he bolted for the neon lights of Vegas. However, cynics speculate that what put the nail in the coffin was Tiësto's ill-advised move from trance to the highly commercialised EDM (the industry abbreviation for Electronic Dance Music, coined when existing European house and techno styles were watered down and exploited via stadium-friendly acts such as David Guetta and Avicii).

The Ibiza trance scene is nowadays centred on big-buck potential, and clubland is well on top of it. Dutch born Armin van Buuren became a big cheese on the island when his A State Of Trance night replaced Tiësto's residency at Privilege. In the summer season of 2014, he brought a second night to new beach hotel venue Ushuaïa in Platja d'en Bossa. Van Buuren's album *Intense* coincided with his Ibiza nights becoming the biggest trance parties of 2013, despite major competition from the techno, electro and deep house nights that now dominate clubland (and a tragic accident involving one of his team being crushed by an elevator at Privilege, which caused the cancellation of his closing party that year).

Van Buuren, who previously worked as a copyright lawyer, is an expressive blonde powerhouse. He has done more than ten thousand gigs worldwide and won audiences by devoting entire nights to the promotion of female DJs. In many ways, he completely embodies the contemporary superstar DJ—'he looked like the ideal son-in-law,' his manager says of meeting him—and he can be seen mounting the stage at some shows on a raised platform with his arms spread-eagled, dramatic pyrotechnics flaring as he lifts his hands in the air, as a gesture of submission to the music. He has been named 'Number One Best DJ' a record number of times—a quantum leap from the days when he was tuning up early tracks like 'Blue Fear' in his bedroom at the family home. He recognises that trance music makes people ecstatic in a religious kind of way, and still claims his proudest achievement is his radio show, which, like his Ibiza night, is also called *A State Of Trance*. Recognising the power of the internet very early on, his first radio show in Amsterdam was streamed online and made him famous all over the world.

Today, van Buuren has a private jet with his name emblazoned on the side, and is one of the faces most often featured on the vast Ibiza billboards. To his credit, he's also one of the few DJs I've ever heard admitting that the life can be very shallow. He first came to the island in 2000, appearing with Judge Jules at Sant Antoni's Eden nightclub. People now watch him at his huge shows like he's a rock star, although he has said he sometimes feels like an oddball in the DJ scene, like he should be sitting in an attorney's office, practising what he learned at law school. For now, though, he's 'living the life', and enormous crowds still flock to his Ibiza nights every summer season. His is a key name on the summer club calendar, his sets combining new electronic soundscapes with echoes of his influences, which include Pink Floyd and Jean-Michel Jarre, one of his heroes, whom he interviewed at Amsterdam's 2014 Dance Event (ADE), an important networking affair on the industry's calendar.

Another important networking event on that same calendar is Ibiza's International Music Summit (IMS). At the 2013 IMS, I too had a chance to sit down with Jarre, who told me of his plans to put on one of his vast shows on the island, and his interested in staging it in Dalt Vila. 'I would be thrilled to be a part of sharing the experience here,' he enthused, 'especially with this old part of the town being a world heritage site. It's a place that would make sense for me to promote, Ibiza being one of the central places for electronic music, even beyond the dance floor.'

Aside from making hugely successful albums such as *Oxygène*, *Equinoxe* and *Zoolook*, he also made the curious *Musique Pour Supermarché (Music For Supermarkets)*, a 1983 album famous for only having one copy pressed. The master plates were then deliberately destroyed, thereby making it one of the most highly collectible pieces of music ever produced. Jarre's first contact with electronic music was with oscillators, 'and some electronic equipment more or less stolen from laboratories and radio stations'. When the first synthesizers arrived, Jarre sold his electric guitar to buy one. It was, he says, 'A big move! I sold my Fender Strat to buy the first EMS VCS3, which was the first real European synth, and it really helped me create my own style.'

A renowned collector of rare equipment, Jarre told me his favourite synth is still the Swedish OP1. Having been something of a loner in the market back when he first put on his extravagant futuristic outdoor music and light shows, he has witnessed the explosion of the electronic music scene in recent years, and a huge peer group, many of whom have been influenced by his performances, now makes up a global community of nerdy technology collectors. 'I recently had the experience where there were a few people on eBay bidding for a drum machine, and I realised that the other guys involved were Martin Gore [of Depeche Mode] and Moby. There are quite a few of us after the same stuff these days.'

Jarre's reputation was made in Paris, but he has built extravagant sets all over the world. He was thinking now of bringing one to Ibiza, the home of so many DJs inspired by him. It's easy to see his influence in the Ibiza club scene, and in the stadium and festival spectacles of the big-name DJs. He seemed tickled by the influence he's had.

I know David Guetta, of course. He was just in Paris with his club scene for years, and now look at him, with this incredible career. It's always nice to feel that you're one of the people who's influencing others, not just in the music but with the audio-visual aspects. I always consider these guys like younger brothers. I did feel quite lonely at the beginning of my career. We were just a very small bunch of crazy guys, but suddenly the whole visual performance side of electronic music is huge.

It was just so much rarer back then. You had to think really carefully about the graphics, the lights, what kind of equipment was available to use … and then work out what you wanted to say with the music, and how to translate its feelings. It's something I've worked on a lot, and to be honest I think something can be lacking these days in the visual aspects of electronic music performance. It's probably harder to find your own visual style. I'm always amazed to see how few people are making relevant visual statements in music, and I don't know why. I think it's all this kind of MTV stuff which killed it, and it's funny because frankly lots of visuals I see from the electronic scene are somehow a bit old school. But I think now is the time and place for re-appropriating a vision of the future. I think after the year 2000 we lost this dream and vision of the future, both sides of it—science fiction and electronic music—and at the moment it's like we're orphans of the future. We need to reinvent the images of the future, and I really do think electronic music is the way to do that.

British-born Mike Oldfield, another early pioneer of ambient electronic music, set up a house and recording studio in the south of the island following the huge success of his albums *Tubular Bells* and *Ommadawn*, among others. His 1996 album *Voyager* features an image of nearby Es Vedrà on the cover. Often cited as the 'godfather' of new age ambient chill-out, Oldfield turned to LSD and alcohol when he became famous, and started to have panic attacks. He believed that, due to a bad childhood, he'd missed out during his teenage years, so he decided to set it straight in his forties in Ibiza. Building his dream house and enraptured by the natural beauty, he threw himself into a hedonistic lifestyle with all the island had to offer, and was spirited away for a few years into the *demi-monde* of the island's clubs and bars. At Pacha, he'd head straight for the DJ booth, where they'd let him spin a few discs.

Oldfield has said that there's 'something in the water' in Ibiza, though, and he certainly fell foul of the island's ability to trick or treat those with a vulnerable disposition. His two-million-pound house was built from scratch near Es Cubells, with a gym and a recording studio, in 1997, close to where Ursula Andress had lived. *Tubular Bells 3* was recorded there, influenced by the island's charms. But his on-off relationship with Ibiza came to a head soon after, and in 1996 he sold the land to Noel Gallagher, then at the pinnacle of Britpop fame with his band Oasis. Gallagher was to successfully sue Oldfield after he discovered part of the property was falling into the Mediterranean. (The Oasis dynamo eventually left the island himself, allegedly mortified by the fact that the singer James Blunt had moved there.)

For Oldfield, whose life had devolved into endless rounds of booze and coke, the time to take his leave of the island came after he crashed his car on leaving a nightclub, way over the legal alcohol limit, and was summarily banned from driving for a year. Despite the dream house, the freedom, the music and the endless parties in paradise, the hangover turned his 'second childhood' into a living hell.

## CHAPTER FOUR
# PACHA: THE HIPPIE CLUB • KU: BASQUES, SHADY POLITICIANS, THE SUNRISE OVER THE DANCE FLOOR
### LA VACA ASESINA: THE IBIZA CLUB PARTY FORMAT · PINO SAGLIOCCO, BRASILIO, FREDDIE MERCURY AND GRACE JONES · THE REIGN OF MANUMISSION · PACHA MAGAZINE, THE PACHA HOTEL AND THE MANUMISSION MOTEL · THE GENTRIFICATION OF MARINA BOTAFOCH · CATHY AND DAVID GUETTA: F*** ME I'M FAMOUS! · PACHA'S POLITICAL SHAPESHIFTING

I t's 1973. Across the bay from the medieval citadel of Dalt Vila and the bustling bars of the port, a quiet *finca*-style building was squatting unloved in the barren marshland near Ses Feixes. It had just been bought for today's equivalent of €11,000. They called it Pacha, and along with another island club, Ku, it would revolutionise the way Ibiza partied. Within a few years, Pacha was epitomising glamour all over the world, mass exporting its club ethic under the twin cherry logo—its crowning symbol of a luscious Mediterranean sensuality and hedonism. Replacing the originally conceived psychedelic eye, Pacha's iconic cherries were devised by designer Yvette Montsalvatge, daughter of leading Spanish composer Xavier Montsalvatge.

The desire to open a new kind of club on the island had been gestating for some time in the minds of two Barcelona brothers, Ricardo and José

'Piti' Urgell, firm believers in the Spanish capacity to party better than anyone else on the planet. The brothers dreamed of creating a space where native islanders could mingle with the stars and the bohemians and the working population. Pacha was born from this dream, the name being chosen after a friend of Ricardo's had told him that he'd soon be 'living like a pacha' with all the money the club would be bringing in. Today it is still the only one of the island's so-called superclubs to stay open all year round, its winter parties catering to residents and showcasing local DJs as well as visiting international names.

The entrenched conservatism of Spanish life under Franco drove the artistic vanguard to look for outlets on the periphery. The first Pacha, which had opened in Sitges, near Barcelona, in 1967, had already proved very popular, and there was naturally a lot of curiosity about the new Ibiza outpost. In the early 1970s, the quiet area around Ses Feixes was still so sparsely populated that the only lights to be seen from across the bay in Ibiza Town were the lights of the new club. Piti Urgell hit the decks for the eclectic crowd of revellers, the new rock'n'roll records that brother Ricardo would fly in from France on the day of release blasting out from his two turntables as ragtag dogs ran around their beatnik owners, under the stars on the outdoor terraces. Cushions were spread between the two dance floors and flowers were scattered everywhere as decoration.

The first Pacha parties were a far cry from the futuristic electronic pageants the club is famed for today. Hollywood-themed evenings, legendary White Parties (where everyone would wear white), and even beauty contests were the order of the day.

'I was in one of the Miss Pacha line-ups,' Tina Cutler remembers of her early summer holidays to the island. 'Pacha's always been really pretty, and in a lot of ways it has stayed exactly the same over the years. I absolutely love the Flower Power party, even though that only used to be once a year. It was always such an event. It's my favourite night because that's the kind of music that used to be played at Pacha all the time, *back in the day*. Then on New Year's Eve they used to play the waltz, and you'd do traditional dancing to that. I remember when they used to bring horses into Pacha.'

Flower Power, which still goes on throughout summer season today, was Piti Urgell's pet night. Drawing on everything from The Monkees and *Sgt Pepper*-era Beatles to 1960s and 70s blues, psychedelia and vintage pop, it's still the night that islanders consider the most authentic to the vibe of the original Ibiza hippie parties. Seasoned clubbers keep going back year after year because of this.

'My favourite club has always been Pacha, and especially on Flower Power nights,' says Pete Gooding, the resident sunset DJ at the celebrated Café Mambo in Sant Antoni. 'And the reason it's fun is because people there aren't staring at the DJ; they're there with their friends just interacting with each other which I think is lovely, and is something that has been lost elsewhere. I love stuff like listening to [John Paul Young's] "Love Is In The Air" when it comes on at 3am.'

Dozens and dozens of interesting anecdotes start or end at Pacha, as it has long been considered a great place to drop in to for a couple of hours, particularly in the *madrugada* hours of 4–6am. 'I went to the opening night of Pacha the year it opened,' party veteran Monica Gerlach recalls.

I was wearing a long Adlib dress. You could only fall in love with Pacha in those days. It had the most beautiful garden around it, with lots of roses, and there were only two dancing rooms. Piti played rock music and Bob Dylan, and there was an area with enormous cushions where you could settle in and relax and have a drink, with flowers all around you. It was so psychedelic, lots of colours and pictures everywhere. We'd always stay there till morning. Young Ibicencos would go, as well as the foreigners. Back then the club just had two record players and some speakers. It was so simple, but somehow perfect. I went back to a Flower Power party not long ago, and I can say it's still unique, totally different to any other night, and best of all, no one cares what age you are.

The French-owned Glory's, across town, was a small bar that also opened in the 1970s, and whose DJ, Jean-Claude Maury, would later move on to the nightclub Ku. The Glory's and Pacha crowds started overlapping as people moved between one and the other over the course of an evening. Pacha had achieved its status as the island's nightclub, although it was still a far cry from the VIP scene it is today. Back then, there was no elitism; the dance floor was pure equality at play. Mick Jagger (whose daughter Jade has lived on the island for years) was spotted dancing alone to the music; Roman Polanski held court on the cushions as barefoot bohemians lay down tripping beside him; and Ziggy, a famous local hippie figure, would dance the night away (and continued to do so until he died in 2003, aged seventy-seven, on the dance floor at DC10). After Pacha closed, which in the early days was at 4am, the Urgells would also have renegade free boat-parties, with food and wine, sailing to the glorious but private island of Espalmador off neighbouring Formentera. This went on until the local authorities fined the brothers one million pesetas despite their scrupulous attempts to conceal all traces of their covert excursions.

Meanwhile, the clubland breezes from the Basque country blew in over Sant Rafel in the centre of the island, to reinvent what came to be known as Ku, the world's biggest nightclub. Until 1978, the Club San Rafael was under French management. Locals and party *cognoscenti* would drop by for food and cocktails, and for a time it was a sports venue where young Ibicencos would come and swim, inland from the more island-bedazzled beach crowds. Then the land was acquired (having allegedly been won in a card game) by three Basque entrepreneurs, whose first Ku club was already making waves in their home town of San Sebastián. They were Javier Iturrioz; José Luis Anabitarte, aka 'Gorri' (the soul of the club who brought in raring promoters Brasilio de Oliveira and Pino Sagliocco); and José Antonio Santamaría, a former footballer with San Sebastián's main team, Real Sociedad.

Named after the bloodthirsty Hawaiian god of war and prosperity, Ku swiftly became the most talked-about and expensive disco on the island. In 1979, the Brazilian-born Oliveira created his first party there. Alongside Sagliocco—the great Italian rock promoter and manager who had arrived at around the same time and soon brought James Brown, Freddie Mercury, Gloria Gaynor, Grace Jones and Bob Marley to the island—Brasilio created the hugely successful La Vaca Asesina night at Ku, the first weekly event to regularly feature trans performers, and attracted drag acts from all over Europe.

'Ku was just a very big piece of land. They had a swimming pool there, a hippie market, a dance floor and a bar,' Monica Gerlach recalls. 'You could buy something from the hippies, and stay at Ku all night. It was mainly open-air and the music wasn't so loud in the early days. It was only when it got louder that the villagers of Sant Rafel mobilised and they had to put a roof on it.'

In 1985, a complaint was issued against the club by locals on account of the noise pollution and late closings, and it seemed there were some vague liquor-licensing issues. The club's powerful lasers could be seen from the mainland and were deemed a danger to night-flying aircraft. Txiki ('Cheeky') Benegas, a well-heeled and well-connected local socialist politician, stepped in behind the scenes to lend a hand, but he paid for this with a damaged reputation when his own government colleagues called him out on it.

Benegas was a known figure in the shadows of Ku's 'private' bar. His cocktails sat on the same table as some of the more reptilian operators that moved through island life in the 1980s. Across the table might be Ferdinando Mach di Palmstein, Giancarlo Parretti, Abel Matutes Juan or, according to quite a lot of murmuring, Bettino Craxi. Mach di Palmstein had been selling arms to the Spanish army, cutting himself in for a fat commission on sales. He was on the run from Italian authorities cracking down on crime associated with mafia money laundering, although, as has so often been the case, 'on the run' in Europe translated to living it large and being celebrated in Ibiza. He was pretty much number two to the notorious Italian socialist fugitive Bettino Craxi, who was believed to be in a supposed self-imposed exile in Tunis. The Sicilian Craxi was a former Italian socialist prime minister whose corrupt ways led to his exile, and to his acquaintances being branded as his 'midgets and dancers'. One of these was his friend Txiki Benegas.

Mach di Palmstein had also brought over the sleazy Sicilian Giancarlo Parretti who, in bizarrely controversial circumstances, somehow managed to buy the MGM film corporation. Parretti had also attempted to acquire the Spanish bank Banesto. His friend and-fellow banker, islander Abel Matutes Juan, whose investments in Ibiza's leisure industry have been considerable, was often at the centre of this group of horse-traders. If Roman Polanski and Prince Albert of Monaco were quartered at a neighbouring table in that same Ku bar, no one would have noticed. The assumed freedoms of social democracy and tolerance meant all bets were off once the nightclub was entered. As the 1980s marched on, Ku became notorious for its lavish parties. Like Pacha, and perhaps more so due to its vast size and inland location, the club gained a reputation for total abandon, under the stars, with the stars.

Island darling José Padilla, later to become king of the sunset gig over at Café del Mar in Sant Antoni, was the first outside promoter to launch a themed night at Pacha. His Moondance parties, which started in 1986, would later include guest DJ luminaries such as progressive house champion John Digweed and pinup house guru Sasha, both from England. By then, the club had doubled its capacity to 1,500, having opened up what is now the main room and adding a roof to appease the newly arrived residents of the slowly expanding area of Marina Botafoch.

DJ Cesar, a King Crimson fanatic who later died of a heroin overdose, and the Italian DJ Pippi, who'd been invited into the fold by Piti Urgell, were among the more popular Pacha resident DJs in the 1980s. Pippi, who had his first residency at Pacha in the summer of 1984, during which he championed the sultry dance floor sounds of Grace Jones and Sade, went on to mix Pacha's first double CD in 1997. Along with other local DJs, such as José Padilla and Alfredo Fiorito, Pippi managed to make quite a bit of spare cash selling his own mix-tapes around the island's beach and bodega scene.

Drummers from all over the island would also huddle in corners at Pacha, contributing rhythms to the music coming out from the turntables, while sophisticated yachting crowds, sports stars and supermodels would cluster and add glamour alongside them. Gangsters, drug dealers, assassins and war criminals on the run added to the mix. LSD and marijuana were circulating from quite early on, later giving way to the ecstasy generation and beyond. A Sunday night party for teenagers was inaugurated in the mid-90s, as were 'Full Moon' parties. Chicago house legend Frankie Knuckles, whose 'Whistle Song' became a Pacha anthem at the time, came over to play at the club, and was utterly seduced by the combination of dance floor magic, lack of inhibition, and the refreshingly pansexual vibe of Pacha's events.

Several of the notorious 'big party' concepts that still play a large part in some of the island's club nights came into being back in the early days of Pacha and Ku. These included the famous Temple of Love nights and the fabulously decadent La Vaca Asesina, both at Ku. The latter was to morph gradually into La Troya and its spinoff night, The Face Of Ibiza, thanks to the presence of Baby Marcelo, one of the island's most well-loved and strikingly costumed drag artists. Ibiza's famous hippie chic Adlib fashion label also prospered well at Ku, alongside outrageously dressed Europeans inventing new looks in dance floor style.

In 1992, promoter Pino Sagliocco orchestrated the filming of the video for Freddie Mercury and Montserrat Caballé's Olympic anthem, 'Barcelona', in the club. Grace Jones and James Brown played to the Ku clique and the trans troupes who danced among them. Spangled stoners and cocaine lovebirds would orbit the club as the live music blasted up, up and out towards the stars, while around the dance floor the freaks and hippies smoked and sold their wares. The naked dance freak Tanit—not the goddess but a notorious French African club bohemian—was a permanent fixture; the epitome of the Ibiza free spirit.

'Ku had people on roller skates going round serving drinks, and they used to have animals walking through the crowd too,' Tina Cutler recalls of her days as a teenage partygoer. 'Everyone would be naked in the pool. Juan Suárez, who's now the commercial director of the *Diario de Ibiza*, used to be the one on the microphone announcing all the various acts. When I was the representative for MTV's large events in Ibiza, Juan was brought on board because he had connections, and I remembered him from being on the microphone introducing Ku's "Mr. Sexy" winner. James Brown played at Ku and I went to that, and there weren't that many people. The fact is nobody cared who anyone was in those days.'

When Faruk Gandji opened the Bar Privé at Ku in the early 1980s, he effectively created the first VIP bar on the island, although entrance was a lot more elastic and uninhibited back then than it is now. Gandji famously unleashed a baby bull at one of his Ku parties. Brasilio had opened the original Coco Loco bar in the port of Ibiza Town, serving a free drink with secret ingredients, and the entire bar was soon transplanted to Ku's second, smaller dance floor, which has been unofficially known as the Coco Loco room ever since. Brasilio's Brazilian past had been awash with carnival and event involvement, and his name became (and still is) synonymous with the most carnival-esque of all Ibiza parties. High camp, fetish, glitter, extravagant period costumes, capoeira, samba and European transvestism are all key elements to his party's image. His La Vaca Asesina (a name based on the Brazilian gay slang term *vaca*, meaning 'bitch' or 'whore'), with its Roman bacchanalian overtures, went on to become La Troya Asesina, and eventually La Troya. Across time, the La Troya party has switched venues several times, but the concept was born and bred at Ku under Brasilio's reign as party king of Ibiza.

Beneath the Ku glitterball, however, innuendo and rumours of corruption had been rumbling, and in 1990, as if symbolically, the makeshift roof of the club collapsed and Ku was forced to close while the mandatory refurbishment took place. Then the club's ex-football star co-owner José Antonio Santamaría, also known as 'Tigre', was implicated in a mammoth drugs investigation. In 1992, Santamaría was murdered in his home town of San Sebastián by Juan Antonio Olarra, an assassin connected to Basque terrorist organisation ETA. Olarra, in disguise as a member of staff, had snuck up on him while he was having supper in one of his favourite restaurants. He shot the forty-seven-year-old club impresario in the neck, killing him instantly.

The venue changed hands again when another Basque businessman, José María Etxaniz, appeared in 1995, taking it over from Santamaría's partners, and Ku was renamed Privilege. Etxaniz brought in the Tiësto trance parties and oversaw the libidinous Manumission nights run by brothers Andy and Mike McKay and their partners, Dawn Hindle and Claire Davies. By the mid-90s, with its twenty-five-foot ceilings, its DJ box suspended over the indoor swimming pool, the Coco Loco room with its huge glass windows looking out to Ibiza Town across the countryside, the famous domed chill-out area, and the queues of traffic blocking the road connecting Ibiza Town and Sant Antoni, Privilege had become a leviathan.

Pacha, meanwhile, was also moving into a new age, and with it came the best of the emerging DJs. In the 1990s, Deep Dish—Iranian-American techno DJ Ali 'Dubfire' Shirazinia and fellow Iranian-American Sharam Tayebi—were invited over to play at the club. Today, Dubfire is one of the best and most popular DJs and producers on the Ibiza club map. But it all began for him at Pacha.

'I guess that pivotal moment where we felt the special vibe of the island occurred as soon as we stepped into Pacha,' he told me at the end of the summer 2014 season.

> It is such an iconic venue, and we'd read so much about its history and seen all of the great photos from those earlier days, that to be there was just … wow! And we were quite nervous but, back then, there wasn't the kind of pressure that DJs feel nowadays in terms of having to totally 'wow' the audience. We were known for our unique marriage of deep house, with a tougher Detroit and European influenced style of techno, and we simply did our thing. I remember that it was an extended set, and the response, from the promoters to the club staff to the crowd, was phenomenal. We had yet to traverse the entire globe, but definitely felt that there was something special about the island, and its magical hold on the locals and tourists who flocked to it from all corners of the world.

Apart from spreading the word and opening satellite Pacha nightclubs all over the world, the Urgell brothers expanded locally in 2003 by opening the swanky El Hotel across the street from the club. They had no doubt what kind of vibe they were trying to create: a maximum stylish, cool and super-chilled space whose central aesthetic was created around an international, luxury minimalist chic. The bar quickly became a hangout for visiting DJs, models and rock stars, and chill-out music was selected from the very best sources. One clever move was to invite the savvy and sophisticated chill-out group Fous De La Mer to be its resident act.

Fous's Marko Bussian is the producer of award-winning acts such as Germany's teenage chart phenomenon LaFee (whose first album, which he produced, went straight to number one in Germany and Austria). Bussian moved to the island from Frankfurt in 2003, and, inspired by the natural surroundings of his countryside residence and the pace of island life, created Fous De La Mer with collaborator Jean-Charles Vandermynsbrugge, a Frankfurt-based French musician, and the Argentinian-born singer Sol Ruiz de Galarreta (described by *Pacha Magazine* as 'the island's most beautiful mermaid'). Fous De La Mer's first album, *Stars And Fishes*, featured the standout erotic lounge track 'Never Stop Loving', which was heard in bars and beach restaurants all over the island in 2004. This was exactly what El Hotel was looking for, and Fous were invited to play a residency in the hotel's newly popular lounge from 2006 to 2008.

'What a great atmosphere, it was so relaxed and here was an audience who were really interested in us just doing our thing,' Bussian told me in 2014, in a beautiful, deserted hotel in Sant Antoni.

'The first picture that comes to mind when I think of my first trip to Pacha is of a girl passing by me in the VIP lounge in high heels, completely naked except for a transparent body suit,' collaborator Vandermynsbrugge adds. 'Then I ran into Skin from Skunk Anansie on the terrace. When Fous De La Mer played at El Hotel, we had Kate Moss and David Byrne as guests.'

As Pacha vaulted towards the apex of clubland cool, Ricardo Urgell's eldest son, Hugo, brought in English electronic music entrepreneurs Danny Whittle and Ben Turner. Turner went on to found *Pacha Magazine*, while Whittle brought in superstar DJs such as Pete Tong, Fatboy Slim, Swedish House Mafia and others to the club. A few years later, Whittle and Turner created an electronic dance music industry conference, the International Music Summit, with Tong. By 2006, the zephyrs of the VIP lifestyle were blowing in to Marina Botafoch, and the makeup of Pacha's visiting echelons was about to change. It was now a superclub.

Francisco Ferrer, its general director, is a popular figure among the night creatures of the port and Marina scene, and is one of those who rode Pacha's cresting wave. A friendly and stylishly creative front man, he gave one of the island's most talented singers, Barcelona-born Rebeka Brown, her first big break in Ibiza. 'The first time I really sang was at Pacha,' she told me, fondly recalling her meeting Francisco as we chatted following her commanding residency at Privilege's outrageously successful night SuperMartXé several years later. 'Francisco gave me this amazing opportunity, so now Pacha is like family to me.'

Displaying an eye for emerging talent, it was Ferrer's 2001 propositioning of a young French couple to come and join the Pacha family and bring the Paris spirit to a night of their own design that effectively galvanised the next revolution in dance music. F*** Me I'm Famous!, which went on to become one of the most talked about parties of the decade, was the brainchild of Parisian clubland doyens Cathy and David Guetta. Their nights at Pacha presented a springboard for what became an international superstorm for the Guetta brand.

By now, America was catching on to what it curiously termed electronic dance music, or EDM (the term had been in use for years but was suddenly taken up as a handy genre brand name by industry marketeers). David Guetta's mix of the Black Eyed Peas track, 'I Got

A Feeling', postmarked the turning point for US acceptance into the mainstream of what had previously been a very underground music scene. As much as anyone else in the industry, Guetta is credited with creating a bridge between the European electronic and American urban music cultures.

The Guettas' Pacha evenings were a triumph of romantic aesthetics (at least until the couple split up in 2014). The club would be decked out in colours and effects reminiscent of a fairy-tale teenage wedding, while the ceiling above the dance floor was ornamented with photographs of the amorous couple. On every poster, the tag 'F*** Me I'm Famous! by Cathy and David Guetta' would accompany loved-up shots of the diva duo.

'Women are the best. That's the most important thing to learn from life. Women are superior to men, and we just have to accept it.' It was spoken like a true believer, and Guetta meant it. I was sat right in front of him at the 2010 International Music Summit, where he refreshingly reminded the often catastrophically sexist dance music world that it needed to get an honest grip on its patriarchal fantasies. Guetta should know. He's managed by powerhouse Caroline Prothero, and his rise to global success is also very much the work of his now ex-wife Cathy, who, among other things, is hugely instrumental in the FMIF! party image.

David and Cathy first met at Saint Tropez's Papagayo club. When David's eyes met hers, he felt instantly that he wanted to spend the rest of his life with her, and he told her so. The Senegalese Cathy Lobé was already a star of the Parisian club scene. She was hanging out with French actor Vincent Cassel and upcoming techno DJ extraordinaire Laurent Garnier, while inventing cocktails at the famous pre-club hangout the Sweet World Café, before going on to manage after-hours parties at the Kit Kat Club, the cellar underneath the legendary Parisian nightspot Le Palace. David was studying law. His mother didn't approve of their wedding; his father got drunk and jumped in the pool at midnight. As David looked on, aghast, his new bride roared with laughter.

When Cathy moved on to Les Bains Douches (along with Le Palace, the bastion of Paris nightclub life at the time), she skilfully learned how to manage VIP sections, with their labelled bottles of fine spirits, while David was doing electro and hip-hop parties at the Rex and Folie's Pigalle. In her memoir, *Bains de Nuit*, Cathy recalls their first trip to Ibiza: 'The star was electronic music. No one said a night was successful because such-and-such celebrity was there, which is how it was in Saint-Tropez. In Ibiza, they said a night was magical because of such-and-such DJ. They talked of nothing else.'

The Guettas quickly considered Ibiza to be 'like one giant nightclub', and they were smitten. David was one of the first French promoters to bring in handfuls of foreign DJs to his club nights in Paris. He and Cathy worked together, 24/7, for a decade. They have always been notoriously hard grafters, and their nights at the Bataclan became the hot ticket of the week. Cathy was always a circumspect businesswoman, using the same staff wherever possible and learning about as many aspects of running a club as she could. Her mother even came on board, selling cigarettes and sweets in the clubs or befriending runaways in need of a shoulder to laugh or cry on. When the Guettas finally moved their act into Le Palace, their Parisian nightlife dream had come true.

Le Palace, run through the 70s by the clubbing virtuoso Fabrice Emaer, was Grace Jones's home from home during the disco era. It was the first club in Paris to mix millionaires with market traders. In the Guetta era, the upstairs bar, Le Fumoir, quickly became known as the hippest lounge in town. Pedro Winter (aka Busy P., who would go on to become the manager of Daft Punk and found his own label, Ed Banger Records, signing up Cassius and Justice in the process) would carry a laundry bag full of music and dress all in fluorescent pink, his face wrapped

permanently in his trademark enormous sunglasses. Winter's friends—
Daft Punk, Étienne de Crécy, Cassius, Dimitri From Paris—made up
the long guest list. Cathy and David brought over Manumission, the
Ibiza night fronted by the island's other famous lovebirds, Mike and
Claire Manumission, whose sex cabaret extravaganzas were the biggest
event for several years at Ibiza's Ku/Privilege.

Pepe Roselló, the mastermind behind Space, eventually invited the
Guettas over to the island to put on a party of their own. Weeks of
work went into planning an after-hours party at the club, which ended
up with the famous outdoor terrace being drowned out by unforeseen
rainstorms, much to Cathy's disappointment. But in the late 1990s,
when Cathy and David were invited to put on a French night at Privilege
by promoter Brasilio de Oliveira (with Mike and Claire Manumission
rooting for them) they delivered Gallic platinum. At the time there was
no other big French night on the island, and here was the sound of
David Guetta, Philippe Zdar from Cassius and Daft Punk. The French
electro musicians had landed. Brasilio was thrilled. The crowd went
wild for them. So Francisco Ferrer finally jumped at his chance, since
Pacha was ready and waiting, and F*** Me I'm Famous! was born.

Cathy and David's glamorous image epitomised the vibe of their
Pacha residency, and within a few years the most expensive VIP tables
being booked at the club were for their parties. World celebrities wanted
to be seen with them, everybody wanted a piece of their magic, and
the only way they managed to keep it all together through the dizzy
heights of the last decade was through their authority and brand as a
couple, and their complete commitment to each other and the party.
With Cathy gone—or at least less visibly a part of things, now that they
are no longer together—there is no doubt that F*** Me I'm Famous!
is a shadow of its former glory days. The vital feminine element of the
party seemed to go *whoosh* overnight, judging by the palpably dejected

vibe the night had taken on by the end of summer season in 2014.

Meanwhile, Roger Sanchez's Pacha Monday-night party, Release Yourself, was the most celebrity-studded of any event on a Monday anywhere in the world by the mid-2000s. Lucien Nicolet, aka Luciano— the Swiss-Chilean techno DJ whose reputation as a god was built at Ibiza's enduringly innovative DC10 club—was also brought in to Pacha to showcase his label, Cadenza Records, and their 'Vagabundos'.

'That whole experience was great,' he told me recently. 'We left a great mark on Ibiza's nightlife.' They did. The splendid Cadenza Vagabundos posters, with all their DJs dressed up as gypsy itinerants, had become the mark of the Ibiza summer by 2010.

Electronic music journalist, editor and manager Ben Turner came to Ibiza in 1993 after being mesmerised and seduced by a wonderful documentary set on the island called *A Short Film About Chilling* (1990). 'I probably watched it forty times,' he claims. Since his first trip, Turner has been averaging ten visits per summer season. His experience of Ibiza clubland has been all-consuming and hands-on, both as editor of *Pacha Magazine* and as a founder of the International Music Summit, which came out of Ibiza and is still an annual event there (with additional satellite events in LA and the Far East). As someone who's had to deal with the everyday realities of doing business on the island, he has stayed realistic about the pitfalls of living in Ibiza full time.

'As much as I love the place, I always felt it was necessary to leave as well,' Turner says. 'The island has incredible extremes of ups and downs.' Turner is an electronic music missionary. After several years working in Britain as a music writer and magazine editor, during which time he felt the electronic music genre was never taken seriously enough, and 'being continually told by people twice my age that this wasn't real music', he shifted his interest overseas. 'When someone opposes you at a very young age, it spurs you on for a whole career, and that's exactly what happened to me. I went from the UK media to trying to show Ibiza what this business was about. You're having to justify to people that this isn't just about people out of their minds listening to some music, it's really so much deeper than that.'

Turner launched *Pacha Magazine* in July 2003. He felt there was only one brand that could carry the message, and Pacha was it. 'The club had been a huge inspiration to me, and it was way beyond just being a dance floor with DJs. It was a lifestyle. The whole cherry brand was like a guiding light for so many people, and it still is. I felt that the island needed some kind of media platform that would drive forward the new era. We were trying to elevate the status of an island that was changing massively. Having visited places like Miami, I felt that Ibiza was a long way behind in terms of restaurant culture and bars, and, dare I say it, even VIP. Obviously in the last few years it has arguably gone too far though.'

Turner's IMS business partner, the visionary Danny Whittle, who joined Pacha as music director in 1999, had by then taken Pacha into a new era. The club, and indeed Ibiza itself, had become a global brand. It was now the era of super-kicks for superstars. The DJs were often calling the shots, and Whittle, who saw their value, backed their whims—much to the chagrin of the Urgell brothers, who take a different view on all this. (Piti Urgell recently told the *New York Times* that 'electronic music hasn't evolved in twenty years, and is for idiots', while his brother Ricardo described the music as 'masochistic'.)

The Whittle era at Pacha concluded in 2012, when he was swiftly replaced by Tallyn Planells, an Ibicenco who'd previously worked as creative manager at Privilege. During Whittle's thirteen-year reign, Pacha had seen big name DJs such as Erick Morillo—who memorably played the hugely emotional closing party of Space after 9/11, ending his set with Frank Sinatra's 'New York, New York'—come into the club's family with his award-winning Subliminal Sessions. Swedish House Mafia also made their global name at Pacha under Whittle's reign. With an expanded capacity of over three thousand people, Pacha was grossing about thirty million euros per summer season, with some DJs were being paid six-figure fees each night. Entrance fees were hitting the seventy-euros-a-night mark for some parties—and that was before VIP fees, which were steadily rising to five thousand euros per table. For Whittle, these top-name DJs and their demands were worth it, because what they brought in was often more than three times that amount, and they attracted other big names as a result. Kylie Minogue, for example, gave a concert at Pacha in July 2010 to celebrate the launch of her album *Aphrodite*.

When the Urgell brothers decided to clamp down, it was the superstar DJs who fell from the club's grace. Out went Luciano, Morillo, Tong and Swedish House Mafia; in came the lesser-known Israeli DJ Guy Gerber and others. There were more Flower Power nights. Significantly, however, they kept Guetta.

Across the street, the new Cipriani restaurant in Marina Botafoch's swanky enclave, to which Whittle was now attached, signed some of the DJs Pacha had dismissed. While Pacha attempted to get back to its more laid-back roots, Cipriani's quickly became the next big celebrity hangout. Lindsay Lohan, Paris Hilton and Puff Daddy hung out there; Orlando Bloom made headlines by walloping Justin Bieber in the middle of the restaurant. The Italian jet-set middle-aged club kid and entrepreneur, Giuseppe Cipriani, soon opened a new nightclub, Bomba, close to Pacha, in the building that had been known as Heaven, Penelope, and Angels at various times in the past.

Rumours began to bounce around the champagne and silver-(coke) spoon circles of Marina Botafoch that the Urgells (who had already taken over the nearby club El Divino, rechristening it Lío) had their eye on Cipriani, and were pulling some weight in the shadowy *sub rosa* committees of Ibiza clubland, in order to undermine Whittle's expansion. Out of the blue, Bomba was declared an illegal name, due to some borderline specious international copyright claim, and the club was renamed Booom! Probably smelling a rat, Whittle moved on. The owners of the property that houses the club filed a claim against Cipriani for €450,000 in unpaid rent, although the club kept going as more parties were announced through the summer of 2014. Then, during Halloween week 2014, Booom! lost its case and cancelled its winter parties. The Urgells, meanwhile, retreated into the shadows and kept counsel.

Tiësto had moved into Pacha in 2012, before being ousted by the Urgell brothers after just one season—but not before Whittle was said to have rebuilt the DJ booth for him. The Dutch superstar DJ then threw his hands in the air and jetted off to Hakkasan in Vegas, leaving a trail of anti-Ibiza sentiment blazing behind him.

The Urgells' recalibration of the weekly Pacha calendar continued with the creation of the techno Insane parties on Friday nights, and their Pure Pacha Saturdays now featured Dutch electro house DJ Hardwell, where once Pete Tong had ruled the booth. The awesome Cadenza nights run by Luciano were replaced with Solomun and his '+1' nights on Sundays. The metamorphosis was complete when Pacha brought in Ibiza Rocks House at Pacha, a weekly house music showcase run by Andy McKay and Dawn Hindle of Manumission, who have established a near empire with their Ibiza Rocks live indie rock-and-dance act gigs in Sant Antoni, cheap package holidays for clubbers, and their more recent acquisition of the legendary Pikes Hotel.

'I guess from doing Pacha for a decade, part of our thing was trying to get people you'd never imagine to come to Ibiza,' Ben Turner tells me. 'Now it seems kind of irrelevant as there are so many celebrities, but I saw that all evolve, from Diego Maradona to Puff Daddy. Part of what we did with *Pacha Magazine* too was documenting these people, trying to understand why they were so fascinated by our culture. Now everybody wants to be attached to electronic music, we're flavour of the month. But the first time Puff Daddy came, and the sort of parties he put on, and the kind of chaos he created, he took all that back to the US. The explosion of interest from the US in our culture could never have happened without people like him coming over and being seduced by the island.'

In 2014, Mike McKay and Claire Davies, Manumission's other couple, returned with a new, cinematically themed party called Phantasmagoria at the ill-fated Booom! 'We made champagne out of shit,' their close collaborator Johnny Golden says. 'Craig Richards was our resident DJ. It was a lot of fun, despite … the club … ' Mike and Claire had become famous with the party they had created 20 years earlier for Privilege: Manumission had been a daring, controversial and exciting club night which set new standards with its outrageous eroticism and uninhibited decadence.

Golden quickly became Manumission's diminutive (he's famously known as 'The Manumission Dwarf') but larger-than-life figurehead. He had first arrived on Ibiza in 1996; a drama teacher from the UK, he'd never heard of Manumission, wasn't from a clubbing background, but when he was told all he had to do, if he fancied a gig working there, was give out fruit at the bar, and drink a lot, he thought he'd give it a go. 'I was told Mike looked like Ming the Merciless, and Claire looked like some crazy gypsy woman with really long fingernails.' But he ended up being shanghaied by Mike's brother, Andy McKay, who had him working for two summers at Bar M in Sant Antoni—now Ibiza Rocks bar. Then, in 1998, the audacious Manumission Motel (formerly Hotel Pereyra) opened. An extension of the Manumission nights at Privilege ethic, except small and cosy, for friends and like-minded people, Golden got to the hotel on a two-week stay and 'ended up staying for four months. The Motel doesn't lead to a very healthy life.'

The site of the motel was the old pink-faced brothel at a junction outside Ibiza Town ironically known as the Cross of Jesus, or Creu de Jesús (Jesús is a neighbouring village), and owned by Eric-Jan Harmsen, who also owns live jazz venue Teatro Pereyra, probably the favourite bar of most island residents. 'That was tempting fate a bit,' Golden continues, referring to the name of the location. 'We hardly left the Motel except for on Mondays, for the Privilege event and the preceding beach parades. It was basically 24/7. When you were getting up, you were never sure if who you were seeing was also getting up or just still going. There were some casualties of war that summer.'

Those casualties included BBC Radio One DJ, Lisa I'Anson, who just never got out of bed to do her crucial radio show, to the cost of her career. 'I had to move beds because she was asleep in my bed,' Golden adds. 'She wasn't a very nice person at that time so I wasn't too bothered that she then got sacked.' Better times were to be had by Fatboy Slim and Zoë Ball, who was also doing her BBC Radio One shows from Ibiza that summer: 'They came to the Motel together and found love.'

The Motel's infamous Pink Pussy Lounge bar was exclusive, and to keep out unwanted visitors, Golden was employed as a bouncer on the door. 'The Ibicencos are very tolerant, but it's their island so we'd get some problems when they turned up, and I'd have to tell them that the place was only for friends. We also had a policy of no cameras. People could get up to things that they probably wouldn't do anywhere else. As did Roman Polanski, Mick Jagger, Kate Moss, for example.'

Manumission parties started in the Coco Loco room at Privilege under Brasilio's artistic direction, but within the space of a few weeks they'd taken over the whole club, with their burlesque shows and various freaks and novelty acts, as well as big name DJs. 'I thought these guys were lunatics,' Golden recalls, 'a lot of people out of their heads saying, I love you. And the whole transvestite/gay thing that I'd just never been exposed to before. By the end of summer, though, I was back in London, going to gay and mixed clubs—it was just a much better vibe, I realised.' Apart from the rumoured live sex shows (they happened, but only a few times), Manumission events relied heavily on theatrical extravagance. The nights could often be a combination of cinema show, contortionism, auto-fellatio, surrealism, and, as far as possible, the unexpected.

The peak year for Manumission at Privilege was probably 2007. Then the doors were locked—bang in the middle of summer season. Etxaniz and Andy McKay had allegedly fallen out over a large unpaid fine that Manumission had incurred due to its parties continuing after legal closing hours at the club. Undeterred, the Manumission crew sped across the highway to rival club Amnesia, where they had the show back on the road a week later, as Golden recalls:

> It was miraculous what we pulled together in a week, as it normally takes the best part of a winter season to work out what you're going to do in a club the following summer. But the Amnesia residency only lasted till the end of the 2008 season. The trouble is that holidaymakers want to go to one club, one time, so we'd pretty much had the franchise on Privilege, but at Amnesia we were in competition with big parties like Cream and Cocoon so clubbers' loyalties were divided. It just really became hard work. I'd be out every night going around the port bars, promoting our night.

Manumission held some tremendous parties over the years, and they were all about concept—a different theme every year, including one featuring a barely clothed Jade Jagger. 'I was once a Manumission character called Johnny Big Dick,' Golden recalls. Their outstanding after-parties on Tuesday mornings at Space in Platja d'en Bossa became known as Carry On parties. 'There were a lot of people who didn't go to Manumission because they wanted to save themselves for Carry On.'

Kris Needs, who'd spent a few years in New York observing the US dance music scene, and went on tour as the DJ with Primal Scream, DJed for Manumission in the Coco Loco room, and at the Motel's Pink Pussy Lounge during the 1998 and 1999 summer seasons.

The one thing New York had taught me was eclecticism. It was very annoying when music got put into little boxes, and thankfully Ibiza had a much more open attitude, as long as it heightened the mood. So when I was DJ'ing at the Motel I could play anything, and if I was in the Coco Loco I would mainly play disco, boogie, hip-hop and electro, but I felt like I was getting away with a much wider cross-section than I could in the UK. And if you put the right record on, the crowd really let you know.

[At Space] everybody would be out on the terrace dancing, and they always broke out a box of party hats, whistles and streamers. There'd be Irvine Welsh, Howard Marks. Fatboy Slim, Primal Scream. It was great, but we knew it couldn't last for long. I was DJ'ing in the Motel bar during the week, sometimes through the night till 11am the next morning, and then sometimes I'd start again the next night.

In the second year I was there, although there were some great additions to the place, such as Sid Shanti's rooftop restaurant, I began to see the harder side of the island. The Motel had already changed. It was losing money, Mike and Claire weren't there all the time, and there were new people around. I'm surprised it lasted as long as it did. It was incredible at first, but like so many of the best things, it was of its time. Some very sleazy guys would start turning up, and that's when Johnny Golden started sitting on the door. But at that point a lot of money was being spent on drugs, in and behind that whole clubland scene, and it affected everything negatively. Something had to give. Coke had really taken hold. There was a lot of room-hopping at the Motel—not for old-fashioned reasons but for doing coke. There would still be those great post-pill moments at 10am when you're levelling off and having a spliff, but there was a hell of a lot of people there obviously hell bent on sussing out who had the bugle.

When British DJ Derek Dahlarge extended his stay at the Manumission Motel despite the fact he had dates booked overseas, the UK dance music magazines started putting out wanted posters for him. He was fine, it later transpired, although he was fried from excessive partying. 'I didn't feel that protected by the island in 1999,' Needs continues. 'If it hadn't been for Johnny and a couple of others ... now, having appreciated the place stone cold sober, I know that it's all down to individual choices. It's what you're fed. So many people were going there and behaving like they were told they were supposed to behave. Rock'n'roll stereotypes crept in, and the same types of characters were, as ever, getting damaged.'

The last ever Manumission club night on the island took place in 2008. 'We'd put a lot of money into it', Golden says, 'because it did cost a lot to put on the type of parties Mike and Claire wanted. Back in the day in Privilege there were no consequences to that spending though, as we were filling the place up. I mean, even if we were filling Amnesia it just wasn't as big as Privilege, and our stage was on the terrace and took up loads of room, so that reduced the potential crowd capacity even further.'

In 2009, the year after Manumission drew its final curtain, my friend Kevin Palmer and I filmed a short documentary feature about Allister Logue, who had been Manumission's stylist during the heady Privilege era. Logue—stylist, club promoter, raconteur, *enfant terrible*—was one of Ibiza's most iconic creatures, and was instrumental to Manumission's enormous success. Born in Belfast in 1954, he had come up as a hair and make-up stylist through the heady days of London's 1970s fashion world, joining the posse of international style creators who defined the era's new *mondo modo* jet-set, working alongside names such as David Bailey, Marisa Berenson and Barbara Daly (who'd done the make-up for Kubrick's *A Clockwork Orange*). Drawn to the more theatrical aspects of the nocturnal, Logue also hung out at Studio 54 in New York, which stood him in good stead for later. After following older sister Daphne (formerly the owner of Daffer's restaurant in Santa Eulària) to Ibiza, Logue instantly made the island his home, inevitably throwing himself into the circus of its club life. Hooking up with Manumission to run the performers' dressing room, he soon became one of the extrovert faces of the party, and was often spotted dancing on Coco Loco podiums into the sunrise at the end of the night. One of his trademark indulgences was gold-painted leaves, which he later clad both himself and his models in, on posters for his own Empire night, which ran through summer 2009.

We caught up with Logue for an in-depth interview on a private terrace that hotelier and island legend Tony Pike threw open for us on a beautiful summer afternoon. Looking back on the early days, he told me:

> I was approached within two weeks of my arrival on the island by Mike and Claire, and they offered me a deal there and then. I did some pictures for them, and then started working for them, which enabled me to stay on the island. I think I always knew in my heart that I would end up in Ibiza, that it's my home. When I came on holiday in the late 1970s/early 80s I loved it immediately. I loved the fashion. I loved how everyone made an effort. You would sit on the beach all day thinking, What the hell am I going to wear tonight? It was all very fashion-oriented. Privilege, which was still Ku then, was the closest equivalent to Studio 54 anywhere in the world. It was renowned as the most beautiful club in the world too, and it had no roof then, so the sun would come up as you were dancing. I remember dancing

one night while a hot air balloon was coming down to land in the club, and the music on the decks was great, it was still the early days of Balearic Beat. It was total escapism.

When I worked at Manumission, our dressing room was usually even more fun than what was going on upstairs. Everyone used to pile down there and we'd just party … then at about 6am I'd have a shower, put my makeup away, and we'd hit the Coco Loco room. It was like a big family, everyone got on, one year turned into the next and I loved every minute of it.

Logue was a totally creative spirit who always prioritised spontaneity and the quest for beauty and originality over the drudgery of business concerns. He was always ready to move on and keep creating. 'You're only as good as your last job,' he said. 'No matter how many great *Vogue* shoots you've done.'

A few years later, Logue quit the booze after a lucky-escape car incident and didn't look back. When his own night, Empire, set up after the folding of Manumission, closed after one season, he turned his sights to TV, making it to the run-up section of the UK *Big Brother* TV series, but not actually into the house.

'Someone once introduced me as a person whose life is like a freight train,' he told me, on that lazy hot summer afternoon at Pikes. 'You either jump out of the way, or get on board and enjoy the ride, if you can hang on that long! And I've lived the kind of life that has been a journey, and I decided that if it's going to be a journey then I might as well have as much entertainment as possible on board, with the people that just kind of pass through my life.'

In a tragic irony, the wildly flamboyant yet softly spoken dog-loving Irishman took his own life in July 2010, jumping in front of a moving train at Charing Cross station in London.

# CHAPTER FIVE
## LA MOVIDA, FRANCO'S DEATH AND SEXUAL LIBERTY • THE FIRST GAY BARS • PANSEXUAL PARTIES
BABY MARCELO AND THE THEATRE OF CLUBLAND ·
SUPERMARTXÉ · SANT ANTONI PACKS THEM IN · THE
RISE OF VIP CULTURE · SWINGERS, SEX PARTIES AND
PRIVATE ORGIES · TONY PIKE, A FREE-SPIRITED IBIZA
PLAYBOY · TOURISM VERSUS THE LIBERTINES · WHITE
LINES AND PORNOGRAPHIC MAKEOVERS · YOUNG
CLUBLAND WORKERS: FROM DREAM TO NIGHTMARE ·
AN AVOIDABLE MURDER IN VIP CLUBLAND

'Don't try to behave as though you were essentially
sane and naturally good. We're all demented
sinners in the same cosmic boat—and the boat is
perpetually sinking.' ALDOUS HUXLEY, ISLAND (1962)

The next cabal to become synonymous with Privilege was the flamboyant SuperMartXé, which arrived in 2008. Following in the tradition of the big theatrical Privilege shows started by La Vaca Asesina and continued by Manumission, but upping the ante in outrageous marketing, SuperMartXé purports simply to be a good-time jamboree where everyone is welcome. And, in the words of William Burroughs and Hassan-i Sabbah that they like to quote in their marketing, 'Nothing is true, everything is permitted.' Bawdily theatrical in their stage presentations, SuperMartXé are one of several club nights to have augmented their evenings with regular guest appearances by Catalan physical theatre groups, in this case Barcelona's masterly and confrontational La Fura dels Baus ('The Ferret from Els Baus'). Priding themselves on using Spanish DJs such as Madrid-born electro headliner

Juanjo Martin, SuperMartXé's marketing tricks employed across the first season (which more than paid off in the long run) included free entrance wristbands all season long for the island's restaurant workers.

In late spring 2008, at the time SuperMartXé were due to launch their first season at Privilege, I unexpectedly found myself involved with them. A close friend, long-term island resident Nikki Bark-Jones, had established some great hip-hop contacts from the UK and US who were looking for a place to play in Ibiza that season, but she was heavily pregnant and needed help with organising some gigs for them. In a matter of days after our initial conversation about me coming on board, we were introduced by Manuel López, manager of Privilege at the time, to SuperMartXé's organisers, who were confident but apprehensive about taking on the sacred Friday night slot of the world's biggest club. On a very informal basis, they gave us the club's Coco Loco room in which to design a night of rap and hip-hop, in the middle of a party otherwise promising (and eventually delivering) a pansexual bacchanalia featuring electro-pop, lasers, drag queens, transsexuals and daring clubbers of all ages. Our trio of performers, Sophisticated Funk, was made up of New York's DJ EQ, Bristol's old-skool hip-hop champion Mo Moniz, and Rod Fame, a US rapper MC who'd previously been one of Michael Jackson's dancers. No one could quite believe we were going to attempt to introduce black hip-hop into SuperMartXé's ostentatious evening, and, as it was the first time such a blatant mix was to happen on the island, it was a bit of a risk. But this was Ibiza.

At 7pm on the day of opening night we were all inside the club making the final arrangements for the evening's show. A few acrobats from La Fura dels Baus were fine-tuning a choreographed routine from the ceilings above the swimming pool in the centre of the main room. In the vast, empty space, under the evening light, the DJ booth perched like an altar above the pool looked surreal, surrounded by enormous props and light fittings, while a dozen organisers scurried around glued to their mobile phones. Our Croatian sound engineer had just been introduced to us, and set designers were attempting to construct a working carousel on the main stage. A gigantic electronic light shaped like the letter 'E' was hoisted up, then down, then up again above the carousel. I'd lost our guest list for that night's opening, and the whole thing looked a bit chaotic, but there was a confident air of calm from the SuperMartXé promoters. Our crowd bailed out with fingers crossed, and headed to Sant Antoni for our necessarily chilled-out pre-party at the beachfront Bay Bar, before heading off to the Underground bar near Sant Rafel, to get dressed for the night.

At 1:30am we headed over to Privilege, still thinking no one was going to show up. In the final hours after twilight, we had sorted out several last-minute hitches (Nikki found my guest list, which I managed to get to the door of Privilege just in time). As we arrived at the club we realised that SuperMartXé had, hook, line, and sinker, pulled it off. The towering atmosphere inside the main room, combined with stunning lasers and a magnificent new sound system, added to the oddly fantastic feeling of seeing the place completely full. In fact, we were told afterwards that the ten thousand capacity was more like eleven thousand, and with another thousand still waiting outside. A half-empty club had been predicted. Nano and Oskar, the powerhouse duo behind SuperMartXé looked elated. All our friends had turned up, and were apparently really enjoying themselves.

The main room was being corralled by Barcelona-born singer Rebeka Brown, whose ability to hold captive a very eclectic crowd of mainly Spanish, Italian, French and South American ravers was to continue the entire season. SuperMartXé's shows were outrageous even by Ibiza standards. The government banned one of their posters for being outside the bounds of decency, an almost impossible feat on an island like Ibiza, so therefore a badge of honour, which only did their reputation a world of good. The owner of Privilege, José María Etxaniz, was quick to defend the party. After all, he pointed out, SuperMartXé had used the same images on a poster in Madrid, with no fuss being made in the more conservative Spanish capital city. The season continued to make headlines with various revues such as Kaos City, Hot Wheels, Moulin Rouge, and, a highlight of that first 2008 season, the Flamenco party. 'The night of the Flamenco show at Privilege I was so incredibly proud to be Spanish!' Rebeka Brown told me afterwards. 'These are the greatest performers. For me perhaps the most inspiring musicians of all, the ones from my own homeland.'

On the full moon that August, SuperMartXé held a hardcore porn cabaret called Peep Show that left nothing to the imagination and still managed to be sexy, thanks to both the enthusiasm and apparently genuine passion of the beautiful X-rated stars specially flown in to perform, and to the party's splendid old time décor—half Weimar, half Paris of the great Revue age. 'It was maybe a bit too much though, even for us, don't you think?' Rebeka Brown reflected in her countryside garden, the following week. She had appeared not only undaunted but somehow, still, the star of the show, when she walked onto the stage as the porn show's climax was reached, belting out 'Big Spender' as well as Shirley Bassey ever did. SuperMartXé was very clever to have booked her for the season. After a notable singing debut at Pacha, she had become a well-respected house singer while performing at Matinée, the Saturday daytime party at Space—when Space was in fact daytime, before the after-hours legal revisions of 2008, imposed by the local Sant Josep council that saw, among other things, a ban on clubs opening between 7:30am and 4:30pm. 'That's what made Matinée special,' she continued. 'Now it's not daytime anymore it's like any other party, and so when SuperMartXé explained to me what they wanted to do, I knew that was exactly what I wanted, too.'

That first season, which had been cautiously entered into by Privilege honchos José María Etxaniz and Manuel López, ended up with SuperMartXé taking over the club's closing party slot, following a riotously successful summer. Even today, it is the biggest party Privilege has had since Manumission. Formed in Madrid by Nano Barea, by 2011 SuperMartXé had established a second night, at Ushuaïa, on Platja d'en Bossa. As with Manumission, their events are crowned by a revue-style stage show, but they have always had live sets as well as DJs. Apart from having Rebeka Brown as their resident for a couple of seasons, they also established Tenerife-born singer Nalaya Brown as an island voice. Then they got involved with Paris Hilton, who threw herself into the mix when Barea and the American heiress set up a SuperMartXé VIP motorbike racing team in 2011, although rumours abounded of Hilton breaching the contract with non-appearances, and then being nearly sued by SuperMartXé to the tune of several million euros.

• ● •

Sexual freedom had gradually fluttered across Spain in the wake of Franco's death in 1975, although it would take several years to settle in, and the homosexual community still suffered a hard degree of marginalisation for some time after. Homosexuality had been strictly illegal under Franco's dictatorship, and homosexual activity resulted in large numbers of people being incarcerated under the 1954 Vagrancy Act, which was only repealed in 1979. Gay men, lesbians and transsexuals were judged as deviants, and treated as such, and incarceration could be in psychiatric institutions as well as prisons.

Things really started to change when a countercultural movement known as *La Movida* came along. Starting in Madrid, then spreading across to Barcelona, Valencia and other cities, with Ibiza being a conspicuous centre, *La Movida* coincided with a period of more widespread drug experimentation, and the 'coming out' of homosexuals. The movement, which saw huge creative changes in cinema (notably in the films of Pedro Almodóvar), music and other arts, reached its height between 1986 and 1990 although, as with so much of the cultural repression of Catalonia and the Balearics, the day the old guard died had been seen as a kind of year zero for the gay community.

The first gay visitors were drawn to both Santa Eulària on the east coast, and Ibiza Town. The *Movida*, along with the growth of the gay rights movement in the rest of Europe and the Western world, was a large factor in making Spain today one of Europe's most socially tolerant places. According to the Pew think-tank, 88 percent of Spanish people of all ages interviewed recently feel strongly that homosexuality should be accepted as a normal part of society.

When Spanish Socialist Workers' Party head José Luis Rodríguez Zapatero came to power in 2004, he was quick to legalise both marriage and adoption for same-sex partners. His desire for change also included passing, in 2006, a bill that allowed for transgender individuals to register as the gender they preferred, even before they'd had sex change operations. Soon after the same-sex marriage bill became law, a member of the Guardia Civil (the Spanish police force) married his partner, and they were allowed to live together in military barracks. This was the first time any police force in Europe had made such an accommodation, and it set a legal precedent.

Soon after the initial visits during the time of the *Movida*, the Spanish gay community was returning to the island in greater numbers. Visitors had started to congregate around the bars of Sa Penya and Dalt Vila, where gay bars were beginning to flourish, and revellers mixed openly with all sectors of the island's eclectic community. At the time, urban centres such as Paris, London, Berlin and Milan were still quite repressive in their views on sexual mores, and Ibiza now offered a sanctuary of open-mindedness, combined with a charmed nightlife under the stars of the Mediterranean sky. Within a few years bars, beaches, hotels and a general air of acceptance turned Ibiza into Europe's premier gay holiday destination. Today, the island is very much influenced by the original ethos of fun and relaxed hospitality that was created by those who searched for a Mediterranean nirvana. Establishments such as the legendary Chiringay beach bar came to be celebrated overseas. Ibiza Town's Calle de la Vírgen, with its quaint cobbled walkways, became the epicentre of gay nightlife, as well as being a favoured meeting point for a diverse mix of people.

Anfora, in Dalt Vila, was one of the first openly gay clubs in Spain. This small and intimate multi-roomed space built into the old rocks was established by the enterprising Fernando Delgado, who had first opened Incognito (now called Soap) in 1972. Delgado had been so impressed by the authentic hospitality he found on the island, and the tolerance of the community there, that he decided to take the plunge and see what happened. Incognito and Anfora were a huge success, and Anfora is still a great favourite among tourists and locals looking for a good night out in Ibiza. With its dance floor built inside a cave, and four bars including a Morocco-styled lounge, and a dark room, it is still one of the friendliest of any clubs on the island. Even Freddie Mercury once gave a spontaneous performance there.

Many club pre- and after-parties are held in the rainbow bars of Dalt Vila and Sa Penya, and the colourful transvestites of the costumed and masked club night parades in and around the medieval alleys are world famous. Other famous gay bars include Lola's, Angelo's (where SuperMartXé had their first vibrant pre-parties), Sunrise and Soap. Angelo's opened in 1968, and the current owner Mitch also owns the

Base Bar down in Ibiza port. Although there are only a few lesbian bars as such, gay tolerance is certainly not restricted to men. As is so often the case, lesbians are just more discreet. Private parties are preferred, although in Summer 2015, Velvet Ibiza, a women-only weekend at Punta Arabí was established.

The abiding success of La Troya, the legendary party which was started by Brasilio de Oliveira as La Vaca Asesina at Privilege, has always been due to the way in which the party confidently captures the spirit of transgression and boundary-blurring that characterised Ibiza during the period of the *Movida*. It started as a word-of-mouth party that soon went colossal; since the Privilege years, it has moved to Amnesia (1999), Space (2006) and back to Amnesia (2009), and it is filled with every type of partygoer, from very glamorous to bohemian. Although, for whatever reasons, it has never been popular with the British community, it has, again like SuperMartXé, attracted a vastly disparate crowd from all over Europe.

La Troya is a cauldron of people trying on attitude and seeing what happens. Born out of the counter-culture it has never really lost touch with its primitive roots, even if they are disguised in carnival-esque costumes and bare-all body stockings. Musically, La Troya has always favoured big beats and electro, and frequent live guest performers. Transvestites in cages, and body-painted dancers mix with the locals and visitors who come relentlessly back, year after year. This is all thanks to Brasilio de Oliveira, that godfather of Ibiza party makers who, apart from inventing pre-party street parades and being involved with Ku/ Privilege since 1978, was also an organiser of one of the famous early electronic music parties in Ibiza, Don't Sleep Till London, which featured British DJs Paul Oakenfold and Nicky Holloway.

In August 2008, Baby Marcelo, the face of La Troya on all the flyers, posters and CDs, and the party's resident, DJ Oliver, both suddenly walked out. Rumours abounded in clubland that Marcelo and Oliver could take no more of the new after-hours licensing rules, and that political infighting had taken over the party vibe at Space. The after-hours laws were infuriating to many clubland professionals. La Troya was one party that frequently went on till nearly midday the morning after, and the new laws were seen as paralysing a crucial aspect of the event. So in mid-season 2008, the party split, along with the faithful followers. For the next week's party, Brasilio replaced Baby Marcelo on the flyers. Undaunted, Marcelo and DJ Oliver set up a new night, The Face of Ibiza, on Saturdays in Privilege. It spoke volumes that both events still attracted huge crowds from the get-go, and for a lot of the La Troya fans there were now two nights to go to rather than one. It was that simple.

'There was a very sexy attitude to The Face of Ibiza, a lot of nudity and irony … and a touch of malice!' Marcelo told me in autumn 2014, after the end of a summer season that saw him perform regularly at the Cafe Olé season at Space. He has become one of Ibiza's most recognisable icons, his face decorated in *Clockwork Orange* style make-up, emblazoned on colourful red billboards all over the island. What he brought to La Troya and continues to bring to anything he touches is a mixture of his own personal style and a helpful background in dance theatre that started when he was very young.

'For me, theatre and dance will always be my first love,' he claims. 'It was a very formative experience to study and then collaborate with the big masters of dance theatre, of the avant-garde. The spirit of this kind of theatre is almost mystical. It really gives you a chance to express feelings and emotions that are normally hidden. It's a totally cathartic art. Lindsay Kemp remains my biggest inspiration. For me he represents genius and pure poetry.' Marcelo arrived in Ibiza in 1994, 'and I was called directly to work at Privilege, back when it was still Ku, to create a group that represented the club in a theatrical form. I wanted to bring my experience of theatre and dance pantomime in. We were called Los Monstruos (The Monsters), and we tried to interpret the *personality* of La Vaca Asesina. It was my first persona in drag, and it came to define me!'

For Baby Marcelo, the makings of a good party mean applying a specific recipe: good music, an international crowd, a live act, and chaos. 'I believe the endemic character of Ibiza is the freak', he declares. Between parties, he can be seen riding his bike in quieter parts of the island, and he is still hugely enamoured of Ibiza's hippie culture, 'the markets, the free love, the respect for nature and freedom, and the flower power! La Vaca Asesina was a completely authentic Ibiza party in just this way,' Marcelo continues, 'and it was one that really promoted freedom in sexual gender identity, and created the idea of the party monster, who came to represent the spirit of creativity and outrageousness of the 1990s. It wasn't a commercial party. It was truly grass roots, and our motto was, *E proibido proibir*—'It is forbidden to forbid', a revolutionary motto Brasilio brought over from his native Brazil. 'I always remember one guy walking into the club completely naked with only his costume in a plastic bag. Then he got up on the stage and just started curling his hair, and of course no one said anything.'

Originally a Saturday morning after-hours event at Space, the event Cafe Olé returned to the club in 2009, with an inventory that included artists such as Dita von Teese, Boy George, Amanda Lepore and Ultra Naté. 'Sharing the stage with Dita von Teese and Boy George isn't an experience you have every day,' Marcelo adds. 'I absolutely love Cafe Olé. That whole show is so incredibly professional, and of course Space is a really unique place. The island has certainly seen a lot of changes over recent years, but sometimes crisis makes room for new energy and new projects.' When I visited La Troya parties during Baby Marcelo's reign, I too was struck by how mixed the crowd was. It seemed like the kind of party absolutely everybody went to (or should have). Ravers mixed with groups of single-sex parties from all over Europe, and public affection was even more on display here than at any other club party I'd been to. I also felt it was one of the few places a woman could go out on her own, and mix freely without there being any agenda.

Down in Sant Antoni however, life can present a different picture. Commercial is the name of the game, and the club nights are resolutely more vanilla and less unilaterally entrancing than La Troya, SuperMartXé or The Face of Ibiza. The two major clubs, Es Paradis Terrenal (once famous for its water parties) and Eden, both with a capacity of about four thousand, have many varied nights between them, but the majority of the punters are younger and more orthodox holidaying club tourists. On some nights the atmosphere in the clubs can be aggressively sexual, and therefore uncomfortably inhibiting. Nowhere is the sun-sea-sand cliché crowd more in evidence than at a Sant Antoni club or bar. Some nights have tried to cater to a more international scene over the years, one example being Pete Tong's Wonderland (a popular night that saw Lady Gaga perform there), for which he left his regular Pacha gig before returning there a few years later. The general vibe promoted among Sant Antoni's club tourists though, is that this is the part of the island to get uproariously drunk and/or pilled up, and then to pursue (in the name of 'freedom') passionless sexual encounters.

There's also a small but active swingers scene in Sant Antoni. Most establishments have mixed reviews, but Beverly's Swing Club, with its fetish area, playrooms and dark room has developed a reputation as a great fun venue, and according to reports, is preferable to sometime competitors the Liberty Loft and Pure Platinum. At the darker end of the scale, organised crime gangs control sex trafficking around the island (and there are known drugs syndicates run by Italians, Romanians and English gangs lurking behind the scene). At the VIP end of the scale, several well-known modelling agencies and concierge services seem to rather vaguely offer extra off-menu services too.

But if Ibiza is supposed to be about 'freedom', it raises the question of how organised fun and sex fit in. The spontaneous aspects of cruising and flirting can be very loaded once you get into clubland, and especially at the high-priced VIP end of things. Everyone has to make a living, and this is actively encouraged, but it increasingly seems that much of this is probably at the expense of the island's once authentically sexy vibe. There's a lot of money and exclusivity being placed in so-called 'high-end' sex parties, too. *Eyes Wide Shut* parties (named after the masked orgy of the Kubrick film) have been happening on the island for some years, and while several visitors have reported 'sexual enlightenment' resulting from these encounters, just as many others have wondered why the organised parties would need to be happening in a space of so-called freedom, as Ibiza is traditionally framed.

According to publisher Martin Davies, 'My friend Marianne tried to drag me along to an *Eyes Wide Shut* party that was in the old underground military building in Santa Gertrudis, and I thought it could be interesting. I made a mask and everything for it, but when we got there the Guardia Civil were stopping all the cars in the middle of the forest and searching them, and we had to get out and be body searched for drugs. Marianne suggested maybe we could park the car and climb over the wall, and it all looked a bit tricky … so I took her home, although apparently the Guardia Civil just gave up in the end because so many cars arrived. Anyway I heard it was an amazing party, and even the next morning people were still drifting around the tunnels.'

Killing Kittens is a sex party set up by British socialite Emma Sayle. Inspired by a wedding-party orgy in Ibiza, she returned to the UK and set up a thriving sex-party empire. In her recently published memoir, *Behind The Mask*, she writes of the Ibiza orgy:

'We were chauffeured to a private villa on the beach for a party to celebrate the wedding of Mr Filthy Rich and Miss Socialite … I expected a hedonistic vibe, but I could never in my wildest fantasies have imagined what was going on inside those doors … Inside there were around 200 beautiful guests, most completely naked, some wearing glittering eye masks … naked people were everywhere, their bodies entirely exposed in every state of arousal … This was a real life masked secret society indulged in ritual orgies … I was amazed and liberated by what I had seen in Ibiza. I had loved seeing women relish their sexuality.'

Inspired by this experience, Killing Kittens now specialises in female-driven events, to which men have to be invited. They offer experiences that aim to turn fantasies into reality, drawing the line at rape fantasies. Sayle went to school with Kate Middleton, the Duchess of Cambridge, and has a vast range of contacts in the UK and on the island, which is where the name of the party was first conceived. During a conversation the morning after the wedding orgy, one of the guests had commented that 'we must have killed a lot of kittens last night', by which he was referring to the US college joke that states that every time someone masturbates, god kills a kitten. The Killing Kittens organisers rented a seven-bedroom villa in Sant Rafel in August 2014, during which, the invites promised, members would 'do what they do best, deep in Ibiza's secluded countryside'. The Kittens also threw a three-day party event at Pikes Hotel in late summer 2014, promising 'a devotion to self-liberation and self-indulgence … kittens will have sex in the pool, on its hot pink tennis courts and wherever else they wish … The party will start at 2pm and will go on all night. If they're brave enough they can play for all three nights.'

Pikes Hotel is not far from the wine regions of Buscastell and Sant Mateu, where the excellent Can Maymó and other popular small vineyards represent a tradition of wine-making that's been on the island since the Carthaginians first introduced the grape in the seventh century BC. The harvest is one of the special events of summer's end in this region; an agricultural island hotspot, with rich fields and vines spread across the fertile soils just inland from the west coast. Fields, one or two charming country restaurants, farms and ancient *fincas* dotted on hillsides still mark the area as special and very unspoilt, as do the stunning citrus terraces which date back to Arab times, at least. And, with a view over the harvest, stands the legendary Pikes Hotel itself.

On a warm November afternoon back in 2008, Tony Pike was being entertained by his new puppy, Marley, who welcomed me in the car park when I arrived to do a biographical feature about the hotelier's life to date. Pike was in fine form, and then in his seventies, and radiated a life of adventure, laced with many colourful anecdotes, which he's happy to impart, one after another.

'How I met Freddie [Mercury], I honestly have no idea,' Pike told me that day.

> He just sort of evolved, and became a big part of my life. But this little hotel is like that. I mean it's not really a hotel, it's a little resort, and people come here and they fall in love with it. Sometimes when they fall in love with it, they fall in love with me. So I've used that to gain their confidence, their allegiance. I never came here to make money, I came here to create a lifestyle, and I did. Some of the world's most famous people: Julio [Iglesias], George Michael, Bon Jovi, all tell me, 'Pikey, you have got a fantastic lifestyle!' Well, that's why I've done it.

One of the most endearing qualities of the hotel is that it is has a pervasive atmosphere of fun, with not a hint of preciousness. It feels cosy and very lived-in. The few rooms are all unique, and filled with character. It is a great place for a party. And you can feel Pike's piquant presence in every corner, even with the recent takeover of the hotel by Ibiza Rocks.

> Freddie was such an impressive person. He wanted five hundred guests for his birthday party: two hundred guests to dine, and then for me to provide tapas for the rest. Well, we ended up seating four hundred in the back terrace alone. I had three days in which to get the party together. They asked for the best private party they'd ever seen. But I could not have done Freddie's party without my good friend Pino Sagliocco. He was a very worldly young boy, having come here from Naples, and he started as a promoter. He became so popular he had all the top stars here wanting him to be their sole agent. He first came here with Spandau Ballet.

Sagliocco, the man behind the Ibiza '92 festival, held in 1987 at Privilege (which was still Ku at the time), was of course the person behind many of the first live acts on the island, including the famous concerts given by Grace Jones, James Brown, Siouxsie and the Banshees, Suzanne Vega, Freddie and Montserrat, and US folk singer Joan Baez.

'I had a bit of a mental thing with Joan. She said she wanted to sing me a love song, and she did. With fifty people watching. They loved it, all applauding. Then she got up and danced for me like Zorba the Greek, with everyone dancing with her round the pool. She made me fall in love with her. I took her to lunch in Formentera. She was terrified of sailing. I convinced her to hold tight and trust me. Grace Jones though, was such a wild person,' Pike recalled, enjoying the memories. They have often spoken of each other with great affection over the years.

> All the stars that Pino brought in, this is where they stayed, at my hotel. Tony Curtis was here. And Wham! was a total bit of luck. Some guy was driving around, looking out for a locale and he spotted me. I was here

working on the place, and he asked me if I'd like to do a video shoot. I said no, I'm not ready for it, but he talked me into it. So out they came. Anyway, funny story, on the plane over George [Michael] was talking to the director, and the guy realised he'd left all the cameras at Heathrow! It cost three and a half thousand pounds for a private jet to bring all the photographic equipment out, and they were doing it on a shoestring budget. Twenty five thousand for the whole deal.

Other beach scenes were filmed at Es Figueral with suggestive rock stack—'Paller des Camp'—in the background, and at a girls' donkey-race at the nearby Can Costa, Buscastell. 'It also made me.' We're talking of course about the immortal Club Tropicana video of 1983, filmed in Pike's pool, and a bestselling single for Wham! at the time. Pike is also in the video, sporting moustache, panama and jaunty bandanna.

Tragically, Pike's son was murdered in Miami in Spring 1998, after flying there to sort out a dodgy contract for a proposed purchase of Pikes Hotel. These days the hotel is owned and run by former Manumission power couple, Andy McKay and Dawn Hindle, although Pike still lives there. The famous Club Tropicana pool has hardly changed, and the ambience remains relaxed and self-confident, like Pike and his hotel. His tales of wild Caribbean drug orgies; the celebrities and titled friends including Prince Ernst of Hanover and his then wife Chantal Hochuli getting 'caught red-handed' by Pike's benighted receptionist while they innocently raided the pool bar fridge late at night looking for sustenance. Pike has been in and out of one type of trouble or another several times over, and has served jail time in Ibiza. 'It was like *Midnight Express* in there,' he says, 'with gypsies catapulting hashish into the prison yard in Dalt Vila so the inmates could have a party.'

• ● •

Sometime around the millennium, some of the more commercial club parties on the island started to become cooler and less spontaneous. This was an orchestrated move, as behind the scenes things were changing. With the endless after-hours and pre-party scene of the time, tourists could indulge non-stop, and even more drugs were mainstreamed into the clubbing ecosystem. Along the way though, the more charismatic aspect of partying in Ibiza got a little bit lost. Commodification was now really settling in, and a lot of the people who'd been coming to Ibiza since the 1960s began to leave, making way for the next strand of invaders; the lifestyle pundits. Way more *Marie-Claire* than *Fortean Times*, the arrival of this new interest group brought a prodigious wave of commercial healers and professed yogis to the island. They embraced the hippie ethic, as dictated by a contrived new take on hippie chic created by fashion magazines produced in their home countries, especially England and Germany. Glamour-seeking yet highly organised in very conservative ways, they came to 'find themselves' in the expensive and status-led new spas and holistic events centres.

While meditation was still encouraged on the island, the more hardcore practitioners began to find themselves confined to word-of-mouth reputation, and in competition against a sort of wealthy, life-enhancement package holiday ethos now on offer all over Ibiza. It was sometime in the mid-2000s that previously rugged and off-beat terrains like Benirràs beach in the north became inundated with an aggressive new breed of bohemian wannabes, and this new semi-resident community became the island's loudspeaker for a few years, trumpeted in society columns and glamour spreads, with goddess Tanit as their faddish icon *du jour*.

Like the social landscape in a J.G. Ballard novel, new adventures in island sex became fairly sterile around this time. Although the porn industry had long had an island presence, it began to be 'celebrated' more, as a sort of pro-porn manifesto also began to pervade clubland. Sometimes this worked, but at most events you got the feeling it was too much about theme partying, and not enough about sincere expression. There was a time when the podiums at Pacha could be occupied by dancers confident enough to make their way up onto them from the floor, and although clubs hired professional dancers too, podium time could be shared by representatives of both groups. With the advent of VIP culture, dance floor podiums started to be reserved for professionals, who were now carefully positioned to be very close to the expensively exclusive tables, and were selected to fit a certain porno ethic: false breasts, in-your-face submissive but gamely gestures, too much make-up, way more vogue-ing, way less funk. There is no doubt that cocaine plays a large part in the lives of a lot of the island's professional dancers, as does the possibility of meeting the eye of someone in VIP, and a chance to continue partying later—for dough.

Italian porn actor, director and one-time *Playgirl* nude centrefold Rocco Siffredi is a known name on the island and has starred in several films made there. One of his more outrageous Ibiza appearances involved him sitting astride a giant manufactured penis on the balcony of Amnesia, which then ejaculated foam all over the audience below. Lots of porn films are made in the ideal natural surroundings of the Ibiza countryside, or on boats, but until recently it wasn't quite so trumpeted. It's all part of a bigger picture, since Ibiza has moved into the age of the more cynical, and many would say more desperate sell when it comes to sex.

'Actually I had a very interesting thought about the whole thing recently,' Martin Davies, who married his partner Toni on the island, reflected. 'In the old days, before Gay Lib, people had sex, ok, and it was kind of furtive and in a way more fun. Now everything's all out in the open, and Ibiza's full of screaming queens who just do not turn you on, it really doesn't appeal to me. I'm so glad I witnessed the gay scene in the late 1980s. That was just so much more exciting. It was far less strident and raucous, and much more laid-back. I mean you could go to a bar and you could talk properly with someone, you didn't have to scream your lungs out. Perhaps it's just become too commercial, and I think drugs do have something to do with the scene changing, too.'

Now everything has to be sexually 'enhanced' or rather enlarged, and made much more manifest. Tabloid stories have abounded with flavour-of-the-month reports telling of the latest experiments in sexual scenarios coming unstuck. In 2013, medics in Ibiza were forced to enlist the help of fire fighters and their chainsaws when it became necessary to free a German tourist from the clutches of a steel sex toy. Emergency services claimed they needed two hours to cut through the metal ring, which was described as a type of 'armour plating', into which the man had placed his penis and testicles. The firemen on hand needed two changes of battery and a second high-speed blade for their chainsaw to get the job done. In 2014, six Swedish tourists were arrested in Ibiza for having group sex in a moving car. The charge: not wearing seat belts.

The British Consulate in Spain issued a recent alert to tourists about the risk of sexual attacks. British tourists are now apparently considered targets for sexual predators in certain of the island's resorts. *'Don't walk home alone or with someone you don't trust, it could cost you your life,'* the flyers cautioned. *'Keep an eye on your drink: It only takes a second for your night out to turn into a nightmare.'* But against the wishes of the British consular director, Will Middleton, hoteliers ripped down the flyers, backed by Carmen Ferrer, Ibiza's councillor for tourism, who was fearful of the impact this negative publicity would have on the resorts. As Leonardo DiCaprio's character Richard says in Danny Boyle's *The Beach* (2000), which revolves around life in a secret paradise trance community in Thailand, 'In the perfect beach resort, nothing is allowed to interrupt the pursuit of pleasure. Not even dying.'

Bar Amsterdam in Sant Antoni was portrayed in the British television documentary *Ibiza:Uncovered* as a sordid establishment where buying drugs was as easy as buying a bottle of beer. Manchester and Liverpool gangsters were revealed to control the drugs trade there, and the documentary also stated that one in three British tourists between the ages of sixteen and thirty-four in Ibiza take drugs during their visits each year. In 2013, the dark underworld of Sant Antoni's West End saw two young tourists connected with the scene around Bar Amsterdam end up in a Peruvian jail. Melissa Reid and Michaella Connolly, both aged twenty, were found in possession of £1.5 million worth of cocaine whilst attempting to fly back to Europe from Peru. They both claimed that they were kidnapped in Ibiza, and eventually flown to Peru, via Mallorca, during which stopover they were introduced to powerful Columbians, at gunpoint. Despite their claims, the head of the organised crime unit in Ibiza, Alberto Arian Barilla, never believed a word of Reid and Connolly's story, and countered that they could have alerted any one of the various passport control officials that they passed on their several-stop journey to Peru.

Melissa Reid had worked in Sant Antoni's Millennium Bar, and both she and Connolly allege that in order to make up for their meagre wages, they were bullied by local gangs into selling drugs to tourists, shortly after they had arrived on the island. This is a common story, low-paid workers being cajoled into purchasing ecstasy pills for three euros and reselling them for ten to tourists. Connolly had worked at Ushuaïa as a dancer, and claimed that after work one evening she went back to a private party with some of the revellers, and ended up having her passport taken. She was then flown to Mallorca the next morning, she said, where she had met Melissa Reid at the airport, before they were both then locked in a house for four days with the Columbian gangsters, who gave them the choice of going to either Thailand or Peru to pick up cocaine for them. Had they chosen Thailand, they could have found themselves sentenced to death if they'd been caught.

In a minor stroke of luck, they decided on Peru instead. In Lima, the Peruvian capital, they claimed they were followed throughout their entire stay by local gang members, who trailed them as far as to the airport for their return flight. But almost immediately upon entering the airport, the two were apprehended by a policeman with sniffer dogs. Some, including Reid and Connolly themselves, claim that they were set up to divert attention from a much bigger load of cocaine going through at the same time. In a bizarre twist, singer Phil Collins's nephew, the thirty-nine-year-old Philip Austin Collins (who had been arrested in 2012 while attempting to smuggle fifty kilos of cocaine across the Atlantic on a private yacht) was at one point put forward as the man who recruited them, despite the fact that he was already in a maximum-security prison in Peru.

Ushuaïa, one of the places that Connolly had worked is usually portrayed as a very upscale venue. The origin of Ushuaïa's popularity was in the wake of the clampdown on after-parties. When the law was passed back in 2008 to stop parties running on for too long, or starting too early in the daytime, private enterprises such as Ushuaïa started springing up. They more or less enclosed their party area, and the local government couldn't really object to the new noise levels coming from the beach front establishment given the amount of money being brought in to the island's economy. Then, a few years ago, a bouncer in the VIP area of Ushuaïa savagely beat another employee, a local man, to death on the premises, after a vicious argument broke out between them. The killer then turned out to be a wanted man in Portugal, although Ushuaïa had either not looked too closely into his background when hiring him, or they'd simply turned a blind eye. A move that didn't pan out at all well for the club's reputation.

## CHAPTER SIX
## McMANSIONS, STRANGE FRUIT OF THE EURO • THE BUREAUCRATIC TROUNCING OF MICHAEL CRETU

ENTER USHUAÏA · MATUTES, THE ISLAND'S GODFATHER · GRUPO PLAYA SOL'S CONTROVERSIAL ASCENT · PLATJA D'EN BOSSA GOES BOOMTOWN · SPACE: THE NEW FRONTIER IN CLUBLAND · DAYTIME PARTIES · THE AFTER-HOURS LAWS OF 2008 · HOW TO BE A WARM-UP DJ AT THE WORLD'S FAVOURITE CLUB · CARL COX AT SPACE · ENTER. RICHIE HAWTIN · QUO VADIS SPACE?

S ometime around the euro launch of 2001–02, word spread on the vine that Ibiza was an easy place to transform soon-to-be-obsolete European banknotes into a nice bit of real estate. A growing huddle of financial refugees from all over the continent, belts stuffed with paper money too big to deal with in their home countries, started to look at the Ibiza countryside as the ideal place to convert sometimes ill-gotten gains into property.

The island actively welcomed this influx of nouveaux riches over the next few years, and a helpfully minimal local code of ethics regarding fiscal provenance greeted them on their arrival. Land and property prices shot up accordingly, providing a washing machine for those quick enough to take advantage, and a spate of 'McMansions' sprung up. Previously run-down rural terraces in idyllic locations became prime targets for conversion into *alcazars* for oligarchs and palaces for playboys.

According to island realtor Natalie Bussian, the market has continued to be steady ever since. The owner of First Inmobiliaria, one of the largest property agencies in Ibiza, Bussian established herself as an Ibiza realtor after leaving her former Frankfurt home and moving to the island with her then husband, producer Marko Bussian. 'In Germany, the real estate business is much more regulated and organised than it is here in Ibiza,' she says. 'When I moved to Ibiza in 2003, the tax offices were less efficient. And a lot of old European currencies were being laundered at first, but in the last few years Russians have been coming and investing, and that continues to be on the increase. One mansion here was apparently sold for fifteen million euros, but that's quite a lot, even for Ibiza. It was a waterfront property and the building itself was more than 1,500 square metres.'

After the millennium, property and land prices increased tenfold in a matter of years, but not before a crop of quickly constructed mansions were built, some more beautifully designed than others. The Romanian musician Michael Cretu, who achieved world success with his new age electronic project Enigma, and also produced his now ex-wife Sandra Lauer's pop hits, came up against the inevitable property backlash when, in 2009 his hillside Santa Agnès mansion was ordered to be demolished. In many ways he was just a victim of timing.

Having lived on the island for a number of years, Cretu had originally established his A.R.T studios in a *finca* outside Santa Eulària, before building the much larger complex in Santa Agnès in a conservation area of 3,150 square metres, allegedly destroying precious groves in the process. Local environmentalists refused to stand for it, and brought down a hail of official complaints against Cretu, which eventually saw the Supreme Court in Madrid step in and declare misconduct. The Ibiza environmental group El Grup d'Estudis de la Naturalesa GEN-GOB won their milestone case against the eighteen-million-euro development, sending out a message in the process.

According to Natalie Bussian, 'We real estate agents could write a book full of mad stories, as sometimes very big emotions are involved in these deals. I have had many crazy experiences, sometimes with so much pressure, when in the last moment it's still unclear whether a deal has gone through or not because some document is missing, or something has not been properly registered, etc.' She believes, however, that the market has now stabilised, especially at the more expensive end, which, since the euro transition of 2001–02, has also meant a need for more lavish leisure development around the island to cater to the new population.

Development in the coastal region of Platja d'en Bossa is a textbook manifestation of the surge in expansion within the island's leisure industry, although it's built on a class premise: as a place to come and show off your money, and for low-budget tourists to enter into that game on the cheaper bar terraces, with their two-for-one happy hours. The close proximity of expensively priced rooms and dirt cheap ones on Platja d'en Bossa beach makes for a curious conflux of the haves and have-nots. Cheap-as-chips apartment blocks line up beside designer hotels along the beachfront, while kebab shops and themed bars line the main drag behind the beach. The flagship d'en Bossa empire is the Ushuaïa Group, effectively run by Abel Matutes Prats (of the Palladium Hotels Group). Named after a city in Tierra del Fuego, Argentina that is considered to be the southernmost in the world, Ushuaïa Ibiza was originally a daytime/evening beach bar run by French promoter Yann Pissenem, and was opened in 2008, coincidentally the same year that after-parties were supposedly declared off bounds. By 2009, Pissenem and the bar had shifted location to further up the beach, and started hosting very popular events, including consistently full parties run by

Swiss-Chilean DJ Luciano and his Vagabundos, on Sunday nights.

Then, in 2011, the Ushuaïa Beach Hotel was born. The Matutes-owned site was previously one of his mid-range Fiesta hotels, and after a winter of complete refurbishment it reopened as an all-new 'high-end' establishment. Now you had to buy a ticket to go to the parties, which would start at 4pm. They brought in Guetta, Sasha, Tiësto, The Black Eyed Peas, Prodigy, Placebo and others, and it became hugely popular very quickly. The next addition to the brand came when the Ushuaïa Tower hotel was opened next door, featuring the only open rooftop terrace in Platja d'en Bossa, The Sky Lounge, amongst other delights. Then a Hard Rock Hotel was opened by Matutes Prats's Palladium Group in the summer of 2014, in a neighbouring building. Rooms at the Hard Rock now cost up to and even beyond seven thousand euros a night in midsummer.

• ● •

Originally from Torres Torres, a small town thirty kilometres north of Valencia, the Matutes family made their fortunes in shipping and banking, and the first of the family settlers in Ibiza were effectively the earliest legal moneylenders on the island, due to the concessions offered to locals by their bank. After studying law and management, Matutes Prats's father, Abel Matutes Juan, joined the world of politics. He was named mayor of Ibiza in 1970, and was Minister for Foreign Affairs under former Spanish Prime Minister José María Aznar from 1996 till 2000. Matutes's business interests in Ibiza include ownership of the construction materials firm Suministros, banking interests, investment in holiday companies and travel firms, ownership of the Fiesta group of hotels (under the umbrella of the Doliga Group), distribution of the island's bottled water, large investment in the locally franchised Pepsi Cola and fruit juice market, and ownership of a lot of private and business property. Matutes Juan is also a director of the huge international banking group, Banco Santander, for which position, according to Forbes, he received an annual payment of $169,000 in 2012.

Matutes was friends with the Basque movers and shakers behind Ku, and when Etxaniz bought in he too had connections to Matutes, via the latter's bank's investment in the club. Responsible for much of the island's recent development, Abel Matutes Juan is loved and despaired of in equal measure, depending on who you talk to. During the controversial construction of the new airport motorway, much was made of the way in which he and his daughter Stella blithely ignored and overruled residents' very noisy protests. He is considered to be a somewhat contradictory personality, viz. for example the fact that he aligns himself to visions of Ibiza as a natural environmental paradise (he was European Commission representative at the Rio Earth Summit in 1992), and yet he is just as keen to be seen as a visionary developer in the tourism sector. His ventures in that direction over the years have included a disastrous attempt to build a multi-storey hotel at the airport, which was deemed unsafe by Madrid and dynamited in 1971. And yet, despite the inconsistencies, and his extensive power reach on the island, he remains in the eyes of those who know him a highly admirable rogue.

According to local historian and publisher Martin Davies:

> He's a very able and ruthless businessman who gets what he wants, although he is quite likeable in many ways. His children are very charming too. But underneath, the bottom line is always money, and of course in the end there's a very high price to pay for sacking a place, although it has been a kind of slow sacking, you might say. His family started out with boats, so in those days they were just kind of carting stuff around the Mediterranean,

whether it was charcoal or almonds, and that had less of a negative impact on locals than blowing music at them, and stopping them from sleeping at night, like he does now with Ushuaïa.

Davies lives in Ibiza Town, not far from Platja d'en Bossa, and like many other locals, is starting to get fed up with the increasing noise levels coming from the ever-expanding waistline of the island's now most popular beach resort.

> Ushuaïa thumps right along the coast. There was a big noise march here recently in Sant Antoni, and a young Ibicenco couple there told me about how people who live in the countryside are getting really bothered about the increase in noise here, and especially around Santa Gertrudis where they're still talking about putting a big disco. They've always been trying to get a big Ushuaïa thing going on there, and the locals have to fight against it continually. There's a new organisation now, which stands up to the increasing noise pollution. It's an ongoing concern with a wide cross section of islanders, who are being more and more affected by it.

According to Ben Turner, one of the partners of the International Music Summit, which since 2014 has been held at Platja d'en Bossa's Hard Rock Hotel, 'Ushuaïa is the modern world we live in.' In Turner's eyes, the fact that Ushuaïa brought outdoor clubbing back to the island is a reason to cheer, as it's 'one of the huge reasons we all fell in love with Ibiza.' The superclubs have gradually all been forced indoors as, one by one, new roof terraces have been ordered to be constructed over the previously beloved open terraces of places like Privilege and Space, whereas, 'Ushuaïa really helped bring that magic back,' Turner continues, 'and we should be very grateful that Platja d'en Bossa has gone the way it has, and I think it's still very much in its infancy in terms of where it's going to end up. No doubt the ambitions for that region are way beyond what anybody can imagine right now.'

Feelings about d'en Bossa's development are hugely mixed, and its chequered present is just a continuation of decades that have seen change come in waves of promise, and desperation. Hotelier Fernando Ferré Cardó who invented and distributed a completely specious bottled water product he called 'Agua de Benirràs' in 1974, nevertheless went on to become one of the biggest hoteliers on the island with his Grupo Playa Sol hotels, enormous 'pack 'em in' constructions booked by tour operators around Platja d'en Bossa, Figueretes and Sant Antoni. Ferré Cardó defrauded on taxes owed to the tune of several million euros, and was charged with grossly exploiting his underpaid immigrant staff. The Grupo Playa Sol hotels are still there, and, unlike so many other hotels, several stay open through winter, although tourists only make up a small percentage of the visitors out of season. On the plus side, their rooms are very good value over the winter, and the Figueretes establishments do provide somewhere cheap to stay for the intrepid out of season visitor.

The fact is that Platja d'en Bossa has had its phases. Until the 1980s, it was considered the island's most desirable beach, with its kilometres of golden sand stretching from the urban end of Figueretes to the Sal Rossa watchtower, and the glorious nudist beach of Es Cavallet a little further south. But, as it is positioned on the wrong side of the island for sunsets (this fact is never, ever mentioned in tourist descriptions of the resort) and is still largely comprised of the concrete jungle of rock-bottom-price package hotels that was being thrown up from the 1980s onwards, recent memories of Platja d'en Bossa are predictably less than positive among locals. The main strip behind the beach is, as with Sant Antoni's West End, full of fast food joints, cheap bar after cheap bar booming out supermarket electro muzak, and public drunkenness on display 24/7 in midsummer. In other words, complete and utter paradise for teenagers away from home for the first time. Thousands upon thousands pour in every year just to prove that.

'Platja d'en Bossa has basically become the new Sant Antoni,' Johnny Golden points out. 'You can do everything there. The whole package holiday, with all the bars you need. I went to Ushuaïa this year to see Placebo and the Prodigy and it was great; I mean, you felt like you were at a proper gig. Although once you left, you felt like you were in Sant Antoni with the type of crowds that were hanging around. I don't like it, but maybe it's because I'm just getting older.'

Apart from being one of the key faces of Manumission's halcyon days, Golden also worked on the door at the Ibiza Rocks Hotel (set up by Dawn and Andy of Manumission) in the centre of Sant Antoni, for a while. A low-tariff holiday package, the Ibiza Rocks hotel deals found huge popularity with young holidaymakers looking for the all-in tourist experience. In many ways a prototype of today's new Platja d'en Bossa-geared holiday package, Ibiza Rocks offered live gigs on-site, and afternoon DJ sets at its Sant Antoni-based hotel complex. They brought in indie rock groups from the UK, thereby becoming the first and only weekly event to feature gigs outside of the electronic music genre. Ibiza Rocks have already moved into Croatia and Mallorca, and their island empire (including their takeover of Pikes Hotel in Sant Antoni and the weekly residency at Pacha) now includes an Ibiza Rocks diner in Platja d'en Bossa.

'Ushuaïa is progress, isn't it,' Golden continues, 'although one of my best friends is a neighbour there, and she can't stand it because they've got all that music constantly blaring. One of the reasons it had to get its live music beach terrace covered, and this is during daytime, mind you, is because of the noise pollution. You've got this massive complex built by Big Brother and his powers that be, blaring music out at half past eleven at night, that everyone can hear, and then there's that whole "we love VIPs" attitude.'

Ushuaïa also ruffled feathers when it made the entrance age to its events eighteen-plus, a move that Golden says was 'anti-Spanish. I think you're normally allowed into clubs when you're sixteen. And to make matters worse, there was a time when you couldn't pay for drinks with cash at Ushuaïa, as they didn't trust the bar staff, so you went to this one person that they trusted, and bought drinks tokens. It doesn't exactly inspire confidence in your staff, does it?'

Next door's Hard Rock Hotel—a hastily constructed giant that was still being refurbished when the International Music Summit was held there at the end of May 2014—is seen as the top end of the Matutes d'en Bossa expansion. It's the latest addition to the family empire that also has properties such as the tranquil and upmarket adults-only *agroturismo* hotel, Sa Talaia, in the Sant Antoni countryside. While there is some economic logic to the island's cheaper-end hotels closing in winter, since they are steadily packed through the entire summer season and, with basic amenities, only require minimal seasonal refurbishment, it's a bit of a mystery how the more expensively maintained establishments such as the Hard Rock Hotel can survive, with all the dust and disrepair that can accumulate and quickly tar a five-star establishment after a seven-month closure. There are only really a maximum of five months of solid tourism, as Ibiza effectively stops between the end of October and the end of May. As with so much of the island, Platja d'en Bossa becomes a ghost town in winter, as all business connected with the entertainment industry shutters down. The ghosts of parties past haunt the empty streets, with their lingering billboards, and abandoned club posters peel off the walls in and around Ibiza Town.

'It's one of the reasons why I don't hang around,' Ben Turner adds. 'I can't sit still, and so Ibiza can get frustrating for me, but I don't think it can become an all-year-round location. It's part of the reason some of the big hotel brands have never come near the island but then in a way that's all part of its magic. It needs to switch off and reignite. Every year April or May come around, and suddenly everybody starts to think positively about the island again.'

DJ Carl Cox is co-owner of the popular Sands restaurant on Platja d'en Bossa beach. 'It's not an easy thing to be doing,' he tells me. 'Thank god I have [partner and owner of local art deco hotel Es Vive] Jason Bull for basically believing in it, though. Jason lives on the island, and he knows everything there is to know about creating a space for entertainment.'

One of the reasons for Sands' popularity is that Cox and co (his manager Lynn Cosgrave is another partner) are known foodies, and their menu is just as important to them as which DJs they book to play afternoon sets there. For this team, the beach restaurant is more than just a place to be seen. There's a whole restorative vibe to Sands, and you can imagine spending the entire day there to your advantage, particularly since they moved their location to further up the beach, away from the more increasingly populated Ushuaïa section. 'Our second location was all about moving away from the big throng,' Cox continues, 'We've seen the progression of the island based on new hotels like the Hard Rock and Ushuaïa, but that stretch of beach is getting kind of swamped now.'

According to producer Lenny Ibizarre, 'People on the island are now clearly voting with their money.' For veteran promoter Pino Sagliocco, the advent of VIP culture on the island has ruined everything. The way he sees it we were all VIPs once, and the new hierarchy is a false imposition. At clubs like Ushuaïa, being a VIP is no simple matter. There are degrees of it and you can now book silver, gold or platinum VIP areas in some locations, the demarcations reminiscent of out-dated credit-card culture, or Vegas slot-machine vernacular. The island is constantly accused of being too expensive these days, with drinks in the clubs costing up to fifteen euros for a small bottle of water in some cases. For a lot of ordinary punters, this is a virus attacking the ecosystem of a venue's natural life force, twisting the knife as non-VIP party seekers get fleeced for drinks, and then shoved around if they dare to approach the VIP sections without being invited. At the Cocoon closing party at Amnesia, at the end of summer 2014, we noted how the otherwise basically perfect experience was slighted by the presence of a 'VVIP' area (one step 'up' from VIP), which was embarrassingly empty, but for a couple of desperate-looking young women in body stockings, brandishing expensive bottles of vodka and fussing over a guest list of 'VVIPs' who never materialised. 'Sometimes it feels like the club owners only care about those VIPs,' Ben Turner agrees.

'It's all about money and prostitutes now,' according to long-term resident Tina Cutler.

I sit there and cringe. VIP in my day was considered where the twits went. I used to get begged to sit in VIP. It just got more and more ridiculous, until the VIP areas got bigger than the actual bit where everyone else went. It makes me feel ill and it's so *not* the Ibiza I understand. It only got expensive about eight years ago, and back then VIP used to mean 150 euros for a bottle, whereas now it's a minimum spend of 2,000 euros. I was still doing concierge services [offering bespoke services to villas, such as providing chefs, VIP club tickets, and boat hire] at the time, and my clients were so bloody rich. I kept saying, 'Stop throwing money at them, you're going to ruin it,' but they still did. So no matter what they charged, people kept paying up, and that's how Ibiza turned into Saint-Tropez. None of it was necessary. In the end, Abel Matutes has sold the soul of Ibiza for money really. There are endless articles about the new places to go in Ibiza. I have journalists calling me up all the time saying, 'Would you like to recommend what you would call the real Ibiza?' I just say no now. I'm keeping my places secret!

The changes she witnessed on an island that had created a childhood idyll for her, eventually drove Cutler to leave and move her base to London.

> It broke my heart, watching the changes. Abel Matutes is just on a mission. He makes millions upon millions, and no matter what he opens up next, people going can't seem to give him enough of their money. When Ushuaïa first opened, they were charging a couple of grand for a table, and people were coming in at about 9pm and then leaving at midnight, so it's hardly a good deal. Prices went up to about 5,000 euros a table, and it still gets overbooked. A lot of the very high-end clients from my concierge days have stopped going to the island now, although even some of them used to send me the most ridiculous emails. I'd just sit there crying, going, 'Where the fuck am I going to get all this specialised vodka, and specialised food?'

This rapid change in the economy of the island is, of course, attracting all sorts of business attention. The Hard Rock Hotel is one of the big names taking an investment risk, entirely built on the premise of Ibiza as a brand, which is exactly what it's become. In many ways identifying your brand with the island is a PR move, rather than a sensible economic one. The short tourist season caps any hopes of all-year round business opportunities, and any serious investors will also come up against the ever-nagging infrastructural problems, such as the recurrent connectivity issues. During the 2009 annual International Music Summit, held at the luxury Gran Hotel in Marina Botafoch, for instance, the Wi-Fi went down for practically the whole event, something unthinkable in any major world business centre by then. But the PR aspect of being associated with the island still can't be overlooked. In 2014, the international motorcade rally, the Gumball 3000, ran from Miami to Ibiza. Platja d'en Bossa also found itself the host to Ibiza's first ever water Grand Prix. A huge platform was built on the beach, with spectators poised to witness powerboats and aqua bikes zoom past them at top speed, merrily strafing the waves with fuel detritus, to the complete horror of local environmentalists.

The undisputed jewel in the crown of Platja d'en Bossa is the visionary nightclub Space. Possibly the most prestigious club in the world, the Space opening and closing (of the summer season) parties have been the acknowledged showcases for the entire season, and for more than twenty-five years seasoned clubbers have made it a point not to miss them. There's a whole aura that goes with Space parties. Situated between the beach and the airport, the club is directly under the incoming flight path, and the party is clearly visible just as you come in to land. The Space Terrace (now closed over with a roof, but for years the most famous outdoor clubbing terrace in the world) has hosted just about every top-name DJ. As the opening and closing parties of Space herald the opening and closing of the summer season, they are therefore also hugely popular with locals and seasonal workers. After the long winter, many residents find themselves craving the fresh winds that the Space opening party blows in, while the closing party inspires a sort of vast communal sigh of relief.

In between the bookends of opening and closing parties, seasonal workers knuckle down flat out to earn a living that will see them through the winter. The opening party is so intense, that a good metaphor for the event would be that scene in *The Italian Job* where considerably more than 'the bloody doors' are blown off, in a manner of speaking. For some reason nearly every Space opening and closing party I've attended has started off as a rainy day, which then gives way to the most beautiful sunshine. Bes is ready, and after the rain the island smells glorious and looks like a troilistic marriage of Rousseau foliage, Cézanne colour and Renoir lushness, and the club's line-up is famously a carefully selected mix of old and new. Foc i Fum, a costumed, spontaneous action theatre group (who have been performing since 1982), lend their iconic look to the opening and closing parties. Their powdered and rouged faces, curly white wigs and Louis XVI-era outfits have been an important part of the poster image for years now.

Traditionally, before the 2008 after-hours changes, a lot of people crowding to Space for the closing might have come directly from Amnesia's final party of the season the night before. And DC10's closing, while effectively the very last club shindig of the season, has always been seen as the Space closing's after-party, and takes place the next day, on the Monday. The post-2008 laws, requiring that clubs do not open before 4pm, have since put enough hours between the separate events that clubbers tend to disperse. Before 2008, it seemed to be more of a giant gang who moved from one club to the next.

Established by Pepe Roselló in 1989 and managed by the friendly Juan Arenas, Space is also where the after-party became a world-famous phenomenon. With a capacity of about five thousand, the club became known as the place where partygoers could continue to rave on after Saturday night parties elsewhere closed in the early morning. The Sunday daytime parties at Space were legendary (and locals would often just pop to Space after breakfast on Sunday for a few hours). But even with the changes in the law dictating later opening hours, the crowds still come. The club has hosted several successful events, such as ENTER., Richie Hawtin's futuristic techno concept party; We Love, the long-standing popular Sunday showcase of eclectic DJ sets; revue-style party Cafe Olé; the underground sounds of Catalan-Japanese joint party Elrow + Kehakuma; and Music is Revolution, the exciting international DJ parade headed up by the island's favourite long-term resident, Carl Cox.

According to Baby Marcelo, 'Space are absolute professionals, from way back in those early days of the after-hours, which I'll never forget. The atmosphere on the terrace back then was so incredible, and it really did have a unique power. Now it's a night-time club it has to compete with the other clubs, but it still has this truly unique energy. It's a real crossroads for people from all parts of the world, and is an undisputed symbol of Ibiza.'

Originally built in 1985 as a convention centre, Space took full advantage of the fact that Spanish law at the time stated clubs were only required to close for two hours a day. But following the furore of the after-hours law imposed by the Ibiza government in 2008, the club found itself in stiff competition with venues such as the Restaurant Blue Marlin in Platja d'es Jondal and parties at the Zoo Project in the abandoned zoo of the Benimussa hills, as well as Platja d'en Bossa spots such as the famous pre-party bar Bora Bora, and of course, Ushuaïa.

The 2014 Space opening party—coming, as ever, at the end of the International Music Summit—delivered a heady mix of local DJs, and Space season favourites. Top names such as Basement Jaxx, Deep Dish, The Chemical Brothers and Marco Loco lined up beside local favourites Camilo Franco, David Moreno, Jonathan Ulysses and Javi Bora. Sets by Carl Cox, Richie Hawtin, Agoria and Disclosure were among the highlights of the closing party in early October. The season marked the twent-fifth anniversary of the club, and both parties were, as always, completely full all through the night.

The early warm-up sets can offer an extremely exciting and well-positioned island debut for DJs on the rise. British-born DVJ (disco and video jockey) Dan Tait, for example, who made his name in Ibiza, went on to release the very first commercial audio-visual DJ mix DVD. His Pioneer radio shows now feature guest interviews with some of the world's top turntablists. Tait played at the Space opening party of 2008, in a warmup slot before DJ and record label owner Yousef. When I interviewed him back in June 2008, he described the importance, when playing an afternoon or early evening slot, of delivering a suitable-bpm set for whatever particular time of day you were on, while also keeping in mind who'd be due on next:

> Doing the warmup is one of my favourite things to do because it's an important job, as you're setting the tone for the entire evening. Space is always a marathon, and you can't burn people out, so you have to just build that tension and anticipation. I started off really slowly, like 121–122bpm, since I came on in the early afternoon, and I was aware it was going to be a long and important night. Anyway, it is nice to build it up in waves like that, although I know some people can get frustrated, because I'm known to give a bit, then take it back down again, like a constant teasing, a constant seducing. So when Yousef came on after me, he could just do whatever he wanted, and carry on what I started. I did feel privileged to do that slot, and my preferred way to shine is to show that I'm not just going to play loads of big tracks, or just come in on a few big spots. I'm playing Space, so that means I under-promise and over-deliver.

Space is home to many local DJs as well as international megastars, and, unlike probably anywhere else in the world, here they play on the same terraces, on the same days. All locals and seasoned visitors have their favourite local DJs. One of the things that is great about the Space opening and closing parties, and represents one of the greatest characteristics of the island itself, is that people who come to these parties will respond to what is good, not what they are told is good.

Being 'in' is not really going to work for this crowd for longer than a season, unless your talent turns out to match your ambition.

It's the Ibiza charm that is at work here for Carl Cox, too:

> Ibiza itself is the island that attracts people, first and foremost. If I wasn't doing Space, or Pacha, or even DJing in Ibiza, I would still go there as a destination because I just love the place itself. It gives me a good grounding, a good idea of how to enjoy life, meet new people, enjoy the food, and just the idea of being in Ibiza with those sunsets! I'm enjoying the best of all worlds, and I've kind of understood the island as much as anyone, I imagine, because I've been going there every year now since 1984, '85. I just love being there. When it comes to my residency at Space, I'm almost part of the island now. You know you can't open the season until Carl Cox has been there and opened up his night!

Carl Cox's image is indeed emblematic of summer season, and for years now, the biggest billboard outside Space, in the car park, greeting the thousands who pile in for the club's opening party features Carl and the announcement of his weekly night. His enthusiastic, beaming gap-toothed smile is part of the island's fabric. His residencies have provided widely eclectic showcases for a host of guest DJs, and Cox still prefers to get behind the decks for very long sets. His seasons have gradually expanded too, and he shows no sign of slowing down for now.

> When we first started at Space, I said I could only play a six-night residency, but it's gone from six to fourteen. Now that's a commitment, to say the least, way over and above anything else I've ever done when it comes to being resident in a club anywhere. I've doubled the amount of time I used to be there, which also makes it quite a long season for me. So I decided I'd open this season by getting behind the decks myself for ten hours. As

soon as you walk in the door, I'm on, and when the evening's finished, I'm still playing. Well, that's a lot of music, a lot of mixes, a lot of thought, a lot of passion, a lot of commitment. A lot of everything goes into that night. The summer 2014 season at Space turned out to be a major success. It's not every night that I did a ten-hour set, but the season this year was very special in terms of how much we all put in.

Cox's passion for music is well chronicled. In his house in Australia, where he spends most of his off-season time, he still has more than 150,000 records stored away in his garage.

I transported them from England in 2004, and I basically racked them up in order, so from 1968 till the time I stopped buying them in 2007, they're all here for me to access. I've kind of moved on from playing vinyl, but one of the main reasons I stopped is because in the early days I would always like to cover my ass in the sense of making sure I had enough music with me at any gig, which usually meant carting around two or three cases full. But half the time they were going missing, or getting stolen, and that kind of stuff gets really stressful. When you put so much time into collecting, as I did, and you build up this really great body of music, and it goes missing, or just doesn't turn up, it really gets to you. I really need to have my music with me, so when the whole CDJ [Pioneer DJ equipment to be used with CDs] player thing came out, it was an absolute godsend. Any music I wanted to play I could just transfer onto CD, and have all my collection with me. Now things have gone even further, and you can play all your music from the library on your laptop.

Besides, a lot of new music is not released on vinyl or CD anymore but as files that go straight to your laptop. If I'd kept on with playing vinyl, I'd have been behind what's actually going on. I mean it looks sexy, it looks really good, right? But if you have a DJ only playing his old favourites you're

**TOP** Kris Needs and Lenny Ibizarre at Ibizarre's home/studio, summer 2014. (*Helen Donlon*)
**ABOVE** Rebeka Brown at SupermartXé, Privilege, 2008. (*Helen Donlon*)
**RIGHT** Flyer for the opening night, first Ibiza season of SupermartXé, Privilege, 2008. (*Helen Donlon Archive*)

**TOP LEFT** Carl Cox, 2014. (*Safehouse Management*)
**TOP RIGHT** Dubfire with bird of prey, 2014. (*Dubfire*)
**ABOVE** ENTER., Space, 2014 closing party. (*Helen Donlon*)
**OPPOSITE, TOP** ENTER., Space, 2014. (*Igor Ribnik/ENTER.*)
**OPPOSITE, BOTTOM** Richie Hawtin at ENTER., 2014. (*Igor Ribnik/ENTER.*)

**RIGHT** Alfredo's 'Balearic' favourites, hand-written for the author in 2014. *(Helen Donlon Archive)*
**BELOW** Cocoon closing party, Amnesia, 2014. *(Helen Donlon)*
**OPPOSITE, TOP** Author James Young in the alley where Nico died, exactly twenty-five years to the day earlier. *(Helen Donlon)*
**OPPOSITE, BOTTOM** Sven Väth and Rosalind Bee. *(FAZ/Olaf Martens)*

JOE SMOOTH - PROMISED LAND
PRINCE - WHEN DOVES CRY
MANUEL GOTTSCHING - E2E4
GEORGE KRANZ - DIN DA DA
GILBERTO GIL TODA MENINA BAHIANA
BOB MARLEY: COULD YOU BE LOVED
JOHN LENNON: IMAGINE
RAZE : BREAK FOR LOVE
KNIGHT OF THE JAGUAR - DJ ROLANDO
EP.
DAFT-PUNK : AROUND THE WORLD

**ABOVE** Pete Gooding, Café Mambo, 2014. (*Pete Gooding/Secret Life Music*)
**OPPOSITE, TOP** José Padilla, Café del Mar, 2014. (*La Skimal/Secret Life Music*)
**OPPOSITE, LEFT** Derrick May's favourite tracks, hand-written. (*Kris Needs Archive*)
**OPPOSITE, RIGHT** José Padilla's first Café del Mar mixtape. (*Helen Donlon Archive*)

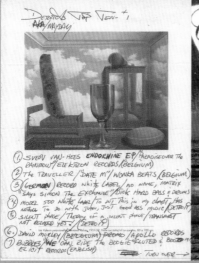

Detroit's Jeff Ten-s
AKA/MAYDAY

(1) SVEN VAN-HEES ENDORHINE EP/PARADISE OVER The
RAINBOW/ELEKTRON RECORDS (BELGIUM)
(2) The TRAVELLER/DATE M°/WONKA BEATS (BELGIUM)
(3) GERMAN RECORD WHITE LABEL/NO NAME, MATRIX
SAYS SIMON The EXCHANGE/DICK HARD BASS & DRUMS
(4) MODEL 500 WHITE LABEL/TO WIT THIS IN MY CLOSET, HAS
NOTHING TO DO WITH JUAN, JUST GOOD ASS MUSIC/DETROIT
(5) SILENT PHASE/THEORY OF A SILENT PHASE/TRANSMAT
NOT RELEASED YET?/(DETROIT)
(6) DAVID MORLEY (BELGIUM) PROMO/APOLLO RECORDS
(7) BUBBLES/WE CAN RIDE The BOOGIE/FLUTED & BOOGIE™
ELIOT RECORDS (ENGLISH)
TURN OVER→

Café del Mar

Café del Mar 4

Café del Mar 4

**ABOVE** Marko Bussian performing on a rooftop in Dalt Vila, 2014. (*Kim Weston Arnold*)
**RIGHT** Tina Cutler in Ibiza, 2014. (*Gypsy Westwood/Tina Cutler*)

just getting to hear a certain person's vision, which is quite selfish. Not to say they're bad records, but people these days like to hear the new music. If I really want something, I can chase it down, get the vinyl and digitise it, and still play it off the computer, but it just takes a bit more rigmarole.

Still, Cox holds the opinion that as a DJ, you should have gone through the realms of playing vinyl.

> Back in the day, when we were all playing vinyl, it really sorted out the wheat from the chaff. You knew the DJs that could play and mix records really well, and you also found out which DJs were rubbish. They'd be struggling to keep up with the beat, and not having fun with it. Then you had DJs that just kind of wallowed in it. If you see Laurent Garnier playing vinyl, it's like watching a ballet. He gets a record, puts it on, cues it up and mixes it right bang into the groove. It's what makes a really good DJ. These days, you can't tell who's a good DJ, with all the machines we use now. The new machines sync up your music, and you can basically pre-mix it all, and have a good idea of what you're going to play, with a pre-planned set list. The DJ who's behind their computer these days, with their hands in the air, going 'wahoo!'—this is easy. It's all made life a lot easier for a lot of people who profess that they're DJs, but the true DJs are the ones who came up playing vinyl. If they haven't, it becomes a bit of a sham.

With all the hard work that goes into Cox's showcase Music Is Revolution nights at Space, there's still a very natural, organic feel to the events, and very different vibes can come through from one week to the next, depending on who he has guesting. Somehow, he manages to keep everything on a really professional level, and to introduce disparate acts who work really well together. For a few years, the residency was just called 'Carl Cox & Friends', and those friends included not just up-to-the-minute big-name DJs, but veteran icons such as François Kevorkian.

Born in 1954, the Armenian, French-bred, New York-based DJ and producer was very well poised to launch his amazing career in house and electro production when he arrived in the Big Apple in 1975, at the start of the disco era. A happy accident perhaps, but the rest is history. In the mid 1990s, Kevorkian set up his own label, Wave Music, and revered New York weekly party Body & Soul. He formed one half of the Cosmic Twins (with Detroit's Derrick May), and then became more involved with techno and dub that led to his eclectic Deep Space NYC parties. His remixes are hugely popular in clubs all over the world, and he is a DJ's DJ, the type of guy that other world-class spinners turn very serious about when you mention his name. When we saw Kevorkian appear as a guest DJ at one of Cox's nights, he managed to hold the Space crowd in his palm all the way through till sunrise. Another special guest was Roni Size, the Bristol-based producer whose groundbreaking musical project, Reprazent, changed the face of drum and bass back in the 1990s. His command of the main room at Space was extraordinary, given the high quality of the techno evening going on in the rest of the club. People were passing from one room to the next all evening, which is typical for Cox's in-demand evenings.

'Musically, I have no manifesto for the season,' Cox explains:

> Our night is eclectic in so many ways; we have drum and bass, we have funk and soul, old skool, house music, techno. It's really an embodiment of all those genres. I never put any onus on any DJ. All the DJs I book, I say, 'Just do your own thing. It's the reason why I booked you.' Rise or fall, it's all about the music. I didn't want to have a particular sound in that club. There's a lot of club nights that say they only play deep house, or only play this or that, but I want people to walk through the door and enjoy something they might not experience elsewhere, because at our night it's all

under one roof. So, say you're really into deep house, and meanwhile you've got a DJ like Andy C playing drum and bass, and you walk through that door, and all you see is this excitement, people screaming and shouting, and the guy's at the 'mic doing his thing? Hopefully, you should feel this energy and just think, 'Wow, I thought one thing about drum and bass, but now I see something else'! It's all entertainment at the end of the day, so I never try and follow any fashion. I never try to be an evangelist for techno music. I just like the idea that people have an opportunity to play, and do what they like, based on what I believe in, and that's what adds to the mystery of the night. You don't know what you're going to get till you walk through those doors, but what I can tell you is you're going to get the very best that I feel can be achieved on the night.

Richie Hawtin's weekly ENTER. techno party at Space is probably the most talked about concept event of the last few years in Ibiza clubland. Futuristic and coolly minimalist in its presentation, its marketing alone is a work of art. Beautifully designed season catalogues, and absolutely stunning close-ups of the irises of the party's main players, with a huge black pupil at the centre, as well as the ever-present black dot that symbolises ENTER. became by far the most iconic graphics of the 2014 summer season. Hawtin, a total perfectionist, made the party all look so simple but, typically, he worked extremely hard to get every detail just right: the lighting, the concept for the different rooms, and the incredible sound of tomorrow he and his stable of visionary DJs delivered. When he devised ENTER. in 2012, he knew that if it was going to happen in Ibiza, it would have to be at Space.

'I'm pretty hands on,' Hawtin told me in December 2014.

We all walked through the club, with the Space management, coming up with creative ideas, and saying we wanted to do this and that. I think they were inspired to see the new perspective, the new energy we were offering. It seemed to energise them. They were a little bit wary though, and to be honest they still are, because it takes two days to build up the production, and one day to take it down. We probably have three times the normal amount of people on staff, to actually make it all come together. That's a lot of time and energy, and budget commitment from both sides. I do believe it's one of the best parties, and certainly one of the most creative events on the whole island, and I'm quite sure it's not the most profitable! We work really hard, and then there are all the DJs that I bring in. Everybody realises that our mission is to create the best experience for everyone involved: DJs, audience and staff, so we're looking really closely at all the details. That includes thinking about exactly how it will all sound, how people will respond to it, and how to make the decorations work. If the DJs and artists feel it's something special, then that's going to translate to the audience, and you'll get a kind of feedback loop, which doesn't happen all the time with events. You can't plan that beautiful moment where the feedback loop materialises, but you can set it up, and then hope the tinder starts to smoke, and then burn, and then turn into an incredible fire. But to get all that to happen, there's a kind of sacrifice required from everyone involved. We all have to put a lot into the pot, in order to create an event that goes way beyond just showing up and playing some record, and getting your fee.

One of the things that's so special about Space is the fact it has several rooms, each with the potential to create a different vibe and pace, and this is the reason it suits showcase events so well. It's also the reason it was such a brilliant after-party spot. You could have one very full on room, still blasting out a more hardcore music for people who wanted to carry on the vibe of the night before. Then you might have the extremely chilled-out terrace, sunlight filtering in, and crash out beds and cushions where conversation could be had in a more relaxed atmosphere. Other rooms would provide something in between.

'When you look at that club in the daytime,' Carl Cox adds, 'it's cleaner than most people's houses, and if you go to any other nightclub it looks like no one's caring for it—they just paint over the walls, and leave chewing gum on the floors. You don't see the wear and tear at Space, because it's so well looked after. How Pepe looks after that club is how he looks after us.' With the different rooms the club provides, the potential for different crowds to find their corner is so much greater here, therefore, than at any of the other superclubs.

For ENTER. ('Music. Sake. Technology. Experience.'), Richie Hawtin took full advantage of the different spaces, creating, amongst other things, a sake bar, and an interactive technology room:

Each year we've had some type of hands-on interactive technology room. And each year it's changed. I'm very aware that the distance between audience and performer has gradually decreased over the last ten to twenty years, and I'm a product of that change. Technology allowed me to tap into my creativity, and become a DJ and musician. Without that technology, I wasn't going to have that possibility. So, to have a room where you can turn the tables, and allow the audience to interact and actually create the musical environment that they're in, is another way of not only just entertaining people, but hopefully it will inspire them to go further into the process. It's another portal, another step in which they can enter a deeper connection with electronic music and technology. Perhaps they come out of the experience of that room and think, 'Hey, that was a fun night.' They might start thinking about it, and get online and download a program, and see if they can make some music themselves.

I've been travelling to Japan for twenty-plus years now. It's a place I feel very in tune with, and that includes with their design aesthetic. And for many, many years the technology in Japan has always been kind of ahead of the rest of the world. They had cell phones really early on, and a lot of music technology. Lots of the technology that records are created with originally came from Japan. As soon as I got there, I just got the most incredibly warm feeling from the people, and from the culture. And as I was going out over the years, sharing conversations over dinner or drinks, I fell in love with sake. The way it was produced, and the way it tasted. The way it was actually so pure and minimal. It's just a perfectly balanced drink, and it gives me a nice buzz. There are so many different reasons why I like it. So, setting up the sake room at ENTER. and creating my own sake, just seemed a perfect way to bring together in Ibiza some of the things I love. I'm curating the line-up of the party, and the sake, and producing the eye images and the black dot, and it's all taking a step into my imagination, where all these things completely make sense together.

It was technology that led Hawtin into making music, which led to DJing and travelling the world, which in turn introduced him to sake.

It's been an evolution of connecting the dots around the world; of friends, of audiences, of artists, of music technology, and that's all wrapped up together within the black dot of ENTER. The core of ENTER. is about sharing the experience, and making sure that the artists were coming in and going to the sake bar, and having a few drinks, and mingling with the crowd, and then going on and doing an incredible set. Entertaining, inspiring, enjoying ourselves together, that's what it's all about, this black dot that sucks us all in. It's perfect for the island, because Ibiza is a place where we all kind of come together in celebration of this incredible technology-based music scene.

In 2016, the original club lease agreement signed by Pepe Roselló is due to expire. No one knows what exactly what will happen, but the likelihood of retaining the electrifying showcase events that have made the club so popular under Roselló's reign is in some doubt.

'I think more than anything what I'm aware of with Space, is that I'm not working for a company,' Carl Cox continues.

> I'm working for a man that has a vision, and belief, and Pepe has been that person from day one. I've been a very integral part of the growth of Space, from the time that he decided I would be a great asset to his vision, and I wouldn't get that with any other manager or club owner anywhere in the world. We've always had a fifty-fifty split on ideas of what my nights should be about, so if it doesn't go well for me, it doesn't go well for him, and vice versa. We've always had that understanding, we are in it together through thick and thin, and with that we support each other in such a way that we've never even had a contract. We've never even had a handshake. It's just a great marriage of ideas.

Roselló has always taken great care to realise all the ideas he and Cox developed when it comes to the production of the nights, the participating DJs, and making sure that the company behind Cox, Safehouse, can deliver at Space.

> I want the best sound system, the best lighting, the best guys that can run a room, the best environment for the people that walk through the door, the best value for money—and Pepe makes all that possible for me. That club is just amazing. But Space will eventually be going, or changing. Pepe's time that he had with Abel Matutes Juan, who actually owns the grounds of the club, was made over twenty-five years ago, and in 2016, when all that ends, Pepe will hand the reins back to Matutes, and Matutes will hand it over to his son, and his son will hand it over to Ushuaïa group. I think you'll find

that the Ushuaïa Group will move into Space, and either carry it on, or knock it down and turn it into an Ushuaïa superclub.

The thing for me, though, is that if Pepe leaves that club, I also leave that club too, because I don't want to work for a company as such, they just wouldn't listen to me. They would want to get more money in, more tables for VIPs, blah blah blah … and I am just not interested. Also, I will have been there myself for sixteen years by then, so it will be time for me to move along on anyway. I like to think Space can carry on as a legacy, but it won't have the same *je ne sais quoi*, because once the new management take over, they won't care in the same way about lights or sound. They just care about how much money they can make from the club itself, and that's where it will all start to go wrong. I mean, commercially it will still be a success, because Space is an amazing place, but you know, if you get rid of Space and turn it into an Ushuaïa club or something like that, basically the club would go into reset mode. What happens next for the future of that club we still don't know for sure, not at this time, but what I can tell you is by 2016, it will all change. In short, when Pepe goes, I go.

While this book was in preparation, Space did indeed celebrate its final summer season in 2016. Its extraordinary legacy will live on forever.

CHAPTER SEVEN
# THE SOCIOLOGY PROFESSOR WHO BUILT
# AMNESIA • FROM AFTER HOURS TO NIGHT-TIME SPOT
THE SANNYASINS SHARE THEIR ECSTASY • ALFREDO
INSPIRES • THE UK INVASION AND EXPANSION:
ACIIEEED • THE RISE OF SASHA AND PAUL
OAKENFOLD • BRITAIN'S SECOND SUMMER OF
LOVE • OUTDOOR RAVES • THE SUPERSTAR DJ ERA •
CREAM • THE CHANGING FACE OF SANT ANTONI
CLUBLAND: EDEN AND ES PARADIS

In 1988 Antonio Escohotado, a forty-seven-year-old sociology lecturer at Spain's Open University (UNED), was sentenced to six years in prison for drug trafficking. The sentence was later reduced to two years when evidence showed he had been framed by the Spanish Guardia Civil. Escohotado had been a known campaigner for drug reform since 1983, a fact that didn't help his appeal. Deciding to make the best of his down time, he brought a computer into his jail cell, along with copious notes, and set about writing up his masterwork, a three-volume *Historia general de las drogas* (first published in 1989, with an abridged version translated into English as *A Brief History Of Drugs* in 1999). And he knew about his subject: in 1969, Escohotado and his wife had abandoned their bourgeois life in Madrid, where he had been working as an academic, and had thrown themselves with ardour into Ibiza's consciousness-expanding world of psychedelics and sexual experimentation. By 1976, Escohotado had rented a beautiful old *finca* near the village of Sant Rafel, and named it Amnesia, partly inspired by the effects of the LSD and marijuana being consumed within its walls. He turned it into a discotheque.

Back in 1970, The Ibicenco Planells family had sold the huge eighteenth-century farmhouse to Countess María Fuencisla Martínez de Campos y Muñoz, who had been living a libertine life of her own making in Ibiza since the 1950s. The Countess transformed the *finca* into a new style of salon for freaks and intellectuals, and hosted art exhibitions and hippie performances, before renting it to Escohotado and his friend Manuel Sáenz de Heredia for 20,000 pesetas (€120) a month. Franco had just died, and Escohotado was first going to call the venue 'Taller del Olvido' ('The Workshop of Forgetfulness') in honour of this, and the type of parties he was holding there. But almost immediately, he decided the simple one word name, Amnesia, would best illustrate his vision for the space. In 1978 the club was passed on to Madrid-born Ginés Sánchez. Despite many ebbs and flows in its fortunes over the decades, Amnesia has become one of the best clubs in the world. At least according to the global electronic music industry, who have repeatedly heaped awards on its Xpanded Amnesia Sound Technology systems, unique club nights, and perfectly formed two-roomed fun palace ambience.

It was during the 1980s that a young Basque called Prontxio Izaguirre crossed the road from Ku, where he had been working, to step in and bring Amnesia into the age that was to make it what it is today. Around the same time, the Kamli Meditation Centre had been opened on the island by sannyasins and followers of Bhagwan Shree Rajneesh, aka Osho, the Indian guru who was famous for his communes in Pune and Oregon. Osho, who was the owner of nearly a hundred Rolls Royces, and who revolutionised dynamic meditation, was a known proponent of the beneficial use of drugs in therapy. He took huge quantities of laughing gas to enhance his own creativity, and encouraged the use of MDMA in his interactive workshops. When Osho was deported from Oregon in 1986 on various charges, including being accused of trying to fix local elections by poisoning voters, he sensibly resettled in India. Plenty of his sannyasins and followers would spend winters in Pune at his commune, sometimes going on to Goa to get involved with the trance party scene there, before moving on to Ibiza where they would spend summers. It is through these itinerants that the use of MDMA in Ibiza's clubs first became a phenomenon.

For a time, Amnesia was just an after-hours club, opening at 3am and going on until 3pm the following day. Ku, Pacha and Es Paradis Terrenal would just be winding down for the night when Amnesia cranked into action. Surrounded by long white *finca* walls, the club had a beautiful pyramid covered in mirrors, which sat in a water pond, in the middle of its open-air dance floor. The pyramid is still the logo on all Amnesia tickets and promotional materials today. Its patrons were a late-night *madrugada* crowd, and more of a freak atmosphere prevailed here than at the other clubs. While the more glamorous of the island's visitors would be across the Sant Rafel road at Ku, a small crowd of all-nighters came to prefer the quieter, more 'bohemian' atmosphere Amnesia offered. During Izaguirre's time, the club's reputation and status started to change, particularly with the advent of a young Argentinian DJ, Alfredo Fiorito, who in the 1980s was to revolutionise the image of the island all over the world, with his highly eclectic sets. These consisted of his own favourite tracks, irrespective of their formerly perceived acceptability on a dance floor. Although low-bpm dance tracks would also come to define the classic sound of sunset bars such as Café del Mar, largely thanks to another pioneering DJ, José Padilla,

Alfredo's became the most famous club night to regularly feature these cosmopolitan mixes.

Alfredo had arrived on the island in 1976, at the age of twenty-three. 'Friends had written me letters, telling me the island was a paradise,' he says, 'and when we arrived, we found freedom. Everybody knew each other only by their first names. We rented a house with no electricity or running water in the countryside, bought a hire car and started to make candles, which we sold at Es Canar [Punta Arabí] hippie market.' Alfredo then opened a shop, and tried his hand at fashion design before being asked to take care of an Ibiza harbour bar called Be-Bop, where he discovered two turntables, a mixer, 'and a huge collection of records'. After working out how to use the mixer, and playing in the bar throughout the winter of 1982–83, he started to dream of becoming a resident at Amnesia. 'It was *the* alternative club,' he continues. 'To tell you the truth, it was a very cool place. They used to have live music, but it was by the underground musicians of the time, with the sannyasins selling food.'

Alfredo started to DJ at Amnesia in 1984. For the first six months he played to a near-empty club, until his girlfriend suggested that, rather than just hanging around waiting to be paid afterwards (at the time he was paid five thousand pesetas a night, the equivalent of thirty euros) he should keep on playing. 'So I started playing music for the workers, like Art of Noise's 'Moments In Love', Manuel Göttsching's 'E2-E4', Marvin Gaye. The people coming down from Ku would be listening from the road. Then they started coming to the club.'

Within ten days, the place was, according to Alfredo, full of 'real nightlife people, people who worked in the other clubs. It was very cosmopolitan, and the age range was eighteen to fifty. The people who came were from all over in the world.' Colourful event-tailored posters for his twelve-hour sessions, which started at 3am, were designed by local artist Sola. Occasionally the club would be invaded by police sent on behalf of other club owners, who suddenly found themselves losing business, but Amnesia always dealt with the complaints and got back on its feet. When Space opened in 1987 though, Amnesia considerably started to close earlier in the day, to make room for the new off-peak hours club.

It was into one of these fabled Alfredo sets at Amnesia in 1987 that a bunch of British DJs wandered, and left so altered that it led them to create what became probably the biggest ever dance culture revolution in the UK. Paul Oakenfold (on holiday for his twenty-fourth birthday), Danny Rampling, Johnny Walker and Nicky Holloway had just taken their first ecstasy trip. They'd started out the evening dropping in to Sant Antoni's Star Club (now Gatecrasher), to see their friend, fellow DJ Trevor Fung, who was working on the island. Fung spun them amazing tales about Amnesia, and this extraordinary new drug called ecstasy. They decided to give it a go. Within half an hour of ingestion, the euphoric 'shoom' hit them. Later, Trevor Fung would suggest Shoom as the name for Danny Rampling's London club party.

As they walked into Amnesia that fateful night, they were struck by the natural ambience of the open-air space. Early morning breezes blew in, and a myriad of beautiful and wild creatures pulsated on the dance floor, entranced by Alfredo's set which included house, rock, hip-hop, reggae and pop. Under the influence of ecstasy, the loved-up atmosphere that pervaded the entire space completely enveloped them. Hooking up with their friends, DJs Lisa Loud and Nancy Noise, they were introduced to Alfredo. After this party their lives were changed forever. The whole experience was taken home at the end of their holiday to the UK, and the British 'Balearic'-influenced acid house scene was born, in what was to become known as the Second Summer of Love.

'I'd started going to Ibiza and Formentera when I was about twenty-four,' recalls Youth, another British face who headed out to the Balearics during the decade.

> The first time I went was with Mark Manning, aka Zodiac Mindwarp. He'd never been on a plane before, and we'd swallowed a load of hash going through security at the airport, so when we got there we just passed out on this beach for two days. It was the early 1980s, and the islands were still the epicentre of the hippie idyll. It was really chilled out, and there were hardly any roads, just a few people on bicycles. All the beaches were nude, and there were a few freaks who'd have parties in villas with rich hippie bohemians. We ended up living in a cave in Formentera. I remember Mark phoning up Nina Hagen, who was playing at Ku, to see if we could get on the guest list.
>
> Then there was this whole 'Balearic' thing that really came to the fore later, in 1987, '88, with acid house, and Oakenfold, and those DJs going out there to hear Alfredo do his sets. That was hugely important. I was popping over to the island around that time as well. It was an amazing time, and it was still very underground, that scene. Even though it was really kicking off in London, it was still unchanged in Ibiza up until the 1990s.

Zodiac Youth, Youth and Manning's joint project, ended up doing a video for 'Fast Forward The Future' in Ibiza, restaging the Last Supper in a villa. 'The moment that English people became a majority part of the dance floor of Amnesia, I had to change the music I played,' recalls Alfredo. Along with fellow DJ Leo Mas, he'd been collecting the kind of records that were available at the time in Europe, and the songs that came to make up his famous Balearic beat mix-tapes might be South American, Italian, French or German, as well as whatever imports were coming in from the UK and US. DJ José Padilla would sell Alfredo's mix-tapes, along with his own, on the beaches and in town, and these now rareties are considered to be practically worth their weight in gold today. At this point, 'Amnesia unified the island', according to Alfredo. 'It was the only club that got people from Sant Antoni and Ibiza Town together in one place.' When Nancy Noise told him he had made the front page of *The Independent* newspaper back in the UK, Alfredo couldn't have been more surprised. The Second Summer of Love had all but made Alfredo a household name by the end of 1989.

Up until that time, UK clubland had been largely soul- and funk-oriented, although hip-hop was making its way to the dance floors. The new wave/post-punk scene had also created a new electronic dance music scene, with bands such as Depeche Mode and New Order paving the way, in the early 1980s, at clubs such as London's Camden Palace, for the coming acid-house scene. On his return from the ecstasy-fuelled trip to Amnesia, Paul Oakenfold started experimental club night Future, later called Spectrum at the Sanctuary (before moving on to the bigger club space, Heaven), where he would play a mixture of proto-trance tracks, such as 'What Time Is Love?' by The KLF (who also did their first live performance at Spectrum), fast house tracks and classical music.

Enhanced by the swirling green lasers and a dry-ice machine, Spectrum is where the term 'Aciieed' was said to have been first shrieked across the dance floor. Danny Rampling and his wife Jenni started club night *Shoom*, bringing in Andrew Weatherall and Terry Farley as residents, and playing Ibiza-inspired low-bpm dance-floor rock, pop and disco, thereby creating the first UK Balearic rave club. Nicky Holloway had been running Special Branch nights in London with Pete Tong, and Gilles Peterson, who coined the term 'acid jazz'. After the famous Ibiza trip for Oakenfold's birthday, Holloway was inspired to launch The Trip, an acid house night at London's Astoria Theatre. Oakenfold, Rampling and Holloway were therefore responsible for turning London on to the Balearic sound, and, in a very big way, ecstasy.

Other DJs and musicians soon followed their example. Mr C. was the frontman for Scottish psychedelic band The Shamen, whose anthemic single 'Ebeneezer Goode' became one of the most controversial UK number ones of all time when it was suggested that, perhaps, the song's title was a play on 'E's [ecstasy pills] are good.' Mr C. (born Richard West) was a resident DJ at the underground acid-house and techno parties taking place at London's former prison dungeon, the Clink. The new music being played at all these clubs was a mixture of Alfredo-inspired Balearic beat, the house music sounds being spun by Ron Hardy and Frankie Knuckles in Chicago, and, in some cases, such as at the Clink nights, the more futuristic sounds being pioneered by Detroit techno DJs Derrick May, Juan Atkins and Kevin Saunderson. The mixture of all these elements—often combined with a new hippie-inflected baggy style of clothing, garish neon colours, and the semi-ubiquitous (at least according to the British press) yellow acid house smiley face—came to define the typical British raver of the time. Within a couple of years, the British media was all over this movement that was causing upstanding Middle Englanders to become extremely uncomfortable. Ecstasy horror stories spread like pandemonium, despite the fact that the new drug had all but replaced drunkenness (and therefore aggression and violence) in clubs. Many of which didn't even bother trying to get a liquor license, dispensing only water to the crowd.

Furthermore, some of the more hardcore UK football terraces, previously known homes to gangs of internationally feared 'football hooligans', started to mysteriously transmogrify. Giant, inflatable Fyffes bananas were being passed through crowds spontaneously launching into loved-up 'Mexican waves', as fist-flying became a thing of the past. This was put down to ecstasy. It wasn't enough to convince the British media though, who were keen to emphasise the 'terrible dangers' they insisted were associated with ecstasy.

Meanwhile Alfredo's mixtapes, and his distinctive nights at Amnesia, had not only catalysed a whole scene in the UK, it had also, as a result of this, created a new breed: the highly-paid DJ superstars, and at first, most of these were British.

Lenny Ibizarre has his own opinions of the British scene:

The English press have completely taken the word 'Ibiza' and rewritten their own history. We're so tired of reading about Oakenfold. I have nothing against Paul, he was very nice to me. But they didn't invent the European acid house scene. They came here to Ibiza to hook up with what everyone else was way, way ahead of already, and then they claimed the rights and went back home to the UK, and tried to sell the story that they invented Ibiza. The English media closes itself off by rewriting history for their own benefit, and you lose out on the reality of the matter. Danny Rampling would be the first to emphasise that. My own career is a product of the English media, because I was here doing what I was doing, and then they arrived needing more material to feed the fucking media cannon, and I was just one more thing to write about. Rob Da Bank [DJ and founder of the UK summer festival Bestival] wrote a beautiful article about me … that was full of lies, although I still love him for it. I was portrayed as this *Ace Ventura* phenomenon, running around with all these animals around me, playing music naked, and singing for them Disney-style. That image caught on, and that's how I became widely known as Lenny Ibizarre, which I had never called myself, by the way.

Meanwhile, back in the UK, a Manchester club called the Haçienda soon saw the city redubbed as 'Madchester' when a whole incredible scene—a combination of high energy live music acts, forward-thinking DJs, ecstasy, improbable business scenarios, risk-taking, rave mentality and a great venue—all came together there under one roof. Tony Wilson, the club's impresario, was a trailblazing and idiosyncratic character. He'd signed the local band Joy Division to his Factory Records label in the late 1970s (the contract was allegedly 'written' by him on a napkin, in his own blood). Following the tragic early suicide of lead singer, Ian Curtis, the band went on to become New Order, to create the record-breaking dance music single 'Blue Monday', and to watch the royalties made from the single being pumped back into the label (and the club's funds), effectively making New Order the financiers of the Madchester scene.

The biggest band to come out of this combination of unorthodox enterprise and cultural energy was probably Happy Mondays. First formed by brothers Paul and Shaun Ryder in 1980, the Mondays were later joined by dancer/maracas player Mark 'Bez' Berry onstage at the Haçienda, and other gigs. His 'freaky dancing' (also the title of his recent memoir) came to emblematise the moves of an entire generation of acid house groovers, and his name gave him a much seized-upon connection with Ibiza's god of dance. After the success of their first two albums, *Squirrel & G-Man Twenty Four Hour Party People Plastic Face Carnt Smile (White Out)*, which was produced by John Cale, and *Bummed*, produced by the mad genius Martin Hannett, Paul Oakenfold was called in to produce the Mondays' third studio album, *Pills 'n' Thrills And Bellyaches*. This featured the spellbinding Balearic anthem 'Step On', with its famous cry of '*You're twistin' my melon, man.*' Oakenfold and Andrew Weatherall's remix of the Mondays track 'Hallelujah' is also one of the most cherished dance floor tracks of the period.

Meanwhile, New Order themselves had long become aware of the Balearic vibe. The summery sound on their 1989 album *Technique* reflects the fact that the band spent four months in Ibiza while making it. It was partly recorded at the island's Mediterranean Studios.

The Haçienda's success is also attributable to DJ Mike Pickering,

SHADOWS ACROSS THE MOON **179**

who had told Tony Wilson that he didn't believe they needed to have live music in order to fill the enormous former warehouse's dance floor. Pickering himself had signed Happy Mondays to Wilson's Factory Records, and he had also started regularly DJing house music nights at the club. These nights represented some of the most famous club rave events of the entire era of British acid house, and certainly contributed to some key 'Madchester' moments. Pickering's name has long been associated with some of the major British acts to have established a reputation over time in Ibiza. He signed Calvin Harris to his own Deconstruction record label, on which he'd released Sasha's spellbinding 'Xpander' in 1999.

Sasha performed 'Xpander' during a mesmerising 2010 show on the medieval ramparts of Dalt Vila, at the end of that year's International Music Summit. Pickering had flown over to appear as one of the keynote interview guests at the IMS panel, and to witness Sasha's show. 'It's so lovely being here,' he said on the night of the Dalt Vila event. 'I've seen so many people from the past twenty-five years of my life. But one night in Ibiza is sometimes enough. If I can make the dash after one night, I'm good. Otherwise I just get dragged along to all the parties, like some naughty schoolboy.'

Sasha, born Alexander Coe in Wales, made his name at Shelley's, a nightclub in the city of Stoke in the north Midlands, with his techno and house sets. He is one of the earliest UK names outside of London to be associated with the new rave music scene that was taking over the spirit of parties in underground clubs all over the country. The first ever DJ to feature on a national magazine cover, Sasha remixed Madonna's 'Ray Of Light' and was a huge influence both on his peers and on the next generation of DJs who came up after him. Pete Gooding, long-time resident DJ at Café Mambo in Sant Antoni, is one such example.

Gooding later went on tour with Sasha and his sometime musical partner John Digweed, but had first come to Ibiza in the heady era of Alfredo's reign at Amnesia.

I was going to Ibiza with my mum and dad for our summer holidays. 1987 was the first time I went there, when I was 14. I think I got no further than the hotel disco, but actually there were two records I really liked from that night, so I got my mum to take me to the record shop in Sant Antoni. Looking back now, I didn't realise how credible I was being, without meaning to, because one was Sven Väth's first record, 'Electric Salsa' [recorded when he was with his first band, Off]. When we went back two years later, in 1989, my sister took me to Amnesia and Es Paradis Terrenal, and she put LSD in my mouth. Then I heard Lil Louis's 'French Kiss' and that was it, I wanted to be a DJ.

My impressions were that those clubs were very weird, yet wonderful. I mean, I hadn't been to any nightclubs at that point in my life, so that was actually my first time inside one. It was a strange mix of very good-looking Europeans, who were far cooler than me, and this exotic sounding music. I was familiar with house music, because my sister, who was older, was into it. I had albums like *The House Sound Of Chicago*, but this was a real mixture. You'd have 808 State's 'Pacific State', A Guy Called Gerald's 'Voodoo Ray', but then you'd have those exotic and unusual records, which I know the names of now, things like Elkin and Nelson's 'Jibaro', and the more down-tempo Balearic stuff that you'd never have expected to hear in a club. Actually hearing those played in a club was the highlight of the night. Overall it was a very exotic experience. When I got home to the UK, I bought my first set of decks. Then my sister started taking me to a lot of the early raves. We went every week to hear Sasha play at Shelley's. When I heard Sasha I was like, 'Oh my god!' This was another level. He *really* made me want to be a DJ. He was so much better than everyone else on the scene.

Kevin Sampson, the Merseyside author of novels such as *Awaydays*, *Powder* and *Clubland*, had worked with band The Farm, who featured heavily in the cult 1990 documentary that he produced called *Ibiza—A Short Film About Chilling*. The film beautifully captures the spirit of Ibiza at the time, and includes footage of wistful Sant Antoni sunsets, as well as evenings at Café del Mar and Ku. Sampson's recent novel, *The House On The Hill*, is partly set in Ibiza.

His partner, fellow Merseyside writer Helen Walsh, set her controversial breakthrough first novel, *Brass*, in Warrington, during the heady days of rave. She was a teenager during the acid house days, and immortalised Warrington's Legends club in an article she wrote for the *Observer*, looking back on the death of acid house.

> The sight of five hundred people, dancing, hugging and grinning—living the night as though it were their last, was simply mind-blowing. I'd fantasised about getting into Legends for so long that the reality just blew me away. I remember walking into the girls' toilets and seeing half a dozen lads with elastic smiles and hard-ons straining through the fabric of their shorts. They were sitting in sinks of cold water, massaging each other with ice cubes. The air was thick with eucalyptus and protestations of undying love, and at last I was a part of it. I was thirteen.

Other UK northern towns were catching on, too. Geoff Oakes launched the club night Renaissance, decorated with gold cherubs and velvet drapes, in Mansfield, in 1991. Back To Basics was born in Leeds, also in 1991, and is still one of Europe's longest-running club nights. A brilliantly energetic and punk-infused DIY underground reaction to the smiley-faced rave scene which had by then become mainstream, the club owes its ethos to its founders, Dave Beer and Ali Cooke. One-time roadie for The Ramones and Sisters Of Mercy, Beer still runs Basics today, and is frequently up against last-minute changes of venue and other bureaucratic hitches, which he somehow always manages to solve. Beer's passport allegedly used to list his occupation as 'Purveyor of good times', and with Basics he and Cooke always promised to take things 'two steps further than any other fucker'. Tragically, Ali Cooke was killed in a car crash in 1993, which Beer himself survived. As a result, Beer promised to keep the club night going for as far into the future as he could, in Cooke's memory. He has toured Basics nights all over the world, but remains faithful to Leeds. ('How can I turn my back on the place that's served me so well? A place with two Es and LSD in its name?' he commented in 2014.)

Carl Cox jumped head first into the scene, seduced by Chicago house music, and eventually moving on to the heart of British outdoor rave culture:

> As soon as I heard 'Time to Jack' by Chip E., which came out of Chicago, I was right on it. Every single house record that ever came out, right from the beginning, whether I liked it or not, I just bought anyway. When Danny Rampling booked me for Shoom, I was playing house music, and then, when the rave scene really started to kick off in warehouses, and eventually progressed to the fields, my name was always there on the agenda: Sunrise, Energy, Biology, Fantasia, I became synonymous with all of those parties. When I was living in Brighton I used to sell tickets for raves, and I believed in that scene wholeheartedly. A lot of people thought I'd freaked out, but I knew *exactly* where I was going. When that music came along, it was only a matter of time before people jumped over from the hip-hop scene into something which was fresh, exciting and new. As it still is today.

The outdoor rave scene was soon sending out signals all over the UK, although the majority of the more well-remembered events took place in the countryside, and many of the London-area ones were only accessible via the newly opened M25 orbital motorway encircling the outer limits of the city (after which 1990s band Orbital took its name). Due to their illegal nature, the parties' locations would often only be confirmed at the last minute. Ravers circling around on the M25 would have to keep driving until the moment came to call a certain phone number, and the party's location could finally be disclosed.

The British prime minister at the time, Margaret Thatcher, comes into the picture in ways she probably never anticipated at this point. One of Thatcher's biggest campaigns revolved around the financial encouragement of DIY entrepreneurship in the UK, opening up all sorts of loan opportunities, promoting meritocracy in the workplace, and encouraging previously low-income workers to start up new businesses. In some ways, the rave scene took full advantage of this new design for living. Gangland was also quick to move in, on its own terms. The period saw outbreaks of 'entrepreneurial' actions such as lorry-jacking (stopping trucks coming into the eastern UK Essex ports, which contained massive consignments of ecstasy from Amsterdam, often unbeknownst to the driver), the distribution of the party drugs, and behind-the-scenes infiltration of some of the better-organised raves. In documentaries covering this period, Thatcher is often given semi-drooling vocal support by renowned 'businessmen' involved in the organisation and 'security' at outdoor raves.

The competitive social aspiration promoted by Thatcher's government during the 1980s meant that, for the first time, class barriers were broken down, at least in terms of a new breed of young people from low- to middle-income families who were now making it into jobs in places such as London's Stock Exchange (which had previously been the exclusive reserve of former public school boys). A character called 'Loadsamoney', who wandered around with pockets stuffed full of cash, bragging about his earnings, was even created by the comedian Harry Enfield. Capitalising on the newly available means for self-starting businesses, the 'Loadsamoneys' would find themselves weighed down with ready banknotes, and looking to party hard, preferably all night, during their well-earned weekends off from their high-earning financial sector jobs.

The rave scene seamlessly merged this crowd with other young people from a wide variety of backgrounds, for the first time since the 1960s. Security for the raves was often provided by gangland, in order to prevent the theft of the huge amounts of entrance money sitting around in bin liners. The drugs coming in from the coast further boosted the cash count. So even the more hippie-minded of the rave organisers found that they sometimes had no choice but to effectively bring back the protection racket, in order to keep their parties and the money safe. Ken Tappenden was the UK National Co-ordinator of Intelligence and Operations for 'acid/rave' parties who the government sent in to clamp down on these illegal outdoor events. However, Tappenden was deeply impressed with the challenge he was up against. Organisers would constantly outmanoeuvre his forces; they would do things like print flyers for fake parties to send the police off in one direction, only to actually stage their party somewhere else, miles away. Time and again they always seemed to be a few steps ahead of the powers that be.

Raves continued on all throughout the 1990s. Never had British man been so publicly emotional in a party setting. On the whole, alcohol was replaced with a new range of 'energy drinks', and ecstasy-enhanced ravers would greet the sunrise with tears of joy. The timeless beauty of the English countryside, with its wistful dawn mists, provided the perfect emotional backdrop to the climax of the events.

'The real rave scene was all about not being inside clubs,' says Carl Cox.

It was about being in amazing unusual venues or in the open air. We'd never really had open-air venues that were catering for this type of music. If you had an open-air venue it would be rock or pop, or something like the *Radio 1 Roadshow*, which was all very nice and clean for the family. But we'd go to Oxford, say, to a field in the middle of god knows where, and put 100k worth of turbine sound in, and lasers and lights. People would have to call a certain phone number on the night to find out the location, and get themselves down there. It would be just one of the most amazing things you'd ever been involved in. You knew there was a certain circuit of DJs who'd be booked for these events, and if you liked that music you'd go. But it was the buzz of not knowing what was gonna happen: was it going to get busted, was it going to get raided by the police or continue to go on into the early hours of the morning when the sun came up and you'd still be there, kicking up dust, listening to Guru Josh or Candy Flip? It was just phenomenal. The whole thing was like a breath of fresh air, even though the Haçienda, and Shelley's, and all those clubs were really amazing. I used to do at least two to three raves a night every week for ten years, and that's how my name got synonymous with the scene.

After his successful club night, The Trip, Nicky Holloway opened the Milk Bar in Central London in 1990, inviting acts like Brand New Heavies and Jamiroquai (who both got signed after their appearances there) and hosting parties featuring Paul Oakenfold, Pete Tong and Darren Emerson. That same year, Emerson became the third member in the revolutionary UK alternative dance band Underworld, taking them into an era which produced preeminent albums such as *dubnobasswithmyheadman*, *Second Toughest in the Infants* and *Beaucoup Fish*, and their single 'Born Slippy', which featured on the soundtrack to Danny Boyle's film *Trainspotting* (1996) and contained high-spirited vocalist Karl Hyde's memorable refrain, '*Shouting lager lager lager lager …* '

Despite the British predominance in a scene that was now starting to spread overseas, Ibiza remained the mother ship to which all the big names associated with the UK rave era kept returning, and commanding higher and higher fees for their club appearances there. In 1991, the Catalan entrepreneur Martín Ferrer took over Amnesia, and the club gradually expanded to include sixteen bars. As with Privilege, new roofs were added after complaints of noise were lodged by local residents. Ferrer also brought in from Barcelona the multi-talented light technician Zeles, whose contribution to Amnesia's club nights cannot be overstated. Alfredo had moved on to Pacha, after several years at Amnesia, during which he had become something of a superstar himself, thanks to the work of the British media, as well as the DJs who had taken so much influence from his parties.

'To tell you the truth, they took the music from me, and they put this name, Balearic, on it, making it into a genre,' he says now. With his newfound accidental hero status he celebrated—and was celebrated— to excess. 'My ego got too big', he says, and, now dealing with various personal and family issues of his own, he was sacked from Amnesia over the winter of 1989. His Ibicenco right-hand man connected him with the owners of Pacha, who came over to London to see him play in Holloway's Milk Bar, and offered him a highly paid residency back on the island. He started at Pacha the following season, bringing in a huge crowd of English followers. For sentimental reasons, he studiously avoided the road to Amnesia when he drove across the island to Pacha, from his home near Santa Gertrudis. Nicky Holloway was asked to set up a Milk Bar at Pacha. When Adamski played at Privilege, Alfredo invited him to come and do a second set at Pacha, which he did, but when Adamski hit the first note of his set, he blew half the system. Nonetheless, Alfredo claims, that was the night they broke not just the sound system but also the supremacy of Amnesia.

Meanwhile, back in England, Paul Oakenfold became a resident at the newly opened Ministry of Sound club that had been set up in a disused bus garage in London, before moving on to Cream, the Liverpool club night set up in 1994 by Joseph Mullen, James Barton, Darren Hughes and Andy Carroll. Cream would soon establish itself as Ibiza's biggest trance event, taking Oakenfold to Amnesia when it did. Oakenfold and Sasha were two of the first 'superstar DJs'. At first earning around £500 a night, within a few years their fees were in five figures, with Sasha earning the nickname 'DJ Rich Bastard', as he flew around the world exporting his musical message to his new global followers.

The UK Criminal Justice and Public Order Act of 1994 had also just been imposed. This was a huge blow for the UK rave scene. While the act covered a wide range of impositions on civil liberties, one part of it, its specifically detailed provision titled 'Powers to remove persons attending or preparing for a rave', seemed designed to close down the whole scene. Once raves were being more carefully monitored, the era of the huge outdoor illegal party began to fade into memory.

According to Youth, 'The acid house thing died down pretty quickly in England, and by the mid-1990s it was on its way out. The big raves were already being shut down. I had been working with Spiral Tribe, who were doing the free festivals. Really what I found was many of the heads from the acid house scene in London and Ibiza were all very quickly disillusioned, and so a lot of them went to India, where of course there was this long connection of freaks living in Goa in the winter, and in Ibiza in the summer.'

By now, the DJs who had already made their names at outdoor raves or club nights were moving on to bigger things elsewhere. Paul Oakenfold was soon creating soundtracks for Hollywood epics such as *The Matrix Reloaded* and *The Bourne Identity*. In Ibiza, nights like

Judge Jules's Judgement Sundays at Eden (now Gatecrasher), We Love at Space and Ministry of Sound at Pacha came to enjoy longstanding relationships with the island, and these came out of that wide international acceptance of the UK scene.

•●•

Before people headed off for these club nights, mid-evening activity would be in the bars around Ibiza harbour. One quirky British pre-party bar, Bar Zuka, was, for some years, a favourite command post of clubbers, DJs and locals including Roger Taylor of Queen and Mike Oldfield. The bar was set up by DJ Nancy Noise, and co-managed by the extrovert and well-connected Mark Hatley with, for a few memorable years, his partner Hazel Lord. Positioned by the medieval walls of Dalt Vila, in Calle de la Vírgen, the passageway otherwise entirely famous for gay bars, Bar Zuka was small and inviting, and decorated with a chandelier, candles, graffiti, paintings and an old piano in an old building with a tiny balcony which overlooked the port. Local DJ Graham Sahara was resident there for a while. On Millennium New Year's Eve, Hatley threw a party in the bar, and accidentally blew up the speakers he had placed out on the passageway. Zuka was a bar that was well loved by locals, who would congregate there all during the summer season, alongside some of the British DJs who had now achieved almost mythological stature.

This new era of the expensive superstar DJ soon led to clubs or club nights becoming pushed as brands. Big money took over with the rise in DJs fees, and drugs became a vital element in this cash nexus. In a few years the omnipresence of ecstasy gave way to cocaine, which was making its way into the scene in a big way. Cocaine was the Molotov cocktail that exploded in clubland. Alongside it, high-priced champagne was quickly added to bar menus, and costly VIP areas were creeping in.

Door prices went up. Two-tier clubbing came in. And in this era, the consumption of drugs became not only more prodigious but, as with the rock and fashion worlds, more flagrant than it had been since the 1970s. People now seemed to live to party and take illegal drugs. Nicky Holloway, like so many others from the scene, would go on to have a rather public battle with cocaine and booze. 'Were DJs less effective on coke? Yes,' says Kris Needs, who DJed all over the UK and in Ibiza in the 1990s. 'And in about 1994–95 some of the music got really harsh as a result, and it continued to do so throughout the decade.'

While many clubbers continued as ever on low budgets, with dance and a good time with friends in their hearts, clubland also became for others an exercise in grandstanding. Binge drinking took over in the 1990s too, and continued through to the next decade, and beyond. 'Clubbing is very hedonistic now,' says Tina Cutler, who lived through the changes she perceives destroyed the great vibes in clubland,

It's all about drugs and alcohol and getting absolutely off your trolley, and the drugs have got very strange, like ketamine. Clubbing in Ibiza wasn't about that before. It was about meeting people, and having a 'heart' connection. I used to dance for eight hours solid. I used to be so fit after a summer in Ibiza. I began to find clubs horribly aggressive. Everyone was turning into monsters, and they were taking too many drugs and you couldn't communicate with anyone. There was just this great cut off. It got to be like *Groundhog Day*. People just doing the same thing again and again and again, and with nothing ever really standing out that much. It started to all merge into the same thing.

'There was still an underground scene back then though, and still is,' continues Kris Needs. 'There was definitely an original element that came out of Chicago and Detroit and other places. Most of those DJs weren't careerists. But as the 1990s went on, mainstream DJs were getting ten grand to put their name on a six-minute remix that some engineer actually did for them. It was conveyor belt stuff. The soul was disappearing. It was big business.'

Tourism on the island had also gone up, from 350 thousand in 1970, to 1.5 million by 1990, and some estimates put the current figure at around six million (the resident population, for which precise figures are very difficult to ascertain for a variety of reasons, is placed at less than 150,000). The British acid-house scene was seen as responsible for some of these numbers, and Amnesia became the club of choice for many British holidaymakers during the late 1980s and through the 1990s. Even after Alfredo had moved over to Pacha, where they would go to see him perform too, their loyalty to Amnesia continued, thanks in particular to the Cream events.

Cream has had a regular Amnesia slot on Thursday nights since 1996. Sasha, Paul van Dyk and Paul Oakenfold are among the top names to have made the party as successful as it is, and it is now the longest standing club night in Ibiza. The famous Amnesia sound systems have seen both Cream and the club itself win several prestigious awards. Amnesia's Main Room and Terrace have afforded this trance and house party a great opportunity to show off the high tech acts that make up its summer roster. During the Cream summer season, the Main Room is a showcase for some of the biggest names in the electronic trance scene worldwide.

Another British night to have made waves in Ibiza was Pete Tong's Wonderland, first launched at Sant Antoni's Eden (now Gatecrasher), in 2008. The venue, originally called the Star Club and later Kaos, was acquired by Salvador and Paquita Salinero in 1998, when it was completely refurbished and renamed Eden. Within a few years it was pulling in large crowds. Café del Mar, Café Mambo and other Sant

Antoni institutions such as the club Es Paradis Terrenal had factored into a lot of the life-changing experiences clubbers in the late 1980s and early 1990s had had. But by the time Tong arrived with Wonderland Sant Antoni was suffering from the bad reputation that rowdy British holidaymakers had brought down on the area. Tong had been performing at Pacha (which was seen as more 'high end' at this point in time) for several seasons. He was also the UK's most influential dance music radio DJ, so the news of him moving to a Sant Antoni club came as a surprise to many.

'It's funny how powerful one's prejudices are,' he told me the year Wonderland opened.

> You find yourself quite ignorant half the time as to why you're making those decisions. I mean when I was offered Eden—and that is how this came about, as initially I would never have chosen it—my reaction was, 'Oh no, anywhere but there!' But then I analysed what I was thinking, and I'd never even been there! Because of what everyone thinks about Sant Antoni, you get carried along by a very powerful current. Then you start to break it down and think about what you could achieve. Sant Antoni has such a strong history with the clubbing scene, and it is this funnel that a lot of our elite clubbers came through at the beginning of their relationships with Ibiza. So, instead of putting the 'cream' at the end of the journey, at Pacha, I wanted to try and put some here at the front.

After a couple of successful seasons, however, Pete Tong returned to Pacha in 2011.

Today Eden, in its current incarnation as Gatecrasher, still attracts mainly British tourists from within the resort of Sant Antoni. While past owners include the Basque Javier Anadón, who owns Café Mambo, the club was recently acquired by the Dutch businessman, Michael van de Kuit, for twelve million euros. He renamed it Gatecrasher, after a joint ten-year deal was concluded with UK promoter Simon Raine's Gatecrasher events of the same name. However, by all accounts, things didn't go too well over the summer 2014 season, and a fight has since broken out between Raine and van de Kuit. British DJ and entertainment lawyer Judge Jules's Judgement Sundays had, since the 1990s, made Eden the busiest of the Sant Antoni clubs. Eventually moving to Friday nights, Jules's night finally slid across the way to Es Paradis Terrenal in 2014, hooking up with the Fiesta del Agua party.

Es Paradis Terrenal, a large one-roomed club next door to Gatecrasher, had originally gained a reputation for drawing a more European than British crowd, particularly Germans and Scandinavians. First opened in August 1975 by the Catalan Pepe Aguirre, the decor of the club was supplied by artist Lluís Güell, who also did the decor for Café del Mar. The centrepiece of the pyramid-shaped Es Paradis was a huge working fountain, which would always be put on at the end of the night, soaking the crowd. That tradition continues in a different format today with the weekly Fiesta del Agua parties, during which the custom-built dance floor is turned into a shallow pool. White decor, Roman columns, and enormous plants have always made Es Paradis one of the most beautiful clubbing spots on the island. José Padilla built his reputation as a DJ here with the all-nighter sessions he played at the club from 1979 to 1982. His dance floor favourites would include music from Ultravox, Supertramp, the Salsoul Orchestra, Pink Floyd and Chic. Later, a weekly slot for British promoters, Clockwork Orange, was set up, with DJs Jeremy Healy, Brandon Block and Alex P bringing in a very mixed crowd by the late 1990s. Owner Pepe Aguirre's daughter, Marisol, who runs the club, is the most prominent woman in Ibiza's clubland.

Hed Kandi and the Ibiza Rocks gigs after-party make up the regular nights there today, along with the new night from DJ Moniz, So Funked. Moniz:

> One of my good friends is Steve Valverde, aka DJ MDK, who has been an Es Paradis resident for many years. He's such a big part of that club and we've always had a good relationship, and he wanted us to do something together, and he's now my business partner there. As he lives on the island, he did all the legwork to set up our So Funked night, and we also do a weekly boat party. Es Paradis have a massive promotional machine, and they bring in a crowd who are really switched on to R&B, but it's a very international one on our nights. It's such a relaxed place, you just feel so comfortable walking in there; it's glamorous, all the trees and plants make you feel so good, and of course they still have the famous fountain.

It is foam, rather than water, that has been the character behind Amnesia's Espuma party nights, a longstanding Ibiza event that sees the main room flooded with soapsuds. In 2013, club owner Martín Ferrer invited Paris Hilton to set up a Foam and Diamonds party there. She accepted. Ferrer is building a new Amnesia club in the port of Barcelona, and he has asked the heiress to be involved in launching it. Other nights which now make up Amnesia's popular summer calendar include Marco Carola's hugely popular Music On house and techno parties; Matinée, which moved over from Space; Cream; and Cocoon, the techno night that snuck in quietly in 1999, and was to be become one of the most electrifying and widely venerated nights that Ibiza clubland has ever experienced …

# CHAPTER EIGHT
# I FEEL LOVE: THE SOUND OF THE FUTURE • DETROIT'S TECHNO UNDERGROUND

A NEW URBAN-INSPIRED MANIFESTO • PLASTIKMAN,
THE ELECTRIFYING MOJO, THE BELLEVILLE THREE
AND UNDERGROUND RESISTANCE • SVEN VÄTH:
CLUBLAND GODHEAD AND IBIZA HIPPIE • THE
LANDING OF COCOON • TECHNO CONTORTIONISM •
EPIC COCOON AFTER-PARTIES • LUCIANO AND
DUBFIRE • CIRCO LOCO'S RENEGADE DJ LAUNCHPAD
• ENTER. AND THE FUTURE

*'The techno rebels are, whether they recognize it or not, agents of the Third Wave. They will not vanish but multiply in the years ahead. For they are a critical part of the advance to a new stage of civilization.'* **ALVIN TOFFLER, THE THIRD WAVE (1980)**

Alfredo's Amnesia parties had radiated overseas to influence UK outdoor rave parties, and later festivals, which were usually celebrated in the serenity of the countryside. But blowing in from 'Motor City' Detroit, as well as from German cities such as Berlin and Frankfurt, were the winds of the next great era of Ibiza clubland: the age of techno. DJs such as Sven Väth and Richie Hawtin are two of the most prominent names in this scene on the island in recent years. The roots of the events they have put on, Cocoon at Amnesia and ENTER. at Space, respectively, are in music that was being made in industrial landscapes in the 1970s and 80s.

When Giorgio Moroder and Pete Bellotte put together 'I Feel Love' for Donna Summer's 1977 journey-across-time concept album, *I Remember Yesterday*, their intention was to create something that sounded like tomorrow. Moroder recorded the entirely synthesised backing track and pulsating bass first, before layering Summer's free-falling vocals on top. For the first time, here was a voice way beyond trying to prove she was rock'n'roll hell-bent on emotional freedom. She sounded like she'd already long crossed the line to joy and transcendence. 'I have heard the sound of the future,' cried Brian Eno to David Bowie, with whom he was then working in Berlin. 'This is it, look no further.' 'I Feel Love''s new and highly driven escapist, timeless sound, which felt like it combined ecstasy with science fiction, took dance music into a new age.

In 1976, Bowie had created his album *Station To Station*, whose icily detached title track, his longest ever studio recording, used *motorik* rhythms inspired by German bands Neu! and Kraftwerk. By 1977, he had recorded his next album, *Heroes*, whose title track was composed with Eno. Along with Kraftwerk's 'Trans-Europe Express', made in Düsseldorf, and 'I Feel Love', which was done in Munich, 'Heroes' was one of the defining tracks of the new European sound that was coming out of Germany. Unusually, 'Heroes' was recorded in English, in German as 'Helden', and in French as 'Héros'.

German music had already been changing, through the experimental music of Cluster, Tangerine Dream, Neu!, Faust, Can, Ash Ra Tempel, Kraftwerk and others. Electronic music was beginning to replace traditional blues and rock in both gigs and recordings. The urban, bleakly industrial post-WWII landscapes of Germany, and the feelings of isolation and social segregation that came about with the era of the Berlin Wall were the inspirations behind a lot of this music. In the case of Kraftwerk, a semi-ironic utopian vision of a return to Germany's status as a nation of progress, and comfortable modern living, played heavily into their meticulously constructed albums.

Their 1975 track 'Autobahn' translated the beautiful simplicity of the German motorways, and 'Trans-Europe Express' the trains that connected cities across Europe. 'Europe Endless', from the *Trans-Europe Express* album, spoke of the continent's timelessly elegant and decadent landscapes, while their 1975 track 'Radioactivity', with its slogan-esque warnings about the dangers of nuclear power plants, name-checked the city of Chernobyl (the very first word in the song), which is eerie considering that for the techno generation it was to become the site of the biggest nuclear disaster in living history, some eleven years later. Kraftwerk would also use custom-built vocoders to give a cybernetic sound to their simple, 'advertising copy'-style lyrics.

When Derrick May described the music he and his friends Juan Atkins and Kevin Saunderson were later creating in Detroit as 'George Clinton and Kraftwerk caught in an elevator, with only a sequencer to keep them company', he was helping to define what can be seen as the next step in the development of the techno music revolution. 'Oh yeah! I can dig that,' Clinton responded, when I asked him how he felt about that now-famous quote.

> You know, when Kraftwerk first came out it was a surprise to hear them played in the US, because we didn't know what that music was. But then later on I worked with Thomas Dolby, and I got a pretty good education in what was going to be happening in music, what the future was. That was the beginning of techno. We could see then that the whole thing of computerised electronic music was the new future. We'd even heard about it by the late 1960s and early 70s—that synthesisers were going to be taking over. With Thomas Dolby, we'd be working with the Mirage synthesiser, and it was when I got with him that I saw exactly what was meant, and he knew how to do all the right sounds for that music. So when they say Kraftwerk and Funkadelic getting together, well yeah, it works.

The city of Detroit, with its huge automotive industry and its rundown buildings served as the urban backdrop for May, Atkins and Saunderson, who came to be known as The Belleville Three, after their local suburb. When May got thrown out of school and moved in with Atkins, the two would stay awake late at night listening to the sounds of pioneering local DJ Charles Johnson, aka The Electrifying Mojo, trying to work out how Bowie and Kraftwerk made their elaborate music. The show would start with the sounds of a mothership being landed, to the music from the film *Close Encounters Of The Third Kind*, before launching into a playlist of tunes which might include Kraftwerk, Yellow Magic Orchestra, Funkadelic, Philip Glass and Afrika Bambaataa. Mojo was considered so influential that even Prince granted him an interview during the mid-1980s, at a time when he was refusing to speak to almost any journalist anywhere.

When Juan Atkins cut his first single, 'Alleys Of Your Mind', in 1981, May stalked Mojo for weeks, before eventually catching up with him and giving him the single, which the DJ then played on his show, effectively launching the Detroit techno scene. Juan Atkins started throwing parties, promoted by local high school kids, in small clubs in the city. He'd allow May, who carried his equipment, to play for fifteen minutes, and pay him twenty bucks a session. May and Atkins would also drive to Chicago every weekend, where the house music scene had taken off, and sell the records they'd started to create. At the time, house music DJs and producers such as Frankie Knuckles, Ron Hardy, Fast Eddie, Farley 'Jackmaster' Funk, Marshall Jefferson and Joe Smooth had taken disco, via the use of new electronic equipment such as synthesisers and drum machines, onto the next level of dance music in Chicago. The sound was soon reaching dance floors in other urban centres such as Detroit and New York.

Derrick May's 'Strings Of Life' is a wistful love song to the three-hundred-year-old port city of Detroit. It was his soundtrack to the sadness of a place that was at the time still caught up in the spectre of its past. The riot of 1967 had seen the city besieged by the National Guard and Lyndon Johnson's troops. Two thousand buildings were destroyed, with a death toll of forty-three and thousands injured. The incident also inspired songs such as local band the MC5's 'Motor City Is Burning' and Bowie's 'Panic In Detroit'.

In the late 80s, times in Detroit were still hard when DJ Jeff Mills and 'Mad' Mike Banks founded Detroit's Underground Resistance record label (often abbreviated to UR) as part of a movement that was to carry the new Detroit techno sound being pioneered by the Belleville Three and others into a more political realm. Underground Resistance's militant dress (which included gas masks) and anti-commercial approach to business was combined with an agenda to increase political awareness in the poorer African American communities that surrounded them. They too were greatly inspired by The Electrifying Mojo who, during his shows, would call for ten-minute gangland truces in the city, and play tracks during which gang members were urged to put aside their differences and get into the music.

Mojo's criticism of commercial radio shows and the kind of mainstream music that was being fed to US citizens, as well as his call to an awakening with regard to the problems in gangland, further inspired Underground Resistance to carry on his message. Detroit techno was a unifying experiment with tones that could be related to on a primal level. Sometimes called Hi Tek Soul, by May, because of the intention to bring a soul vibe into the music, it was seen as a universal language whose deep beats were meant to contain the keys to the universe, taking humans forward, beyond their differences. 'Beyond The Dance', May's 1989 track, recorded as 'Rhythim Is Rhythim', on Transmat, the record label he founded in 1986, was devised as a message to convey this unifying sentiment.

Juan Atkins first used the word techno, inspired by Alvin Toffler's 1980 book *The Third Wave*, which had coined the term 'techno-rebels'. Other names to have come out of the scene include Stacey Pullen, Kenny Larkin, and Detroit 'techno ambassador' and Ibiza favourite, Carl Craig. Initially, the Detroit techno scene merged the musical influences that Mojo had been introducing the city to. UR's Jeff Mills was also guesting as 'The Wizard' on Mojo's show, and his contributions became just as influential. Eminem, the Detroit rapper who starred in *8 Mile* (2002), the hip-hop film set in the city, name-checked 'The Wizard' in his song 'Groundhog Day'. 'Detroit techno has been important to all of us,' says DJ Luciano, 'it's where our music originated. It's still very relevant to me. The tracks on my label Basaec were inspired by the Detroit sounds. You can hear a lot of that influence in them.'

'We were really trying to create a soundtrack to this future that was just at our fingertips,' says Richie Hawtin, who grew up in nearby Windsor, Ontario, and got involved in the neighbouring Detroit scene as a teenager.

Not the far, far future, just a more modernised future, connected and created or sustained by mechanics and technology. That really came from the atmosphere of growing up in or around the Motor City. Detroit was always a city on the edge of tomorrow, always poised to become the next big centre point of North America, which the car industry never really grasped. We'd spend a lot of time driving through Detroit, or doing events in incredibly landmark warehouses, like the one where the 'Model T' automobile had been created, the Packard automotive factory. We were re-appropriating these spaces to make use of them for music events and parties, so in a way it was a land of optimistic opportunity for us. The city had seen so much upheaval, especially in the 1960s and 70s, but somehow, in this ever-decaying city, there was always an incredible spirit of looking towards tomorrow, towards a brighter future. I think that's what you hear in the mechanics and entanglement of music and technology that came up in those first Detroit records.

'Techno is an approach,' adds DJ Dubfire, whose seamless, futuristic deep house sets have provided Cocoon with pitch-dark, controlled landscapes of sound that add a stark, chromatic edge to his music. 'It's a means of exploring a type of creativity that is driven by the desire to achieve something sonically challenging, or radical, not only to oneself, but to the listener. Techno inspires, influences and sets the bar. Techno can be a wall of gritty sound, it can resonate with emotional melody, or it can be utterly minimalistic. It is the way forward.'

For Hawtin, who studied film, elements of science fiction and cinema came to be integrated into the music he made, and the shows he put on.

I was going into special effects and cinematography, and I was very much interested in film when I was a teenager. Many of my early tracks were inspired by sci-fi films or just the idea that there was some kind of cinematic approach to music. Most of my albums are recorded in a way that there's more of a storytelling. There's very little space between tracks. Each piece moulds itself into the next. I was trying to create a tapestry, to create an alternative reality that people step into, and listen to for seventy or eighty minutes. I think all of that is also found in the events that I produce. From the early days in Detroit doing warehouse parties, up to what we're doing now with ENTER. at Space, it was always about changing the location, modifying the environment and trying to make the experience as immersive as possible. That experience was always based upon music, but I felt very strongly and from very early on that if you played with the environment, and the structure of the rooms, you could take people on a deeper experience.

Hawtin, known in the early Detroit days as Richie Rich, created albums and shows as Plastikman, using 808 and 909 drum machines on tracks such as 'Spastik' in 1993. He would cover the inside walls of the club spaces he performed in with black plastic. Also influenced by bands he admired such as Skinny Puppy, Nitzer Ebb, Front 242, Kraftwerk and Tangerine Dream, Hawtin was an introverted kid who enjoyed the quiet status DJing afforded him, being the centre of attention without having to sing or play a guitar. With his friend John Acquaviva, he set up the Plus 8 record label from their studio in Canada, and signed artists such as Speedy J from Rotterdam, and Detroit's Kenny Larkin, as well as issuing Plastikman releases and other side projects by Hawtin and Acquaviva themselves.

Claiming to be 'the future sound of Detroit', Plus 8 ruffled a few feathers, since Hawtin and Acquaviva were a self-proclaimed unit of 'two white kids from Canada', while Transmat (Derrick May's label) and Metroplex (Juan Atkins's label) were coming from the heart of Detroit, and had got there first. Over time, Plus 8 has come to be seen as one of the most revolutionary record labels on the global techno scene. Hawtin's pioneering early work as Plastikman was hugely influential in party zones such as Berlin and Ibiza. And also in Frankfurt, where the musician, DJ and producer Sven Väth had opened the popular Omen club.

Cocoon is an Ibiza party, a one-time Frankfurt-based club, a booking agency and a record label all headed up by veteran techno exemplar Väth. The Ibiza nights have routinely showcased the talents of many of the established techno giants, including Richie Hawtin, Luciano, Dubfire, Ricardo Villalobos and, most prominently, Väth himself, since 1999.

The name Cocoon was inspired by a show Väth had witnessed, staged in Berlin by Catalan theatre group La Fura dels Baus in 1994, in which they suspended water-filled cocoons from the ceilings, representing metamorphosis. He was struck by the image, and felt it represented what he was trying to create with his newly evolving techno night.

When Cocoon arrived in Ibiza in 1999, it was allocated the unpromising Monday night slot at Amnesia, which, up until then, had been the only night the club remained closed. In the face of this inauspicious beginning however, Cocoon went on to entirely defy expectations. At the time, the only really big Monday-night club event on the island was the Manumission party at Privilege. Cocoon started attracting a different kind of crowd, a gathering of young European techno and deep house fans, and a lot of DJs. Väth would play new tracks like Rolando's 'Knights Of The Jaguar' (recorded on the Underground Resistance label) and Wassermann's 'W.I.R.', as well as releases from his own Eye Q and Harthouse record labels.

Following a short four-week experimental season in 1999, Cocoon came back for a complete summer season in 2000, and has continued, ever since, to run completely packed-out parties every Monday. These attract an extremely loyal following of thousands of techno and deep house followers, as well as many locals for whom the party provides a highly innovative and enormously fun experience. Ricardo Villalobos, Magda, Luciano, Cassy, Richie Hawtin, Josh Wink, Dubfire, Adam Beyer, Marco Carola, Loco Dice, Alter Ego and Väth himself are among the names that have regularly come together on the decks at Cocoon across the seasons.

Nothing interrupts a Cocoon party. In 2005, Amnesia was forced by local authorities to close its doors at 6am, for two hours, after which it could reopen at 8am. Amazingly, Sven's sets were being recorded and broadcast on a local radio station during those two hours, so the party would just move into the car park and continue, with the radio blasting from car stereos, until it was time to get back to the dance floor again at 8am.

Väth has always had a reputation for throwing himself into the audience, crowd-surfing and generally engaging in every way he could, in between setting up his tracks. This means that the atmosphere at Cocoon feels extremely intimate. 'The best thing I ever did was gather a great team around me,' he says. One of his early party tricks was to hang upside down, suspended like a bat above the crowd, while the dry ice cannon filled the dance floor. The Cocoon after-parties had, by the early 2000s, become the most talked-about after-parties of the week, and would take place on beaches, or in private villas, until eventually moving to new establishment Destino. Performers such as contortionist Rosalind Bee, aka Rose the Snakewoman, were also billboard headliners over the years at Cocoon, and added a colourful performance art aspect to the parties.

'I first performed at Cocoon in Amnesia in 2000, with my Angel show,' Rose told me.

Sven always knew what he wanted, and he already knew most of my performances. He would give me an exact description of his concepts. For my Tinky show, where I came out of a futuristic egg that was especially made for Cocoon Ibiza, Sven had wanted a techno dragonfly to come out of the egg, and I'd already conceived of a techno Tinkerbell coming out of a rose, so we had more or less the same idea. I chose Alter Ego/Sensorama's track 'Projektor' to perform that one to, and Ricardo Villalobos edited it a bit for me in Ibiza. For three months I watched films like *The Fly* and studied insect behaviour and moves, and that's how I created the choreography and character.

Sven had seen Rose, the first ever 'techno contortionist', perform in 1989, at Frankfurt's Tigerpalast. 'Then months later Jean-Charles Vandermynsbrugge [of Fous de la Mer and Señor Coconut] took me to Sven's Omen club. Sven asked me to create a performance there, and that one eventually led on to others. When I did my Ice Princess performance, where I balanced a glass with blue liquid in it on my forehead in the middle of an elaborate contortion move, with the bass pumping madly away and making the stage bounce Sven said he was nervous just watching it.'

On the night of her Shiva performance at Cocoon, for which Rose was using Alter Ego's track 'Betty Ford', Alter Ego themselves (Frankfurt techno aces Jörn Elling Wuttke and Roman Flügel) were performing a live set in the Main Room, which meant that, at Väth's suggestion, she got to perform to their live version of the track. 'My six-armed performance,' she continues, 'for which they kindly played a six-minute version of "Betty Ford".' Later, DJ Ata (who runs Frankfurt's Robert Johnson club) invited Alter Ego, Rose, DJ Heiko MSO and others to his *finca*, where a brilliant Mediterranean storm—huge pulsating sheets of lightning, which can knock out all the electricity in the countryside, known by locals as 'God's disco'—broke out. 'So we stayed over and watched this spectacular natural light show. Three days later we were still there.' Rose and Jörn Elling Wuttke then became, for some years, one of Frankfurt's most famous techno couples.

Dubfire recalls a Cocoon after-party he put on himself:

A close group of friends and I rented a beautiful all-white villa back in 2008 or 2009, and had arranged to do the official after-party there as I was playing Cocoon the night before. When we arrived and got a tour of the villa, the owners told us that they'd recently renovated the entire place, and that we could not so much as lay a single drop of wine on the floors for fear of damaging them, let alone host a wild after-party. Of course we didn't pay any attention to this, and had already hired security, bought all of the alcohol, spread the word, et cetera. After they'd left, and our sound system rental guy came and tested the gear with the first track, our neighbour ran over and angrily told us (in French!) that he was there on a quiet holiday, and would call the police if he so much as heard a single noise from us that even smelled of a party. We of course politely heeded his warning, but went right back to the business of finalising the remaining logistics, and deciding on the right number of people we'd invite, which ended up being about forty to fifty. To make a long story short, throughout the night at Cocoon we had collectively ended up inviting about four hundred to five hundred people, and actually letting in about three hundred of them. And I mean *everyone* was there—Luciano, Loco Dice, Marco Carola, et cetera—and I ended up playing all day for them.

Of course, the police came:

> But we managed to find someone who was celebrating a birthday that day, and told the police that this was their birthday party, and not some wild after-party. They left, never came back again, and we continued to party on all day. At some point late in the afternoon, a few of my roommates asked me to come into the kitchen/main area of the house to look at the filthy mess that had piled up all day. The place was a shambles. Then a girl who was there said she knew of some amazing Brazilian cleaners who she could summon to thoroughly clean up. In the end, miraculously, we returned the villa to its original spotless condition and then spent the next two days in bed recovering. But the party was epic!

Dubfire is one of several DJs to have helped the Cocoon sound evolve over the seasons, with his stark, organic techno sets providing a dark groove to the parties. Luciano, another important part of the Cocoon sound, adds a different tone. Born Lucien Nicolet, he had been a promoter in Chile at the heart of a scene that included Ricardo Villalobos and Señor Coconut. 'My Latin roots and my growing up in Chile are a major influence,' he says. 'Those sounds flew into my music. They're a part of my self.'

After becoming a DJ in 1993, Luciano first came to Ibiza to visit Villalobos, before becoming a regular himself at DC10's Circo Loco party, and Cocoon. 'Ricardo is a mentor, and an inspiration,' he says, 'and he's the one who showed me Ibiza for the first time! Musically, he's so unique. I learnt so much from him.'

Luciano's own music is the winning combination of deep techno and Latin rhythms that made him perfect for the chilled-out, minimal vibe at DC10, and also brought a funky element to the Cocoon family. 'Well, in a way, Sven and his gang brought the underground techno sound to Ibiza, having myself, Ricardo and Richie on stage with them. They really made a statement. Now times have changed, but they are still a relevant force. Sven is a friend, a great entertainer and has always had an amazing vision for his parties.'

One of the most in-demand DJs in Ibiza today, Luciano won the 2014 and 2015 DJ Awards category for tech house, and his parties attract a vast crowd every time.

My Origins party in Ibiza created a lot of buzz, as did the Luciano & Friends events at Destino. And now I'm releasing new music under the Luciæn alias on my new label, Basaec. 2014 was a year of change, and for the better. For Origins, we wanted to focus on quality instead of quantity. We played less gigs, we chose a strong visual concept and we went for it, no compromises. We wanted also to bring back a sense of unity that's been lacking recently in Ibiza. Too many parties, too many arguments, and bad politics were destroying what the real Ibiza is. Ibiza for me is music, love and freedom.

The new Destino in Talamanca has also been the host to Cocoon after-parties, so, along with Luciano's night, the venue has become the latest techno hub and another place for fans of the scene to enjoy all-night revelry. 'Destino is beautiful,' he adds. 'The sound is great and the vibe is just magical. On top of it, the team there is amazing, and the crowd is one of the best you can get in Ibiza. Classy and ready to rave! It's so good that it has opened, and offered a new spot in the island's club life.' Like many of today's techno DJs, Luciano uses Traktor equipment, 'with four decks running at the same time. And a cappellas and synth melodies on top of a very punchy groove.' But he still uses vinyl whenever possible. 'Of course! I did play a few gigs this summer with vinyl only, most notably the one at Rumors at Plan Be near Ibiza Town, and the closing of Amnesia, back to back with Ricardo. Loved that!'

Luciano also runs the successful record label Cadenza, which he put together 'very simply: to have a label to release my own music, and to welcome artists who shared my influence'. The Cadenza Vagabundos, a concept that came out of the label, and inspired his Pacha residency 'were like a bunch of travelling music makers, techno and house gypsies. The name was very fitting to our vibe and to our lifestyle.'

His six-piece Cadenza live Aether project involved different performers who each played sounds using Ableton Live software. 'I was standing like a conductor with my back to the audience, selecting which sounds would be ultimately heard by the audience. The musical symphony of these performers and a percussionist was coupled with a visual aspect, where each sound had a denominated synchronised colour. Todd Graft and Loki of Micro Chunk helped me control the visuals throughout the performance.'

The Cocoon DJs, led by their ringmaster Väth, have managed to create one of the most successful parties the island has ever seen. Where other longstanding iconic parties are now consigned to the past, or have seen fragmentation or relocation jolt their reputations, Cocoon is still there in that now packed-out Monday night slot at Amnesia. In the Main Room, and particularly on the Terrace the atmosphere in and around the DJ booth is uniquely celebratory, and Väth is known for bringing out behaviour in DJs known to be more sedate in their behaviour elsewhere. 'Every society needs its charismatic visionaries, and animating spirits,' he says. The Cocoon family has always been known as that: a family, as Väth is one of the DJs most known for rallying like-minded DJs and organisers, who all celebrate and promote each other.

Väth first came to Ibiza in 1980, at the age of sixteen. He slept on a sun-lounger in the middle of a forest for three months, and fell in love with the hippie ambience of the clubs at the time. He went back to Germany, and started DJing in a club run by his parents. Subsequent trips back to Ibiza over the decade saw him become 'the wildest one on the dance floor,' and included life-changing trips to Amnesia to see Alfredo perform. 'I'd be climbing up the walls trying to get to him. Meanwhile they'd be handing out a bowl of mescaline on the dance floor.' Amnesia owner Martín Ferrer's son Mar-T offered him the 1999 residency, which saw around 1,200 people attend the first night.

The free Cocoon after-parties were started almost immediately too. Väth became legendary for playing extremely long sets. 'A twenty-hour set for me in Ibiza is normal,' he says. Known today as Papa Sven, he also practices ayurvedic nutritional and lifestyle principles for several months every year (like many of the top DJs he is now in his fifties), which first started in the early 1990s when he lived in Goa.

'I approach my life in a different way throughout the year,' he says. 'I am still an endlessly searching jungle beast when it comes to the music and people I love, but I have found a balance that works. Without these experiences, and the ability to relax, I discovered I could not pull off the heavy schedule.' These healthy annual interludes mean he's ready to set the island on fire by the beginning of every summer season, when he takes up his place on the decks at Amnesia and gives it everything he's got, revelling in a barrage of spontaneity. 'Improvisation is my biggest art form,' he says.

'Cocoon is where I have had some of my most amazing Ibiza nights,' says Richie Hawtin.

It is a very small, tight-knit family, and we'd all be there celebrating that. Sometimes I'd be behind the booth DJing or next to Sven as he was playing, or sometimes we'd climb down from the booth, and jump onto the dance floor and dance, and you'd end up making new friends, and creating relationships over the summer that would become long-lasting friendships, or became people who work for you. It was incredibly inspiring, and especially with the new relationships and connections. In my mind, Cocoon was one of the more vibrant parties which crossed really incredible techno music with a bit of theatre, and performance art.

It has to be said, though, that the stage-diving for which Väth is famous goes hand-in-hand with an incredible commitment to his sets. While he is no doubt a 'superstar DJ', the respect he commands from his loyal crowds in Ibiza is due to his complete professionalism when it comes to getting behind the decks, along with the consistently wide selection of incredible music he plays, and his abiding love of vinyl.

'I simply cannot imagine DJing with anything else,' says Väth. 'Vinyl is the medium for anyone who sets high values on good sound.' Along with the way he whips up the Cocoon crowds, this has led to him being recognised as perhaps Ibiza's number-one DJ shaman. It's a role that is celebrated in Ibiza clubland, although if you want to be taken seriously by clubbers who know their stuff, it has to be earned, and in recent years it's the techno DJs who have monopolised the market, including Dubfire, who recalls:

> I made 'Diablo' with Oliver Huntemann, which was sort of a tribute to Cocoon on Mondays, and specifically Sven and his wild antics in the booth and at the after-hours. And I would be lying if I didn't tell you that there have definitely been countless times where I feel shamanistic in my control of the crowd, and my ability to visibly create incredible waves of emotion within them. For me, the symbiotic relationship between DJ and crowd is all about control and submission, tension and release.
>
> Each techno night or club on the island represents a particular sound or vibe, and of course we see the same faces at Cocoon or DC10, but they're all musically varied and equally important to the techno scene's dominance on the island. I was in a very fortunate position for many seasons to be able to play for Circo Loco at DC10, Cocoon at Amnesia, and both ENTER. and Carl Cox's night at Space, et cetera, and yet play a completely different set for each, factoring in the differences in sound, lighting and crowd, and succumbing to each unique environment.

DC10 is of course the famous techno daytime club whose Monday Circo Loco parties not only provided, until the after-hours legal revisions of 2008, an after-party to We Love … Sundays at Space, but also a warm-up party of sorts for clubbers going on to Monday night's Cocoon party at Amnesia. Despite the changes in the law it has remained just as popular. It therefore always contains a highly eclectic crowd, some coming down from, others on their way up to one party or another. DC10 is also extremely popular with locals. The minimal techno party Circo Loco, run by Andrea and Antonio Pelino, has always been the

most talked-about party DC10 hosts. They often throw a Circo Loco
New Year's Day party, when permissions allow, and for January 1st 2015
they even managed to secure Carl Cox, whose loyalties usually belong
to another club:

> Over the last fifteen years I've obviously belonged to Space, and I don't tend
> to play anywhere else. DC10 for me has always been like a playground,
> where I can go and hear other DJs play their music. But the vibe in DC10 is
> just awesome. Every year, I've been asked to play there. I asked Pepe [Roselló]
> and he was a bit reluctant, as he didn't want to take away the essence of what
> I am at Space, but DC10 is so special for me, because the music that gets
> played in there is unbelievable. You don't hear the sound of DC10 in any
> other club on the island. That's the reason it's so popular. Plus with that, it's
> not all about big name DJs. It's about DJs who have a heart and soul, and
> the spirit of the dance floor, and I love that. If I get to play DC10 my set is
> entirely different from the one at Space anyway. And with DC10, my fee,
> the length of my sets, everything is just the same as it is for other DJs that
> play there. And at the end of the day, you get to play to a very knowledgeable
> crowd, who are there for you to deliver! I mean that crowd will just stand
> there with their arms folded if you don't. You have to be of a certain calibre
> to be able to play there in the correct manner. I pass with flying colours
> because I've been going there as a punter for so long now, and I know the
> scene there so well. So I know as a DJ exactly what to play, and how to play it
> there. Times have changed obviously from back in the day when DC10 was
> the after-party club, that you went to only when everywhere else had closed,
> until of course the local government decided that no club should open until
> 4pm, so that kind of killed the after-hours buzz.

DC10 opened in 1990, in a run-down building near the airport, beside
Ibiza's salt pans and close to Salines beach, although Circo Loco really

got the venue going when their parties started in 1999. Some of the DJs that have come up through the famous Circo Loco Monday sessions include Luciano, Magda, Ricardo Villalobos, Cassy, Loco Dice, Arpiar, System of Survival, and Tania Vulcano. The club's capacity has grown to 1,500, which includes its now-covered Terrace, although the Pelino brothers have had much-chronicled run-ins with the local Sant Josep authorities, including the imposition of a €300,000 fine in 2008, and the club being closed for a whole season in 2009.

Then, to the delight of the legions of local and international DC10 fans, the club was reopened in 2010. Over the years, huge inflatable aeroplanes would be passed around the dance floor, and the DJs would sometimes wear masks and other ad hoc finery, while the crowd would often dress in highly elaborate costumes. The parties at DC10 have never stopped being outrageous, and as Carl Cox says, the music delivered is always expected to be of the best standard available.

'I remember going to DC10 a few times after I'd just woken up,' says Manumission's Johnny Golden, 'and people would come up to me and say, Johnny, you look fucked! Even though I was probably the only one in there who'd been to bed before arriving in the afternoon. It must be the atmosphere of that place that makes everyone look that way.'

'After a HOLY SHIT moment on the dance floor of DC10 listening to Loco Dice,' says Dubfire, 'I went back home to Washington DC and swiftly made my track "RibCage", which was fully inspired by that trip to Ibiza. In fact I could go so far as to say that every trip to Ibiza has inspired my studio output to some degree.'

DC10 still maintains its after-hours atmosphere, no matter what time you're there. The often-minimal techno sets are designed to keep the atmosphere cool and smooth, and it always feels like a private party.

'It's not dark or moody, or anything like that,' adds Carl Cox, 'it's more of a summery feeling, a feel-good sound. It still has its energy and pump, and its funk, but when you're seeing people in their sunglasses there all dressed-up, and looking so cool, you know they're there to just have a good time. There's nothing better, and that's what DC10 is all about. I'm able to play a lot of old-skool records as well as new music, but most of all I'm able to play what I believe in. So I'm really pleased that I'm able to slot myself in there. I wouldn't want to change a thing about DC10.'

ENTER. opened at Space in 2013, and elevated the techno scene in Ibiza onto a new level. Unapologetically futuristic in concept, Hawtin's new night brought what was happening at Cocoon at Amnesia, and Circo Loco at DC10, into some kind of new age, although all three still work beautifully together. Alongside Carl Cox's Music Is Revolution, ENTER. is living proof of why techno works so well at Space, with its multi-roomed format.

Ben Turner has been with Hawtin every step of the way with the ENTER. project, as his manager, having known him for more than two decades:

> I've known Richie since before I went to Ibiza. I went to Detroit in 1993 to interview him for *Melody Maker*, and we really hit it off. We had a very similar outlook on electronic music. I was completely inspired by Detroit at that point, and he was obviously living close to Detroit and taking his inspiration from there. We reconnected in Berlin after he'd moved there, and I reminded myself of why he was such a visionary back then. We started to work together on certain areas, and now I'm fully involved in all of his career and everything he's got going on, which is a huge amount. It's a relationship I take incredibly seriously. It's very intense, and very full on, but he's always striving to do very futuristic, very progressive, very forward-thinking things.

After being a big part of the Cocoon story, Hawtin was ready to take the next step and create a night that fully represented his own vision, as Turner recalls.

> When I think back on the history of the island, I'd never really appreciated things like Manumission at the time. I had a very strange, very negative perception of it very early on, but actually, as time went on and then it finished, I started to realise how much they'd delivered in terms of creativity and ideas, and conceptually. Very few people have genuinely tried to create a concept on the island. ENTER. came along just at that right point when underground music was huge, but it was all very one-dimensional. Of course there's the beauty and simplicity of DC10, and its entire magic, and but I guess ENTER. is the other extreme of that. It's absolutely focused on uncompromisingly cutting-edge music, but you can make that fun, you can make that appeal to a wider audience.

Hawtin:

> We had some meetings with some of the other clubs, but when we walked through Space for the first time it was like, Whoa! What we liked about Space was probably what other people *don't* like about it, which is that you actually have a lot of rooms to fill. It's an advantage, but also a disadvantage. At Amnesia, you only have the two rooms to fill, so you can book some DJs and … perfect, but at Space I had to find a lot of DJs to keep everybody entertained in all the different rooms. I decided to make them into different zones, and create different atmospheres. As soon as I walked in, I knew I could do the Sake Bar, and knew that could be a very cool thing to see as you step inside the club. But then I had to decide what to do with the Terrace, and all the other rooms … and eventually I could see that this would all become a highly creative project which I could experiment

with; bringing different DJs and different music types together, playing with decoration and lighting, building up some of my own projects that I hadn't had the time or energy or budgets to delve into before. For many years I asked myself, 'Why do a night in Ibiza?' But it eventually became apparent that the only place in the world where we could really create such a theatrical show for a whole season, and be able to deliver a deeper experience to people, was in fact Ibiza.

For the ENTER. concept Hawtin and crew played with a number of names, partly inspired by Gaspar Noé's 2009 film *Enter The Void*, which starts with what are probably the most techno opening credits of all time. Over a rapid animation of cast and crew names, LFO's track 'Freak' introduces the often highly psychedelic energy of a film that includes an animated DMT trip sequence, and a neon-drenched Tokyo, as perceived by the disembodied spirit of the protagonist.

Our event was going to be called 'Enter The Void' at one point, or just 'Void', because of this space that is Ibiza: It's really just a black hole in the middle of the world where anything is possible. But it's only possible if you bring something to the table. You have to participate, and that in the end is the challenge for ENTER. It's welcoming, but it's also saying, cross the threshold, leave everything behind and see what we're doing, and let's create something unique and special together. Not only as a party, but also within the context of Ibiza, because I think Ibiza has been pretty stagnant for a long time. The island's not really very edgy at all. Maybe it was in the early days, probably even before I went there. There's still some kind of hedonism, but I think in the 1970s and 80s it really was a place to release yourself, with other freaks, and the outcasts of society. After a while it just became about nightclubbing and dancing and less about theatre, less about art, less about fashion, and we tried to think about all those things when we started planning ENTER. The black dot is connected to the idea of the void. In German, you'd say, 'ENTER. Punkt.' It's to the point, and again it's a challenge, more of a statement than an invitation. Our event is a point of entry into my take on what is interesting in electronic music and what an event should be. It's like a portal.

The striking iris close-ups of the ENTER. DJs, seen on all the marketing material, provide the most psychedelic and visceral design concept the island has seen for years. The black dot of ENTER.—the period after the name, the close-up of the pupil in the iris images, black dots on merchandise and clothing, Richie's tiny round black earring, and so on—is the central totem of the concept, as Turner recalls.

> That whole vision—the Sake Bar, the dancers, the black dot, the marketing, every single aspect of it—makes underground music slightly more appealing to a wider group of people. You can see that from the kind of numbers we have in there; you've got your die-hard fan, but you've also got a whole group of people who are just coming to experience this incredible concept they've heard about. We hope people will walk out of that experience and dig a little bit deeper, and look for more challenging forms of music. That to us would be a great result. Everything Richie does is about the smallest of details adding up to being just incredibly well thought out. When you look at the simplicity of the marketing, and how engaging that was. The Ibiza landscape looks so beautiful with its trees, and green hills and just the colourfulness of the island, but once you add those huge billboards with the DJs faces on them it's just very unimaginative, very uninspiring, so the eyeball really seemed to capture people's imaginations.

Hawtin's ENTER. nights have produced stellar DJ line-ups which feature many of his M_nus label artists, as well as the names from Ibiza's coalition of techno commanders, including Väth, Dubfire and Luciano. 'Me and Richie have a lot of respect for each other,' says Luciano, 'It's a long-time friendship, and we have a great connection between the two of us. We've both gone on to create our own sound too: the Cadenza sound and the M_nus sound, in which we've carved out our own musical identity, each one of us with his own influences and personality.'

'Everyone uses the word *tastemakers*,' says Hawtin, 'but DJs are really international travellers touching on different cultures, bringing that to a wider audience, and trying to bring people closer together. I want to give people new experiences. It's something that I've always felt was important. When I started to play records for people in the early days, of course I wanted to see people dance, but I was always excited to play a record for the first time, and to hear people go, *Wow—what is this*? I think opening people's minds to new experiences can go much further than just music though. It's about introducing people to the wider variety of things in the world.'

On ENTER. nights at Space, the centrepiece enormous metal ring in the Main Room, the darkly minimal lights, often evoking a *Close Encounters Of The Third Kind* feel, and the ice-cool techno being mastered by the DJs there have sealed the party's reputation as the most visionary setting in the island's contemporary nightscape. Australian DJ Bella Sarris, who worked for the ENTER. team before stepping behind the DJ booth herself, has become one of the popular faces in ENTER.'s Sake Bar. Gaiser, Paco Osuna, Tale of Us and Matador, all M_nus artists, have also added to the ENTER. roster, as has British-born Maya Jane Coles, and Richie's brother, the DJ and visual artist Matthew Hawtin's many contributions.

Both brothers are involved and interested in the world of visual arts, as Richie notes:

I've read a number of biographies on famous artists like Rothko, James Turrell and people like Robert Irwin. Artists who are actually working in between being installation art and sculpture, using three dimensions to express themselves. Apart from that, a lot of my general philosophy comes from early sci-fi movies I would watch. I'd be thinking about an optimistic future where less is more, a sort of streamlined design aesthetic that I could define in much of what I create musically, or in the events, or even in the marketing or the promotion. Like with the black dot of ENTER. It's pretty stripped-down. I think that also came from what I took as a teenager or young adult from Juan and Derrick and Kevin and the other Detroit guys.

ENTER. was a breath of fresh air for an island whose best parties are traditionally believed to be the ones that have been going for several years, when it opened in 2012. No other club night has seen the installation of an interactive room, like the one Richie has created at Space, and in which visitors can contribute, via a specially designed technology, to create the music in the room. Hawtin cuts a well-recognised figure, with his curtain of blond hair, and his slender frame dressed in black. His application to every aspect of the design of the ENTER. night has brought unprecedented levels of sophistication into Ibiza's party scene.

The island has opened up over the last five years and welcomed better music, but it's also become homogenised by a lot of the same type of music. I'm sure there was a little thing in the back of my mind for a long time about doing my own night, but it definitely wasn't a focus. I was quite happy to fly in and out and play under other people's concepts. When the opportunity came up, I felt there was no reason to put together another music-only DJ party. I didn't really feel I wanted to just have my face on a whole load of billboards and have a straightforward Richie Hawtin residency. It made me think about what we used to do in Detroit, and it was fantastic to now have the opportunity to do something like that in Ibiza, instead of just flying in and out with a set amount of time and a set budget. I've been stepping up my game on a production level since 2008 anyway, doing a lot of festival tours and having visuals and a lighting guy. But when we got the chance to create a night which could run for fourteen weeks, we could create more of a storyline, more of a tapestry, and actually build things for the club. That's when it became something more than just another party.

## Summing up the appeal of ENTER., Dufire concludes:

I think the success of ENTER. lies in large part to Rich's clear vision about the concept and the imagery surrounding it. I can't recall a time *ever* where you had legions of followers running around Ibiza wearing all black, and with black dot tattoos plastered all over their bodies! And then there's the amazing team that he's gathered; beginning with his core touring crew which have brought an unprecedented level of quality, in terms of production values, to the island.

Then there's Rich's dedication to the whole project; I mean he's there every week for twelve-plus hours, not only playing, but present from the pre-party, through dinner, onto the Sake Bar and then once the rest of the club opens, rotating between each room. I can't think of anyone else who's committed *that* much time to an Ibiza residency and it's a testament to the night's huge success.

## CHAPTER NINE

# PINK FLAMINGOS AND SALT PANS • SA TRINXA • THE QUIET CHILL-OUT SPOTS

MANEL, CAVE LIFE AND THE SUNSET ASHRAM · FOUS DE LA MER, OPERA, AND HOW TO BE AN IBIZA CHILL-OUT PRODUCER · SANTA AGNÈS AND THE ALMOND VALLEY · DAVID LYNCH'S MUSIC AND A QUIET HOTEL IN THE CAMPO · TALES OF PARADISE TODAY · THE IBIZA FILM FESTIVAL · EL DIVINO'S EVOLUTION · THE CROISSANT SHOW, HOME OF THE DEMI-MONDE · THE INTERNATIONAL MUSIC SUMMIT · SANT ANTONI SUNSETS: FROM THE CLIFFS AND COLOURS TO CAFÉ DEL MAR AND CAFÉ MAMBO

The ethereal dawn over Salines nature reserve lights up paths formed over decades along the rocks by the shore. Slivers of rosy sky, with golden flecks near the horizon, announce the approach of the rising sun, as flamingos settle on the silvery salt pans nearby. Mists from the tranquil Mediterranean drift across the island, past sheltered coves, through hills and valleys, and over fertile plains scented in winter with almond and orange blossom, as well as jasmine, wild herbs, and resinous pines.

Salines beach itself has long been considered one of the island's chill-out zones. Chill-out in Ibiza is a culture and absolutely a daily way of life, all year round. It's not just a type of music for which the island's bars have become world famous. Chill-out is the island's favourite after-party. The one that takes place after the last of Pan's disciples have re-entered the earth's atmosphere, and alighted into the quiet stillness of the morning. Finding breakfast, heading to the beach for a swim or just gazing at the misty vapour floating in across the land are all traditional ways to close a night out in Ibiza. This is why all veterans of Ibiza clubland know they mustn't forget to bring their sunglasses with them the night before.

Along the main drag of Salines, where shallow waters roll gently against the beach, is Sa Trinxa, a well-kept wooden shack covered in palm fronds, which is a celebrated chill-out restaurant and beach bar. Its resident DJ Jonathan Grey, or Jon Sa Trinxa, is one of the most well-loved DJs on the island, and has been ever since he arrived in the mid-1990s. His deeply chilled eclectic afternoon sets at the sandy haven have provided the soundtrack to thousands of holiday bliss moments in Salines' shallow waters. The story goes that he drove to Ibiza in 1994 on a hippie bus, carrying his sound system and a bunch of records, then got separated from the friends he'd driven over with, used up all his cash, and ended up living in a forsaken apartment in Sa Penya, with no gas, water or electricity. Ibiza's two faces of violent energy and opportunity struck when, while hitchhiking one day, he got thwacked by a car and knocked into a ditch. Fortuitously, the very next car that came motoring by was driven by Nito Cardona, the owner of Sa Trinxa. Nito took pity on the roughed-up English lad from Cheltenham, and drove him back to the shack to feed him and let him get cleaned up and restored after the accident. Amazingly, it turned out that Jon's sound system and records had been left by his absent friends at the bar anyway. So the next day, when the regular Sa Trinxa DJ didn't show up, Nito asked Jon if he would break out his sounds and take over. Never looking back from that moment, he's been there ever since, and now has his own custom-built DJ booth.

'Jon Sa Trinxa is such a lovely guy,' says Pete Gooding, the resident at

Sant Antoni's sunset bar Café Mambo. 'And what a brilliant DJ!' Tales of Jon's breezy afternoon sets cram so many peoples' mental scrapbooks of golden Ibiza holiday memories, and have done ever since he made Salines a mandatory beach stop for afternoon chilling, by combining two of the island's most colourful aspects—a hippie undercurrent, and an awareness of nature as a backdrop to music—in his perfectly serene and picturesque setting. It's an environment that rests beautifully between nocturnal pleasures.

'When me and Sharam came over with our girlfriends for the first time, as Deep Dish,' says Dubfire, 'we were put in a beautiful villa, and quite spoiled from the get-go. We'd go to Salines beach during the day and the clubs at night. Ibiza is, and always has been the epicentre of our collective scene, and now more so than ever. The location, the climate, the natural beauty, freedom, the hippie vibe. That openness and free-spirited nature of hippie culture is an integral part of the island, especially as it relates to its evolving dance music.'

Most of the beaches around the island, especially the smaller ones, are very peaceful, although some cater to people wanting more, with beach restaurants and bars renowned for their ambient music and vibe. Inland it's hills, valleys and forests. In winter particularly, the level of tranquillity is enormous, but even in summer the fact that so much of the island is still quiet is a much-cherished blessing. No matter what goes on behind the scenes, and notably in the heady competitive arena of clubland, no one will interfere with you choosing how to spend your days inland. Ibiza has a reputation for being expensive, but for the best of the island you actually don't need more than a few euros a day spending money to have a beautiful natural holiday.

Whether you're a tourist or a local, stopping in at one of the small, locally run village shops which often double up as bars, tobacconists and newsagents can provide all you need for a picnic on the beach or in the middle of the countryside. Fresh bread, *aioli*, serrano ham, cheese, fruit (especially the locally grown figs and oranges), and *flaó* (a delicious local variation on cheesecake, with herbs) as well as drinks of every variety, can be purchased at budget prices, saving a potential fortune on eating in a restaurant.

The whole island has its daytime charms, although most of the more beautiful locations are away from the main resorts and towns. A clockwise whistle-stop tour of some of Ibiza's coastal gems, with a few inland highlights thrown in, along with some extra commentary from local artists and other island characters will help us navigate through some of the best of them.

Starting at Salines, a scenic walk around the headlands of this southeast bay of the island, or back along the salt lagoons, takes you to the clean strand of Es Cavallet's gay beach, where surfing can be possible, depending on the day's winds. The popular beach bar Chiringay and the elegant S'Escollera restaurant are there, beside the clusters of sand dunes popular for cruising. Further along is the southern tip of Platja d'en Bossa, which in winter is a far cry from its summer incarnation. Since the 1950s, d'en Bossa and neighbouring Figueretes have been locals' favourite beaches for long walks in winter, when the hotels and raucous beach bars have all shuttered down.

In summer, the choice of places to stop and have a drink or a meal in this area is vast: Sands (Carl Cox's restaurant), Ushuaïa, Sankeys, the elegant Nassau Beach Club and the party bar, Bora Bora are all widely recognised hot spots. Or, for something completely different, a refreshingly original Caribbean soul food bar and restaurant has popped up in the middle of all the d'en Bossa action. The Jam Shak, where they play reggae music and serve house specialities such as jerk chicken, rum cocktails and coconut water, is run by Nikki Bark-Jones and her husband Stevie McIntyre. Originally from Jamaica, McIntyre has enlisted the skills handed down to him by his mother Jeannie, to bring a completely unique (and decently priced) culinary experience to the island. 'I'd be happy going to the Jam Shak every day,' DJ Moniz says. 'Stevie's food from day one was absolutely bangin'. Whenever I have friends over, it's the first place I take them.' (In fact, the Jam Shak has now expanded and moved round the coast to Sant Antoni).

Starting out clockwise in the other direction from Sa Trinxa takes you along Salines beach to the Jockey Club, an island favourite restaurant which has been there since 1993, and at one point was one of the only beach establishments open on Christmas Day, which made it a fashionable hangout for island chefs. Further round that headland is the magnificent Cap d'es Falcó, which has a steep walking route that offers spectacular views of Es Vedrà, and looking behind you in the other direction, beyond Figueretes, Dalt Vila.

Behind the beach at Cap d'es Falcó it looks like the planes at the nearby airport are taking off and landing on the salt pans, and there is a huge salt hillock in front of the pans around which, depending on the time of year, a flurry of pink flamingos can be seen gathering. Carrying on along the coast eventually gets you to Es Codolar, a pebbly beach very popular with locals, just east of what was the Phoenician settlement of Sa Caleta (the archeological site that is there today is also easy to reach, and well worth seeing). Sa Caleta's own beach (also known locally as Es Bol Nou) is famous for its red cliffs, its glorious sandy bay and its fresh fish restaurant, which is also open in winter.

A bit further along, Platja d'es Jondal is a favoured spot with the yachting fraternity, and the Blue Marlin beach restaurant there offers a sublime menu and international DJ sets. Heading further west, the tranquil cove of Es Porroig is an idyllic spot for a quiet swim. The nearby tiny village of Es Cubells offers stunning cliff-top views of Es Vedrà, as well as a place to stop for a drink or some food, while below the neighbouring bay at Cala Llentrisca provides another secluded beach ideal for swimming. The other southern beaches include Cala d'Hort (directly opposite Es Vedrà), with neighbouring Atlantis a brave, steep cliff walk away, Cala Carbó, Cala Vadella, Cala Tarida, Cala Bassa, and Platges de Comte, home of the enticing Eastern-influenced restaurant, sunset bar and wedding venue, Sunset Ashram.

Sunset Ashram is run by Manel Aragonés, who arrived on the island in 1969, and soon became part of the hippie scene in the clubs and around the island. He helped design the decor at Amnesia, and legend has it that he spent time there with Alexander 'Sasha' Shulgin, the man credited with introducing MDMA to psychologists. When his son was killed in an accident, Aragonés went to live in a cave with spring water and a small allotment opposite Es Vedrà. He stayed in the cave mourning the loss of his son for seven summers, travelling in the intervening winter months. Aragonés opened Sunset Ashram in 1996, and turned it into one of the most popular sunset spots on the island.

The former hippie bar Kumharas is further along the coast, at Port des Torrent, just before Sant Antoni's main bay. Although this is still a popular spot with local and international visitors, the restaurant Chiringuito Es Puetó on the beach further up the road towards the restored windmill of Sa Punta d'es Molí is even more special, and it is one of the best-value fish restaurants on the island, situated in the small bay, with tables in the sand. Keeping things chilled, the main bay of Sant Antoni can be avoided by heading straight around to the quieter and more beautiful sunset spots of Cala Gració, Punta Galera (arguably the most magical place on the island), Cala Salada, and a hidden favourite, Ses Fontanelles.

'I love that beach at Ses Fontanelles,' says sunset DJ Pete Gooding, 'I mean, you have to walk for quite a bit over the rocks to get to it, but it's well worth it.'

Nearby Cap Negret is where producer and musician Marko Bussian has his quiet house and studio. 'This is one of my favourite spots,' he says, 'especially out of season, when no one's around. I also love the rocks and cliffs in Santa Agnès, and the freshwater streams inland at Es Broll—an unusual thing for Ibiza, as so many of the rivers are dry now. But I also love to go to the top of the highest mountains here, and get that 360-degree view of this tiny island. And, of course, Dalt Vila also has a certain magical vibration.' And it's these vibrations as well as the calming effect of the beautiful island locations he lives surrounded by which play very much into the chill-out music Bussian has become famous for.

Bussian and his musical collaborator, Jean-Charles Vandermynsbrugge first came to Ibiza in 2001, straight from Barcelona's Sonar festival, where they had been performing deep house sets as Glissando Bros. On that first trip over, they stayed with their friend, fellow musician and producer Ingmar Hansch, in his old *finca* in the heart of Sant Mateu. 'I fell in love with the different natural aspects here,' continues Bussian, 'and I began to think about the way that I saw the sea, the mountains and the trees, and how it could be harmonised in some way into electronic music. If music affects me, then it's because I'm influenced by certain vibes, waves, feelings—all of which I could also feel in the natural surroundings of the island.' Bussian and Vandermysnsbrugge then created Fous de la Mer. (Vandermynsbrugge had, prior to the Glissando Bros., been working in Frankfurt, in the 1990s, for projects including Earth Nation, which was released on Sven Väth's Eye Q label).

'The hippie heritage which still pervades the island, especially in winter, really makes you feel you can be yourself here,' says Vandermynsbrugge. 'When I first came here, I rediscovered the quieter vibrations of the Mediterranean, which reminded me of my upbringing in the south of France, and I felt the urge to express these feelings of peacefulness in the music I create with Marko. Our songs are recorded in Marko's Hacienda Studios, with its view over Sant Antoni's beautiful bay—songs that I think convey both the superficiality and the depth of life.'

Bussian and Vandermynsbrugge went on a crawl of clubland on that first trip, dropping in at the Manumission Motel rooftop bar, where Sol Ruiz de Galarreta was singing over a set being played by the DJ Arian 911. She hooked up with them, and eventually they recorded the first Fous de la Mer release 'Never Stop Loving', which saw the musicians move towards an island-inspired more down-tempo groove. Subsequent album releases saw them become perhaps the most famous chill-out group on the island, as well as achieving success in Germany.

Bussian came from Frankfurt, and for a time he worked in the same building in Offenbach as Sven Väth, creating music for adverts, 'back when Sven was doing his first recordings. I knew all those guys, but I was always completely engrossed in my own music.' Like Vandermynsbrugge, who took the name 'Fou' from the tarot and started working on the early Fous de la Mer tracks in his own Frankfurt studio, inspired by the view over the Main River flowing down below, Bussian is motivated by being close to water.

> Even before I lived in Ibiza, I had the strong feeling that I needed to be here. The whole feeling of the island sucked me in to a certain atmosphere which I can't leave. I still feel that way. I've never been involved in the nightclub scene, or tourism, I'm living in my own space, interacting with colleagues and creating things. You can have a beautiful life on the island, if you choose the spots to go to, and the right moment.

Vandermynsbrugge, who is still based in Frankfurt, but visits the island regularly, sometimes despairs of the city he currently calls home. 'It's all about money,' he says, 'and with its cold weather, the finance sector and the accompanying skyscrapers it provides a sober background for the European cradle of techno.'

After moving to Ibiza in 2003, Bussian says he met

> mostly foreigners, who had all been living here for several years. We had a special community of very welcoming and interesting people, and it was no problem making new contacts as everyone here is interested in one other, and what experiences they've had. I started playing some live sessions with Thomas Feldmüller from Sant Llorenç. He was playing guitar, me piano, and we invited friends like Chris Smith, with his flute, or some percussion players, and we'd all meet up and do improvisations. I'm a classically trained piano player, and these sessions really helped inspire my personal style, picking up melodies from the other musicians, exchanging phrases, and so forth. So after moving here, my piano style developed into this dreamy, floating, wavy style and that's a key element in the music of Fous de la Mer, too.

Aside from Fous de la Mer, Bussian has been involved in some other interesting projects since moving to the island, such as *The Journey*, an opera-inspired album created with German drummer and producer Wolfgang Filz and British soprano Olivia Safe, under the name La Mia Bocca. Filz had taken over Michael Cretu's old *finca* outside Santa Eulària when Cretu moved to his ill-fated mansion in Santa Agnès. The old Santa Eulària *finca* though still had the original studio where Cretu's bestselling Enigma project had been recorded, and in it Bussian and Filz started mixing electronic music with traditional opera arias. 'We took all the original harmonies and melodies, and processed them with synthesisers, before inviting Olivia Safe to come from London to do the vocals on the album,' says Bussian.

When it was ready, *The Journey* was previewed live by La Mia Bocca on the rocks in front of Café Mambo, in Sant Antoni.

I had never seen a live concert before at Mambo. They installed a stage on which we were set up, facing the sunset. We checked the sunset times in advance, so we had maybe twenty minutes of the sun starting to set, and then right at the moment of the sunset itself we brought in a beautiful peak in the music. People were really applauding, so we continued well into the night. I really loved it, because this was probably the closest gig to the water that I have ever played. We were only two or three metres away, and you could hear the waves in the background. The tempo of the songs is pre-scaled, and some elements of the music are run by computer, but just hearing the sea really affected us. We were in our own bubble— Olivia singing, Wolfgang on the drums, and we'd invited Jean-Charles [Vandermynsbrugge] to play bass for the gig. I think we created an evening that the audience really responded to, because it was so unusual.

One of Bussian's other side projects was engineering teen superstar LaFee's recordings. Her first album, *LaFee*, went straight to number one in Germany. 'I worked with Wolfgang on this album too,' he says. 'We used a variety of effects, from chill-out to Rammstein-like heavy metal phrases, which was a unique combination.' Bussian has now started a project of live sessions on the island with bassist Matthias Wahl, vocalist Eva Martinez (formerly of Fragma), and Ulysses Tas, a guitar player from Brazil. They started out playing sessions in a basement in Santa Gertrudis, but when Wahl moved to the ancient streets of Dalt Vila, they decided to take the project outdoors.

Matthias is living this kind of Krautrock lifestyle. You know, with his long hair, having a quiet beer in the evening … although he's working professionally as an electrician too, on solar power systems. Anyway, after he moved up to Dalt Vila, he invited us to play on a roof terrace there. We do Krautrock-style improvisations, sometimes with Pink Floyd influences, and with either Spanish or English vocals, and this takes place every two weeks in summer, up on the top of an old building.

The first time the guerrilla rooftop gang performed, the neighbours called in the police within twenty minutes.

So our singer Eva went down to talk to them, during which time our sound came together beautifully, so the police had no complaints about it. In fact they said, 'OK, you can play for one-and-a-half hours more, and if you behave yourselves, then no problem!' It's all very Krautrock—floating guitars, building up rhythms with no song structure, sometimes jamming on two chords, everyone interacting.

Hacienda Studios is now one of the most famous on the island, and Bussian is happy to provide a quick behind-the-scenes of the renowned chill-out studio.

I have moved house several times since I've been here, so, apart from anything, my studio does have to be transportable. I have a very good microphone, good loudspeakers, and I also did some acoustic treatment of the room itself. Nowadays you can do everything on your laptop, but you do need to have a professional studio environment if you want to work properly, it's just not enough to listen on headphones in some hotel room, as some DJs do. Acoustic treatment of the room means you don't get too much echo. And you need a good speaker system to listen back. Apart from that, I'm using an Apple Mac with a TC Electronic sound card, and external equipment like a Lexicon 300L reverb effects system, or an Eventide H3000 harmoniser. They have certain effects I haven't yet managed to find on any plugin. I'm very traditional, because I came from recording with tape machines, then sequencers with audio recording capabilities came out and I used those. Since I've lived in Ibiza, a lot of stuff like Ableton Live has come out, but I've never been so interested in those. They're for people who are not playing with musicians. They can just grab samples and grooves, and mix them together, and they can make for brilliant tracks. But I always play my harmonies, and Jean-Charles plays his bass and records his own vocals, so this more manual way of putting our tracks together is what makes Fous de la Mer so special. And this all comes together right here, in Cap Negret.

Stepping outside, you can see that the location—with its sea views, sweeping cliffs and charmed sunsets, provides a kind of perfect cocoon for Bussian's creativity. The entire area in all directions is lovely. Continuing onwards then, just north of Hacienda Studios and Cap Negret are some of the most arcadian sites for countryside picnics. Cala d'Albarca, a beautiful cove accessible by sea (or by the intrepid walker), is one such perfect place to stop, as is the heavenly Ses Portes del Cel cliff-top—both close to Santa Agnès.

The valley of Santa Agnès is home to a vast display of almond trees, which, in early February, produce heady white blossoms that fill the air with a musky scent. The sight of the inland valley in bloom is among the most stunning and sublime views on the island, although almond trees are in evidence in smaller groupings, all over the countryside. These trees, and the whole unspoilt area which heads north-east from Sant Antoni towards the village of Sant Miquel is still a rural splendour, and old white farmhouses or *fincas* dot the landscape, while pine forests and stunning sea views from the coastal cliffs have kept Ibiza one of the most treasured islands of the Mediterranean for nature-seekers.

Martin Davies remembers bringing some friends from Romania for a walk between Sant Mateu and Sant Miquel, up in the hills:

> We were just feeling our way slowly, when we got to this incredibly beautiful spot overlooking the coast, with cliffs, and pine forests all around. And it was one of those moments where Tanit had just kind of arranged things, so that the sun was sinking into the sea at that very minute we arrived. We sat there with our beers, looking around, and I thought in that moment that the island reminded me of *The Plains Of Heaven*, a wonderful painting by John Martin, that's in the Tate Gallery. And then one of the friends I was with looked at me and said she could quite happily die, there and then. That sums up Ibiza for me. We all want to share the island when it's like that. It's like a religion. You want to tell everyone else about it.

Es Cucons hotel in Santa Agnès is a pastoral retreat, where Ben Turner spends a few days recovering from the excitement of his International Music Summit every year. In 2010, he was sitting quietly by himself on the hotel's terrace, when he remembered that Jason Bentley, a Californian DJ who works closely with the Summit, had earlier handed him an MP3 on a USB stick, which he had placed in his bag for later and then forgotten about. It contained a track recorded by film director David Lynch.

> It's amazing that it was Ibiza that made that whole connection with David Lynch for me. Especially since he's somebody who's a huge inspiration in my life generally. Jason Bentley had given me this USB stick earlier, telling me it was a new electronic track by David Lynch, but I didn't realise he meant *the* David Lynch. I played it, and thought it was an incredible piece of music. The minute his voice came in, I was like, 'My god, it really is him!' I couldn't believe how good it was. So I emailed Jason straight away, and

he told me it was available for signing up. About two weeks later, I was out having a curry in London, and I got a call from David Lynch's office on my mobile phone. I was put straight onto him, there and then! And I had ten minutes to sell my record label. As a result of that call, they trusted us to safely take this record and put it out into the musical landscape.

Turner's label, Sunday Best, is co-owned by British festival promoter Rob Da Bank. 'We've had a four-year relationship with Lynch since then,' continues Turner. 'We've released two albums and are currently working on a third one. It's been a great privilege. Every time I go to LA now, I get into a car and go up to David's house and spend time with him. He's been so appreciative of what we've done for him and his music. It's been a great relationship, and it was all Ibiza that made that happen, from that moment in the Santa Agnès countryside.'

Further northeast is an unspoilt cove, accessible by a path that starts 150 metres above sea level, and leads down to the bay. Martin Davies:

Some friends came over to visit Ibiza, and I took them here. When we got down to the shore, this local guy gave us all some delicious fish, simply because I swam out to a yacht and got ice for his whiskey. Then Pep, the guy from the bar Can Sulayetas came by with a friend of his from Bar Grial and they invited us to come out in their boat. We had an amazing, relaxing time with them, fishing and sunbathing, and we went round to another cove you can only get to by boat. It was so peaceful. Then, out of nowhere, these louts from Sant Antoni came sailing in on their pleasure boat, with music pumping out and everything. In this beautiful natural amphitheatre! Eventually, I swam over, and circled the boat a few times, like the shark in *Jaws*, until building up the courage to ask the boat's top dog to turn the music down, after flattering his boat first, of course. I told him, 'Look, we're in a very special part of Ibiza, one of the great secret bays, and we've come to enjoy the tranquillity.' To my amazement he said, 'Yeah, you're right, mate, I'll turn it right off.' And he did, and we ended up having a really nice chat about the magic of Ibiza, and all sorts of other stuff.

The town of Sant Miquel is one of the most authentic and least touristy villages on the island. The celebrated inlet of Benirràs nearby is where Nina Hagen married her teenage lover on the beach in 1987, and where drummers still gather at sunset. A bit further north, the beaches outside the village of Sant Joan include Cala de Xarraca, Portinatx and Cala d'en Serra. This remote part of the island is still something of a hippie enclave, and the Sant Joan weekend market is a smaller version of the Las Dalias market in Sant Carles. 'If I ever get to feeling like the season's catching up with me,' says Pete Gooding, 'I'll just go and sit in that market in Sant Joan. Then I can feel just like I'm in the Ibiza of decades ago.'

Around from Portinatx, the northeast of the island's coastline is full of remote valleys, quiet farms, and former communes. The actor Terence Stamp, who became an Osho sannyasin in 1976, set up an organic farm in the area in the same decade. Cala de Sant Vicent is the beach where French assassin Raoul Villain was murdered in 1936. Leif Borthen's 1967 book *The Road To San Vicente*, republished by Martin Davies's Barbary Press in 2007, describes this episode and many of the colourful Sant Vicent characters of the 1930s and 1950s—periods when that whole area was cut off from the rest of the island—the road out to Ibiza Town from Sant Vicent was only finally opened in 1964. In former days, locals would rush down to the beach to greet the boats bringing market wares back in from Ibiza Town. Today the beach is a tranquil oasis to stop and have lunch after visiting nearby Cova des Culleram (Tanit's Cave), for example.

Moving down the east coast, Cala Boix offers a glorious walk around the rocks with a steep descent to its grey sands, and a view of the island of Tagomago. Close by, the traditional Restaurante Pou des Lleó serves fantastic paellas. Neighbouring Platja de s'Aigua Blanca also offers spectacular views from its clifftops, and the beach itself is a locals' favourite, as are the mud baths a bit further along. The closest village to these sites is Sant Carles, where Ca n'Anneta (Bar Anita) is unchanged since the 1970s, its traditional bar and restaurant (serving everything from fresh fish, tapas and pastries, to their own home-made *hierbas*) containing walls of functioning post office boxes, and local art.

The next big town heading south from the village of Sant Carles is Santa Eulària. It is also Ibiza's second cultural centre, after Ibiza Town, hosting a congress hall that puts on ballets, recitals, theatre, conferences, and, for a few years, the Ibiza Film Festival (IFF). Radically different from Cannes, the IFF bestowed Falcó d'Or (golden falcon) awards, and let guest celebrities mingle freely in the auditorium and at the attendant events, with island visitors.

'It's such great fun, and it's been very relaxing,' Bill Forsyth, the director of films such as *Gregory's Girl* and *Local Hero*, commented at the 2009 event, which marked his first visit in Ibiza. 'Ibiza's a pretty wonderful place. It wasn't hard to accept the invitation to come out here.'

Cuba Gooding Jr, who along with Forsyth was invited to appear as a judge at the 2009 IFF, was also clearly impressed with the very laid-back format of the event, which differed a great deal from the pace of his normal Hollywood schedule. 'This is a festival made for me!' he cheered. 'I'm not a morning person. Yesterday I saw my last film at 2am and had dinner at 5am. Woke up today at 1pm. But I just go with the flow, you know. It's island life. It's controlled chaos, and I think it's great.'

Terry Gilliam, one of the patrons of the festival, was involved in every annual IFF, working behind the scenes, helping to choose the films that made the selection, and joining the panel of judges. 'The IFF is such a funny festival,' he observed, 'because it's very small and it's still learning to walk, but the people I've met here are just fantastic. You have time to talk to each other, time to relate normally and relax.'

Relaxing in this case often meant quiet afternoons in hilltop villas, such as actor Terry Thomas's beautiful *finca* high in the hills above Sant Carles, converted by his son into the *agroturismo* hotel Can Talaias, or heading out for a swim at the beaches between Santa Eulària and Ibiza Town. Of these, Sol d'en Serra, Platja de s'Estanyol and Platja de Talamanca are all great for swimming, and for lunch, and the often dramatic coastal drive between Santa Eulària and Talamanca Bay makes for a great day out with these colourful en route pitstops.

Talamanca Bay leads round into Ibiza harbour, where the town area starts. The yachts in Marina Botafoch (the other side of the harbour from the famous port bars) can include some of the largest in Europe during summer season, including a few owned by billionaire Middle Eastern royalty, which pull in specifically for the Space opening and closing parties. The elegant club situated on the rocks by the marina, and known today as Lío, was formerly El Divino. Built in 1992, when Fellini's set designer Paolo Galia purchased an old bar with two French colleagues and glamourised it, El Divino was known for its sannyasin-organised hippie parties, as well as for club nights such as Defected, Release Yourself and Hed Kandi. One of the owners, Claude Challe opened Buddha Bar in Paris in 1996, and also ran Paris's Sweet World Café, where Cathy Guetta had worked, on her way up to superstardom.

By 1996, El Divino had been sold to Khalid Rodan, who also owned the famous landmark Hotel Montesol. The club continued to host its regular parties, as well as special one-off events, such as the one where Eric Burdon performed a crammed late-night set at Christmas 2001, rocking the stage with a talented local pick-up band till 5am, as the mists rose behind him on the elegant terrace-on-the-rocks which looks out across the harbour to Dalt Vila. In 2010, El Divino was sold on to the Pacha Group and renamed Lío (allegedly after the headaches the chaos of refurbishing caused new owner Ricardo Urgell: *lío* is Spanish for complication or mess). Ulises Braun, now the flamboyant host of Lío, has been involved in Ibiza clubland since the end of the 1970s.

By the ancient entrance of Dalt Vila itself, with its headless Roman statues and medieval walls, sits the great Ibiza landmark of The Croissant Show. Taking its name from the idea of hot croissants ('Show' representing the French *chaud*), this early morning favourite breakfast spot home to the demi-monde was run for years by local French character André Quidu, island-famous for his Dali-esque moustache. Sunrise over the ancient bricks and drag artists drinking hot chocolate, warm croissants with locals as the fruit-and-vegetable market opposite sets up, hustlers and gypsies slipping through the shadows into the medieval fortress walls, and the bustle of local boutiques and hairdressers going about their day—all make this spot at the foot of the old town entrance the heart of Ibiza Town, whatever the season.

On the terrace of Croissant Show you can sit with a glass of cava and listen to the sounds of the annual summer Jazz Festival, or witness the electronic chords and lasers of the IMS closing party. At Easter, the Good Friday parades are a costumed spectacle made up of what appear to be Klan-hooded penitents bearing giant candles and carrying Jesuses—some as statues in a box, some live and in chains, some mock-crucified—through the Old Town from the cathedral at the top, all the way down to the market square.

The nearby Plaça del Parc is another longstanding meeting place, full of charming cafés offering great-value light meals and drinks, around a tree-lined square with benches, and views of the massive Renaissance walls. In July 1988, the singer Nico died after falling off her bicycle just past the square, and suffering a probable brain haemorrhage, but not being treated quickly enough after being picked up by a passing taxi driver. She had left her son Ari in the house of Russian George, a friend they were staying with in a hidden valley off the Sant Josep road. Ironically, having finally successfully quit her heroin habit, she had been surviving on methadone and marijuana on the island, and gradually getting her health back. Peter Hook from British band New Order was allegedly one of the last people who saw her that fateful day, as she cycled calmly across Plaça del Parc on her way home from town.

During the 1960s and 70s Nico's favourite beach had been Figueretes, the strand connecting Ibiza Town with Platja d'en Bossa, a favoured spot for the freaks and artists living in town, a short walk away. Platja d'en Bossa in summer is now a tourist enclave that couldn't be further removed from that halcyon idyll. Back then, the foreigners were travellers, a very different breed from modern-day all-in tourists.

'Tourism is the great soporific,' the character Kay Churchill says in J.G. Ballard's apocalyptic 2003 novel, *Millennium People*. 'It's a huge confidence trick, and gives people the dangerous idea that there's something interesting in their lives. Today's tourist goes nowhere.'

In other words, something meaningful has been lost in the transition from the well-travelled observer's point of view. Mass tourism, especially in areas such as Platja d'en Bossa, has led to an aimlessness that tends to funnel holidaymakers into drinking and spending money just to be seen.

Feeling that the island, and the electronic music scene in particular, had something more to offer than this, is partly what inspired the creation of the IMS by Ben Turner and his partners Pete Tong, Danny Whittle, Mark Netto and Simeon Friend. They were also at the point where they weren't getting anything from the industry's Miami Winter Conference, which had been set up as a business event with peripheral parties, before its emphasis got heavily reversed a few years in, by which time it was starting to seem a bit confused as to its actual purpose. So Turner et al decided to use Ibiza as a base to create a new conference, and from the start they were emphatic that the IMS would be about business first and fun second. 'We wanted to show these bastions of Ibiza politics that electronic music is actually a global billion-dollar business,' says Turner, 'and it is a forward-thinking and progressive one. And we've tried to make people look beyond the nightlife here, and at the more futuristic qualities which we're all obsessed with.'

The first IMS was held in Ibiza in 2007. 'Everyone was surprised,' Turner continues, 'from the newspapers to the councillors, that people were interested in actually getting out of bed and going straight to business panels, in Ibiza, by 11am.'

Against various odds—the improbability of a global business summit on the island, given Ibiza's notoriously rinky-dink infrastructure, being the main one—the summit worked, and has continued to be an annual event ever since. Events and panels now run over three days at Platja d'en Bossa's Hard Rock Hotel, and include keynote interviews with the biggest names in the electronic music world, from musicians and DJs, to producers, promoters, record label heads and other industry professionals. They even managed, at the first IMS, to get the heads of all the superclubs to sit down together, a momentous event that took a level of cajoling and persuasion you might expect to endure when arranging the sit-down with the heads of all the 'families' in *The Godfather*— something Turner says they quickly decided never to try again:

> It was so hard to get them all to sit together. There used to be an Association of Discos in Ibiza, which was a group of club owners who did meet and talk regularly, and at one point I had been invited to one of those. You didn't need to follow the Spanish that was being spoken there though, as the body

language and the posturing said absolutely everything. It's fascinating what goes on behind the scenes of clubland; all these strong, powerful people who've been fighting for decades now to stay alive.

It's a deeply political island, and it's a very stressful environment to work in. It's so hard to get stuff done. People are ready to stab you in the back at any minute. It's an unfortunate reality of the island.

Other IMS guests over the years have included François Kevorkian, Sven Väth, David Guetta, Nile Rodgers, George Clinton, and Alfredo, who still lives on the island. When he was interviewed by Turner at IMS 2014, Afredo was keen to emphasise the restorative chill-out areas of the island that he would seek after long nights at Amnesia back in the 1980s.

'After twelve hours of music,' he said, 'to go to the beach was, for me, a dream. To listen to the birds and the sea, and bathe, with no *boom boom* at all. And that was what most people would be looking for: silence.'

Many of the summer DJs and club workers have winter schedules elsewhere to get to once the season ends, although the more experienced ones have learned how and when to stop and take a conscious intermission.

Carl Cox enjoys motorbiking around the island, especially at sunset:

Just getting the bike out at sunset, in that early evening warmth, go to some of the real deserted beaches in the north, for example, and then ride home … I really enjoy that, although I try and stay kind of incognito when I ride around, which can be difficult! I have to pull away and take time out to do something else. Go fishing, go camping … I mean if you look at Marco Carola's schedule, he is everywhere! He is special, of course, and it's his time now, his Music On nights are so great, but, as he'll tell you himself, his sole purpose, as far as he's concerned, is that he's out there doing what he does.

He does it to keep himself alive, but that is going to bite him in the bum, and nearly did in 2014. He had an ear infection which basically damaged his eardrum, and the doctor's orders were for him to take himself away from the scene for four weeks. He listened to his body for a while, but after three weeks he went straight back in, put in his earplugs, and carried on!

It's the kind of thing the DJs who work all summer long in Ibiza may do once or twice … before they realize that winter is definitely best spent in down time, whether on the island or not. And even in summer, Ibiza is a place where chill-out is incorporated into the summer party timetable anyway.

Sunset chill-out is almost synonymous with Sant Antoni's Café del Mar, and its veteran DJ José Padilla, who moved to the island in 1976, and made his name by DJing at Es Paradis and selling his mix-tapes on the beach. Back in the late 1970s, he had lived almost next door to Café del Mar, and at barbecues he would put on specially prepared mix-tapes that his friends loved, and this led to him making lots of copies to sell. By the mid-1980s, he was selling hundreds of them a day. He became resident at Café del Mar in 1991, and still compiles their popular annual compilation CDs. According to Pete Gooding, who now manages Padilla, 'José's a very melancholic chap at the best of times. He can have a real fiery side. His taste was shaped by Franco controlling what came into the country in mainland Spain, and he couldn't find the Stones, but ended up finding Tangerine Dream, Brian Eno, Penguin Café Orchestra, and Latin jazz.'

Gooding discovered Café del Mar in 1991, the same year Padilla took up residence there.

I'd read in *Mixmag* about this great DJ, whose name I incorrectly assumed was pronounced 'Joce'!! So I went up to the DJ box and said to José, 'I've

read about this DJ called Joce—can I buy one of his tapes?' He just kind
of smirked knowingly at me and said, 'Well … how about if you have one
of mine?' How embarrassing. I was really blown away when I heard José's
tape, though, and I started collecting them immediately. I've got sixty-four
now, I think.

Café del Mar, designed by Catalan artist Lluís Güell (he of Es Paradis
fame), has stayed very true to its chill-out roots. Although still hugely
popular, largely because of its legacy as the first Sant Antoni sunset bar,
it's actually the neighbouring Café Mambo which sees bigger crowds
gather once the sun's gone down. This is partly due to Mambo having
bothered to put together a great food menu, and also because it started
as an industry hangout in the days when every tourist in Sant Antoni
would be blindly hogging the tables next door at Café del Mar—which,
according to Gooding, now the resident DJ at Café Mambo, is 'actually
dead by ten o'clock':

> Once the sun's gone down, Café del Mar don't really give anyone a reason
> to be there. The owners of Mambo are a very different kettle of fish. Javier
> Anadon and his sons are the very public face of Mambo, and they really
> know how to make people feel really welcome. It feels more personal
> somehow, and it always has. Before I became resident there, I was running
> my own club in Solihull, booking all the world's biggest DJs—Erick
> Morillo, Tony Humphries, and I went to school with Steve Lawler, another
> DJ who's big in Ibiza now because of Mambo. Groups of us would come
> back to the island on holiday in the mid-1990s, and one night the queues
> were so big at Café del Mar, so we went next door to the quieter Café
> Mambo, but we noticed straightaway that the big DJs were actually all
> hanging out there—Sasha, Carl Cox, plus all the aspiring DJs.

Lawler got his DJ spot at Mambo the classic Ibiza way—by accident. He had given one of his mixtapes to a woman who ended up working at Mambo. Owner Javier Anadon had heard the tape there and after being suitably impressed, offered Lawler his first gig. When Lawler unexpectedly had somewhere else to be during the season, he recommended Gooding as his replacement, to Anadon. 'I got really lucky,' says Gooding. 'I did the stint as the main DJ for ten years, literally every night, nine hours a night.'

Although he still does the compilation CDs every year, Gooding is doing fewer hours and nights DJing there these days, as he's so busy, managing José Padilla and running his label, Secret Life, among other things.

Café Mambo is now the official pre-party spot for Pacha parties, but before that people like Sasha would pop in and ask if he could play some tunes. I'd always be totally terrified of even standing anywhere near him, and José for that matter. They were my DJ idols! They would come and play music they couldn't play anywhere else. Now of course we're all mates. In the early days I was playing to a very busy bar at 3am, even 4am, but that's never the case these days. Noise restrictions came in, although we're still jammed till 1am now, and then it's time to go to the clubs anyway.

In the face of all the chatter of Platja d'en Bossa becoming the new Sant Antoni, the one thing d'en Bossa's east-coast location can never lay on is a sunset. The whole of Sant Antoni bay is one gigantic sunset bath. For this reason, the number of tourists booking into Sant Antoni hostelries remains as high as ever, and, according to Miquel Costa, cultural director at the council of Sant Antoni, figures appear to be still on the rise. Costa himself was born bang in the centre of Ibiza, in an apartment above Bar Costa in Santa Gertrudis, a location opened by his father, and famed for its eclectic art collection made up of gifts from local artists to compensate for their bar bills. The ham, tomato and cheese *bocadillos*, made from the noble and commanding gigantic smoked ham legs hanging above the bar, are widely considered to be the best on the island.

Costa is also heavily involved in the organisation of cultural events around Sant Antoni, such as the visual arts festival Bloop, which takes place every summer, and which he describes as 'a benchmark in cutting-edge urban art. The exhibitions are a showcase for a wide range of pro-active art and media interaction, and the events reinforce the whole creative aura of Ibiza.' He grew up in Dalt Vila, in the 1970s, and remembers seeing art forger Elmyr de Hory's studio as a boy, while he continues to believe that the region of Sant Antoni is unbeatable, anywhere, in terms of its glorious sunsets. 'There are so many points on the west coast that I like, and each has its charm,' he says. 'The sunsets from Punta Galera, Sa Torre de Cap Negret, Cala Salada … they're all so spectacular, and you get the feeling they transmit some sort of power, and peace.'

'It's by far my favourite part of the day,' Pete Gooding adds.

Especially if I'm DJing at Mambo. Putting on a sunset DJ set is like watching a film, you're putting on music to match the mood, you know, like if the sky goes dark I'll play a slightly moody track, or if what I'm seeing puts me in a certain mood, I'll pick a record that reflects that. It could be opera, classical music, soundtracks. I normally play off a laptop when I play at Mambo, because I generally have about forty thousand tracks ready, and of course being a total geek, I remember them all! I've done the sunset thing for so long now though that I don't need to do any preparation for it. I grew up with that music, so even at my most self-indulgent, I can provide what's perfect for Mambo. All of this though comes originally from watching José and others in action.

'People are looking for quiet holidays as well now,' says Martin Davies. 'The whole outdoors thing is taking off in Ibiza, with walking, cycling and all these different countryside activities. This is where a lot of the Ibiza council's tourist office thrust is going, to encourage people to see this other side of Ibiza.'

This 'other side' was beautifully captured in actor/DJ/director Jimi Mistry's 2009 film *And the Beat Goes On*, which premiered on the island at both the IMS and the International Film Festival. The film admirably covers both clubland life and the chill-out culture, and combines them in a way that shows how the two sides blend so naturally together in Ibiza.

The film was originally conceived as a celebration of the twentieth anniversary of the UK acid house revolution of 1988, 'but it very naturally turned into something else' says Mistry, who filmed at Benirràs and Es Vedrà, as well as in clubland. Danny Rampling, Johnny Walker, Nicky Holloway, Paul Oakenfold, Alfredo, Lenny Ibizarre, Sven Väth, David Guetta and other island DJs feature in the film.

Mistry wanted to interview the four British DJs who had made that fateful trip to Amnesia in 1987—Oakenfold, Holloway, Walker and Rampling—reuniting all four on the island for the first time:

I met the legendary Tony Pike, and he said, 'Bring the interview here, no problem.' He cleared the Club Tropicana pool bar for us, and I sat and did the interview like it was a TV show, with hotel guests watching beside the pool. It was a perfect setting. Of course they were like a bunch of school kids; Nicky and Paul put eyeliner on and you could really see their personalities coming through, which is exactly what I wanted. The interview was three hours long, and we emptied several bottles of champagne.

The film also includes clips from *A Short Film About Chilling*, and

Mistry himself got a chance to investigate the chill-out culture when he was invited to a full moon party in the hills.

> A friend called me, and said, 'Jimi, you've got to meet Akoo, he's having a full moon party and you should be there.' So I did, and we met in Santa Gertrudis, and he read my eyes to see what my spirit was about. I went up to his house which is just amazing, on the full moon, and it just blew me away. He has a music temple, just for his instruments, up there on the mountain. Drums, synths, maracas, and anything else you can shake. He just said, bring food and drink, and share in this musical journey. We had a jam session that lasted five hours, and all the hippies came. It was incredible. I'd never been to anything like it. It reminded me of how Ibiza embraces you or spits you out, which everyone will say. If you're willing to just let go, you'll be OK. I remember going to Amnesia when I first came here, and I'm a really outgoing person, but for some reason I was finding it so hard to just let go, and it took me a while to be able to do so, to lose my self-consciousness. But it happened at Akoo's, in the same way it had at Amnesia for me. The drums are a great catalyst. They unlock any insecurity that you have about that stuff.

After sunset, the magic of outdoor get-togethers is very much what Mistry describes. For Luciano, 'Ibiza is still very romantic and free-spirited. As it's still naturally wild, it is really inspiring to me—it's an island to express your feelings, your sexuality, and your dreams.' The community who live here all year round will venture out, even in winter, for various types of social events, although quiet nights in restaurants or just hanging out round at each other's houses is a valued pastime in the early, colder months of the year. The night-time skies are clear and almost completely pollution-free, which makes stargazing and moon watching almost a necessity, and particularly when you live in the countryside where there is no white light to guide the way home, just the moon in its various phases. On such nights you can feel completely disconnected from the rest of the world, and yet connected to everything the island is about.

'These days when I'm in Ibiza,' Tina Cutler adds, 'I'll quite often just sit and look at the stars at night, and interact with the sounds and the aromas around me in the natural surroundings. It's interesting that I feel very beautiful in myself in that environment.'

When the last club tourists have gone home after the season has folded, and the frogs have disappeared into winter retreat with the cicadas, and the shutters are rolled down across the beaches, and the winter oranges hang in the night breezes, and you're walking at midnight through the deserted pastures of Santa Agnès during the headily scented almond blossom season, or you're gathered with friends from all over the world for multilingual home-made feasts in a house in the depth of the forest, or you're just watching the sun rise on the Mediterranean as the first bars open in the port under the morning mists ... Ibiza is always the place where you can just stop and peacefully dissolve into the environment. And then this ancient island is timeless; its past, present and future quietly infusing the landscape all around you, mercurial and yet, somehow, always the same, always just itself.

# OUTRO

In the last twelve years, I've spent more time in Ibiza than anywhere else on earth, and witnessed not only the dizzy heights of the blazing summer seasons but the semi-mystical winter repose, which unofficially starts for residents once the restaurant oasis Bambuddha Grove has held its spectacular annual Halloween party. I've been privileged to have gathered a close-knit group of international and Ibicenco island friends over the years, all of us with some involvement in the arts: writing, acting, painting, making music, design, cultural administration, cooking—and all bound by a profound love of language, books, cinema, music, food, nature, dancing, European travel … and Ibiza.

Outside of summer season, we've spent long afternoons walking in remote areas, cooking meals with herbs that grew wild outside our countryside homes, picking oranges from the gardens in the morning mists, taking dogs to run up and down the beach or across the hills at sunset, planning elaborate costumes for secluded parties in the countryside, gathering for nights at the cinema, swapping books. For several summer seasons I worked as a clubland correspondent, as well as dipping into club promotion, and being asked to be a cultural curator/

organiser with Sant Antoni Council. All of this combined experience led to my being asked to write this book.

Like many of my friends I was terrifically bored of staring at the gigantic chasm between the 'serious' books on Ibiza, which scrupulously avoid discussions of clubland, and, on the other hand, the mountain of literature which consistently promotes partying on the island as a mindless and superficial escape. Hopefully my book will bridge that gap, and correct a few prejudices about this very special place, where, as I put the finishing touches to the text, the almond trees are all in blossom in Santa Agnès, and the island looks like paradise on earth.

**HELEN DONLON, SPRING 2017**

# NOTES AND FURTHER READING

*Catalan place names have been used throughout the book, for consistency.*

## INTERVIEWEES

ALFREDO DJ, chapter 7, 9: interview at Hard Rock Hotel, May 2014; extra comments from keynote IMS interview, May 2014

ALLISTER LOGUE stylist, party creator, chapter 4: interview at Pikes Hotel; quotes from a short documentary I made with Kevin Palmer of Kuschty Rye Productions, 2009

AUBREY POWELL filmmaker, photographer, designer and co-founder of Hipgnosis design group, chapter 1: from my interview with Powell and the late Storm Thorgerson of Hipgnosis at Pikes Hotel, Sant Antoni and in Ibiza Town; quotes cited here previously appeared in 'Helen Donlon Interviews Hipgnosis', *London Grip*, September 2009

BABY MARCELO performance artist, chapter 5, 6: email interview, November 2014

BEN TURNER writer, manager, original editor of *Pacha Magazine*, label head, creative director, co-founder of the International Music Summit, chapter 4, 6, 8, 9: phone interviews, December 2014

BILL FORSYTH filmmaker, chapter 9: interview at Hotel Aquas de Ibiza, during the Ibiza Film Festival, 2009

CARL COX DJ, party creator, chapter 3, 6, 7, 8, 9: phone interview, November 2014

CUBA GOODING JR actor, chapter 9: interview at Can Talaias during the Ibiza Film Festival, May 2009

DAN TAIT DJ, VDJ, producer and radio presenter, chapter 6: interview at the Hotel Fenicia, Santa Eulària, 2008

DUBFIRE (ALI SHIRAZINIA) DJ, producer, chapter 4, 8, 9: email interview, November 2014

GEORGE CLINTON producer, musician, chapter 8: interview at the Hard Rock Hotel, Platja d'en Bossa, during the International Music Summit, May 2014; quotes first appeared in 'Paint The White Isle Black', *The Quietus*, 2014

JEAN-CHARLES VANDERMYNSBRUGGE musician, vocalist, writer, producer, chapter 4, 9: interview by email, September 2014

JEAN-MICHEL JARRE musician, pioneer of large-scale electronic music events, chapter 3: interview at the Gran Hotel Ibiza during the International Music Summit, 2012

JENNY FABIAN author, chapter 2: interview in London, Summer 2009; quotes cited here previously appeared in 'Leaving No Stone Unturned', *London Grip*, 2009

JIMI MISTRY actor, director, DJ, chapter 9: interview at Hostal Talamanca, May 2009; quotes cited first appeared in 'And The Beat Goes On', *London Grip*, summer 2009

JOHNNY GOLDEN (AKA THE MANUMISSION DWARF) clubland figurehead, chapter 4, 6, 8: interview at the Hotel Montesol, September 2014

KRIS NEEDS journalist, author, DJ, chapter 3, 4, 7: interview at home, November 2014

LENNY IBIZARRE producer, musician, co-founder of the DJ Awards, chapter 2, 3, 6, 7: interview at home near Benirràs, September 2014

LUCIANO DJ, producer, party creator, chapter 4, 8, 9: email interview, November 2014

MARKO BUSSIAN musician, producer, chapter 4, 9: interview at the Hostal La Torre, Cap Negret, September 2014

MARTIN DAVIES publisher, writer, historian, chapter 1, 2, 5, 6, 9: phone interview, November 2014

MARTIN GLOVER (AKA YOUTH) musician, producer, chapter 2, 3, 7: phone interview, January 2015

MIKE PICKERING DJ, label head, party creator, chapter 7: interview at the Ibiza Gran Hotel for the International Music Summit, 2010

MIMSY FARMER actress, chapter 2: email exchange, August 2014

MIQUEL COSTA Cultural Director, Ajuntament de Sant Antoni, chapter 9: email interview, January 2015

MONICA GERLACH teacher, former Ibiza party girl, chapters 2, 4: interview at the Hotel Montesol, September 2014

MONIZ club owner, DJ, chapters 7, 9: phone interview, January 2015

NATALIE BUSSIAN realtor; chapter 6: email interview, October 2014

PETE GOODING DJ, producer, label head, artist manager, chapters 4, 7, 9: phone interview, November 2014

PETE TONG DJ, radio presenter, party creator, co-founder of the International Music Summit, chapter 7: interview after the first IMS, May 2008; quote first appeared in 'Helen Donlon On The International Music Summit', London Grip, Summer 2008

REBEKA BROWN singer, chapters 4, 5: interview at home in Ibiza, 2008; quotes first appeared in 'Ibiza Mid-Season', London Grip, Summer 2008

RICHIE HAWTIN DJ, musician, label head, producer, party creator, chapters 6, 8: phone interview, December 2014

ROSALIND BEE contortionist, chapter 8: email interview, October 2014

SVEN VÄTH DJ, label head, producer, party creator, chapter 8: quotes via Väth's manager, Maurizio Schmitz, February 2015

TERRY GILLIAM filmmaker, Python, chapters 1, 9: from my interview with Gilliam at the late actor Terry Thomas's Ibiza house, Hotel Can Talaias, June 2009, during the Ibiza Film Festival; first used in a short documentary I made with Kevin Palmer of Kuschty Rye Productions, 2009

TINA CUTLER vibrational healer, Ibiza fashion stylist, former party girl, events management and concierge services, chapters 2, 3, 4, 6, 7: phone interview, October 2014

TONY PIKE hotelier, party creator, chapter 5: interview at Pikes Hotel in Ibiza, 2008; quotes first appeared in 'Ibiza Finale 2008', London Grip, 2008

## CITATIONS
## CHAPTER ONE

Burroughs, William Destroy All Rational Thought (video), 1988

Camus, Albert, from Semi-Invisible Man: The Life Of Norman Lewis by Julian Evans, Jonathan Cape, 2008

Crawford Flitch, J.E. Mediterranean Moods, 1911

Enright, Damien Dope In The Age of Innocence, Liberties Press, 2010

Homer Odyssey, Book XII, c. 800 BC

Journal Of The Royal Geographical Society Of London 1830–31, Vol. 1

Leary, Timothy Jail Notes, Douglas, 1970

Mellen, Joe Bore Hole, Glucocracy, 1975

Palau, Francisco, letter to the Reverend Ildefonso Gatell, from Ibiza, February 22 1864, from Francisco Palau Writings, Editorial Monte Carmelo, 2006

Pliny the Elder Naturalis Historia, Vol. VI, c. 77–79 AD

P-Orridge, Genesis, jajouka.com

Selz, Jean *An Experiment With Walter Benjamin*, from Benjamin, Walter, *On*

*Hashish*, Harvard University Press, 2006

Siculus, Diodorus *Bibliotheca Historica, Book V*, Loeb Classical Library, 1935

**CHAPTER TWO**

Editorial *Diario de Ibiza*, September 5 1963

Enright, Damien *Dope In The Age Of Innocence*, Liberties Press, 2010

Irving, Clifford *Fake! The Story Of Elmyr de Hory, The Greatest Art Forger Of Our Time*, McGraw Hill, 1969

Irving, Clifford *The Hoax: How The Authorized Biography Of Howard Hughes Almost*

*Fooled The World*, Mandarin, 1989

Mellen, Joe *Bore Hole*, Glucocracy, 1975

Phillips, Neal 'Yohimbina Diaries', *Oz* #30, October 1970

Verd, Sebastián *Policías Disfrazados de 'hippies' Realizaron, Por Primera Vez, Una Aprehensión de Heroína*, ABC España, September 15 1971

**CHAPTER THREE**

Gobello, José *Crónica General del Tango*, Editorial Fraterna, 1980

Khan, Inayat (Hazrat) *The Mysticism Of Sound And Music*, Shambhala, 1991

Lester, Paul 'Mike Oldfield: We Wouldn't Have Had *Tubular Bells* Without Drugs',

*Guardian*, March 20 2014

Maloney, Max, and Verpoort Oscar (dirs.) *A Year With Armin van Buuren*, 2012

Shakespeare, William, *Twelfth Night*, Wordsworth Editions, 2001

Toffler, Alvin *Future Shock*, Amereon, 1970

**CHAPTER FOUR**

Barrionuevo, Alexei, and Sisario, Ben 'Trouble Stalking Night-Life Paradise', *New York Times*, April 7 2013

Guetta, Cathy, *Bains De Nuit*, Editions

Fayard, 2008 (translations my own)

Guetta, David, keynote interview conference at the International Music Summit, Gran Hotel Ibiza, 2010

**CHAPTER FIVE**

Consell de Sant Antoni *Enjoy And Respect* safe tourism campaign, 2014

Sayle, Emma *Behind The Mask*, Harper Collins, 2014

**CHAPTER SEVEN**

*Criminal Justice And Public Order Act Of 1994*

Walsh, Helen 'My First Love', *Observer*, February 22nd 2004

**CHAPTER EIGHT**

Bowie, David, quoting Brian Eno, liner notes to *Sound & Vision*, 1989

Cosgrove, Stuart, liner notes to *Techno! The New Dance Sound of Detroit*, 1988

Cosgrove, Stuart 'Seventh City Techno', *The Face*, May 1988

Toffler, Alvin *The Third Wave*, William Morrow, 1980

**CHAPTER NINE**

Ballard, J.G. *Millennium People*, Flamingo, 2003

## FURTHER READING

Armstrong, Stephen *The White Island*, Black Swan, 2005

Bazin, Claire, 'Sea, Sex And Sun: Janet Frame's experience(s) in Ibiza', *Journal Of New Zealand Literature* #29, 2011

Blacker, Terence *You Cannot Live As I Have Lived And Not End Up Like This: The Thoroughly Disgraceful Life And Times Of Willie Donaldson*, Ebury Press, 2007

Borthen, Leif *The Road To San Vicente*, Barbary Press, 2007

Byrne, David *How Music Works*, McSweeney's, 2012

Cervera, Rafa *'El Enigma de Nico'*, Rolling Stone Spain, July 18 2013

Cox, Joseph 'The Woman Who Drilled A Hole In Her Head To Open Up Her Mind', *VICE*, August 14 2013

Cremer, Jan *I, Jan Cremer*, Panther, 1971

Cremer, Jan *The Big Kick* (typescript), property of Jan Cremer, 1960

Las Dalias editors 'So What Have You Done With My Hippies?' *Las Dalias* #3, 2012

D'Andrea, Anthony *Global Nomads: Techno And New Age As Transnational Countercultures In Ibiza And Goa*, Routledge, 2007

Davies, Paul R. *Ibiza And Formentera's Heritage: A Non-Clubber's Guide (Second Edition)*, Barbary Press, 2014

Donlon, Helen 'Highwaymen And Other "Great" Essex Outlaws', *Thaxted Bulletin*, Autumn 2012

Enright, Damien 'In Search Of The Beautiful Ghosts', nthposition.com

Escohotado, Antonio, *Brief History Of Drugs: From The Stone Age To The Stoned Age*, Park Street Press, 1999

Fabian, Jenny *A Chemical Romance*, The Do-Not-Press, 1998

Fajarnés Ribas, Enrique, et al *Grupo Ibiza 59: Passat i Present*, exhibition catalogue, Museu d'Art Contemporani d'Eivissa, 1992

I-Voice 'Where Is Our Ibiza? What Is Happening To The Island We Love?' ibiza-voice.com, September 2011

Kaufman, Emily *The History Buff's Guide To Ibiza*, Libro Azul, 2008

Ku, *Kiss Me Darling*, Ku, 1992

Mehagian, Nancy *Siren's Feast: An Edible Odyssey*, Cielo

Mellen, Joe 'The Hole To Luck, Dr. Bart Huges Interviewed By Joe Mellen', *Transatlantic Review* #23, winter 1966–1967

Michaud, Yves *Ibiza Mon Amour*, NIL, 2012

Odzer, Clio *Goa Freaks: My Hippie Years In India*, Blue Moon Books, 1995

Perez-Sanchez, Gema *Queer Transitions In Contemporary Spanish Culture: From Franco To La Movida*, State University of New York Press, 2007

Rettig, Ottavio *Bufo Alvarius, El Sapo del Amanecer-La Historia*, OTAC, 2014

Riera, Toni *Pacha: 40 Años de Historia*, Lunwerg Editores, 2008

Sampson, Kevin *The House On The Hill*, Jonathan Cape, 2014

Stewart, Ian, and Davies, Martin *The Mini Rough Guide To Ibiza And Formentera*, Rough Guides, 2001

Škvorecký, Josef *The Bass Saxophone*, Washington Square Press, 1985

Toribio, Múria Tirana 'A Punk Called Pedro: La Movida In The Films Of Pedro Almodóvar', *Contemporary Spanish Cultural Studies*, edited by Barry Jordan and Rikki Morgan-Tamosunas, Oxford University Press, 2000

J.Z., 'El PSOE Balear Dice Que La Amistad Entre Benegas Y Matutes Les Perjudica', *ABC España*, October 24th 1987

## PLAYLISTS

*These playlists were originally conceived to help my German editor and translator Kirsten Borchardt understand the island's vibes, characters, and influences better, chapter by chapter, as she worked on the text. All of these tracks contain great Ibiza memories for me.*

### CHAPTER 1

Cream, 'Tales Of Brave Ulysses'
Miles Davis, 'Concierto De Aranjuez'
Ry Cooder, 'The Hashishin'
Moody Blues, 'The Best Way To Travel'
Brian Jones and Joujouka, 'Take Me With You My Darling' (Goat Mix)

Philip Glass, 'Koyaanisqaatsi'
Pink Floyd, 'Sheep'
Jimi Hendrix, 'Third Stone From The Sun'
John Coltrane, 'A Love Supreme'
The Beach Boys, 'Sail On, Sailor'

### CHAPTER 2

The Beatles, 'Tomorrow Never Knows'
Joni Mitchell, 'All I Want'
Crosby Stills & Nash, 'Marrakesh Express'
Traffic, 'Paper Sun'
Julie Felix, 'This Wheel's On Fire'

Nico, 'I'm Not Saying'
Georgie Fame, 'Yeh Yeh'
Pink Floyd, 'Ibiza Bar'
Can, 'Oh Yeah'
The Beatles, 'Hey Bulldog'

### CHAPTER 3

Eric Burdon, 'Winds Of Change'
The Rolling Stones, '2000 Light Years From Home'
Faust, 'Krautrock'
Suicide, 'Dream Baby Dream'
Louis Prima, 'Buona Sera'
Augustus Pablo, 'Keep on Dubbing'

Sylvester, 'Mighty Real'
Herbie Hancock, 'Rockit'
Paul Van Dyk, 'Love Stimulation'
Dimension 5, 'Psychic Influence'
Juno Reactor, 'Laughing Gas'
Jean-Michel Jarre, 'Music For Supermarkets'

### CHAPTER 4

Wild Cherry, 'Play That Funky Music'
Cher, 'Gypsies, Tramps And Thieves'
Van Morrison, 'The Way Young Lovers Do'
Jean Paul Young, 'Love Is In The Air'
Grace Jones, 'Libertango'
Third World, 'Now That We've Found Love'
Donna Summer, 'Down Deep Inside'

Stevie Wonder, 'Another Star'
Fous de la Mer, 'Asi Vas'
Daft Punk, 'Harder, Better, Faster, Stronger' (Neptunes Remix)
Sebastien Tellier, 'La Ritournelle'
Les Innocents, 'Danny Wilde'
U2, 'Miami'

### CHAPTER 5

John Roberts, 'Sophisticated Funk'
Grandmaster Flash and Melle Mel, 'White Lines (Don't Don't Do It)'
George Michael, 'Faith'

Pet Shop Boys, 'Being Boring'
Funkadelic, 'One Nation Under A Groove'
Caetano Veloso, 'E proibido proibir'

Earth Wind & Fire, 'Fantasy'
Chris Isaak, 'Baby Did A Bad Bad Thing'
Jocelyn Pook, 'Masked Ball'

Wham, 'Club Tropicana'
Nine Inch Nails, 'Closer'
Giorgio Moroder, 'Chase'

## CHAPTER 6

Felix da Housecat, 'Money Success Fame
   Glamour'
Tiefschwarz (featuring Cassy), 'Find Me'
Henrik Schwarz, 'Leave My Head Alone
   Brain'
The Chemical Brothers, 'Setting Sun'
The Orb, 'A Huge Evergrowing Pulsating
   Brain That Rules From The Centre Of The

   Ultraworld' (Orbital remix)
Rob D, 'Clubbed To Death'
Fatboy Slim, 'Weapon Of Choice'
Paul Oakenfold, 'Ready Steady Go'
Luciano, 'Pasando Una Puerta'
LCD Soundsystem, 'Get Innocuous'
Shirley Bassey and Yello, 'The
   Rhythm Divine'

## CHAPTER 7

Focus, 'Sylvia'
Vanilla Fudge, 'You Keep Me Hangin' On'
Bruce Springsteen, 'Blinded By The Light'
Donald Fagen, 'New Frontier'
Marvin Gaye, 'Mercy, Mercy Me'
Zodiac Youth, 'Fast Forward The
   Future'
The KLF, 'What Time Is Love?'

The Happy Mondays, 'Hallelujah'
Sasha, 'Xpander'
Lil Louie, 'French Kiss'
Elkin and Nelson, 'Jibaro'
Marshall Jefferson, 'Move Your Body
   (The House Music Anthem)'
Orbital, 'Adnan's'
Underworld, 'Pearl's Girl'

## CHAPTER 8

Underground Resistance, 'Amazon'
Derrick May, 'Strings Of Life'
Aufgang, 'Sonar'
Joey Beltram, 'Energy Flash'
LFO, 'Freak'
Jeff Mills, 'The Bells'
Plastikman, 'Spastik'
Laurent Garnier, 'Acid Eiffel'

Underworld, 'Juanita/Kiteless'
Radio Slave, 'Grindhouse' (Dubfire
   Terror Planet Remix)
Kraftwerk, 'Radioactivity'
The Human League, 'Being Boiled'
Nine Inch Nails & Aphex Twin, 'At The
   Heart Of It All'
Suicide, 'Ghost Rider'

## CHAPTER 9

David Bowie, 'Memory Of A Free
   Festival'
Gilberto Gil, 'Super Homem'
The Orb, 'Little Fluffy Clouds'
The Doors, 'Riders On The Storm'
   (Lenny Ibizarre Mix)
Caetano Veloso, 'Cucurrucucu Paloma'

Grace Jones, 'La Vie En Rose'
Donovan, 'Season Of The Witch'
Bernard Herrmann, 'Theme From
   Taxi Driver'
Damien Rice, 'The Blower's Daughter'
Van Morrison, 'Madame George'
Pota Lait, 'Sa Botiga De Dalt Vila'

*To listen to these playlists, visit www.jawbonepress.com/shadows/*

# INDEX

# ACKNOWLEDGEMENTS

Firstly, a massive thank you to Kirsten Borchardt, whose dedication and attention to detail when editing, translating and preparing the first, German edition of the book made this such a pleasure to be doing. Her subsequent advice for this English edition was also invaluable. Another massive thank you to my dear friend and ally Martin Davies whose years of scrupulous editorial work for his own Ibiza-based Barbary Press made him a perfect editor in every way for this English edition of the text. My warmest thanks to Nigel Osborne for his clear-sighted long-term enthusiasm and commitment to becoming my UK publisher at Jawbone Press. Tom Seabrook at Jawbone for his professionalism, dedication to detail and wonderful editorial and design suggestions. Matthew Hamilton for providing early guidance and enthusiasm and Dave and Lee at Faber for their time and interest during the early stages of the English manuscript.

Untold thanks to all my interviewees, who are listed above separately, and several of whom took precious time out from busy international touring schedules to talk to me. And to James Young and Lutz Ulbrich for their help with interviews for our Nico project—parts of which contribute to my introduction to this edition. Very special thanks go to Richie Hawtin for writing me a beautiful foreword, and to Ben Turner for his continued faith and assistance. A huge thank you to Miki Williams at Dubfire's office, Francesco Bergomi at Cadenza, Maurizio Schmitz, Johannes Goller and Teresa Martini at Cocoon, Nicole Trigo at Paul van Dyk's office, Meryl White and Joel Davis from Graphite Media, Ian Hussey, Lynn Cosgrave and Steve King at Safehouse Management, Thomas Nau at M_nus, Kitty Lester at Mission PR, Wiltrud Schwetje, Frank Weyrauther, Frank Fabian, and Monika Koch, Hollow Skai and the much missed Eckhard Schwettmann at Hannibal.

For endless hospitality, a big thank you to our Ibiza crew including Augusto Rigo, Vera Rigo, Henning Lange, Anja Liebow, Orietta Sala, all our Italian friends at The Coffee Shop in Figueretes and Boris at Autos Marí. Big thanks as well to both *Data Transmission* and *The Quietus*, whose journalistic reputations on the island blew the hinges off a lot of backstage doors for us along the way. To two beautiful and brilliant Ibicencas—Maria and Anna Ramon Planells. To my Colombian yogini soul sister Liliana Galvis, for so much powerful and ongoing shared magic over the years. Bernadette, Sabine and Ian provided huge support on a summer's night outside the Rock bar, and I wish them the very best for bringing their spectacular Magic Bus ('Half vintage clothing store, half after-party') to Ibiza next year. Warmest eternal hugs for all my other long time Ibiza friends, who have always been completely sure about who they are. Thanks for the wild and loving island memories go to my amazing but now sadly absent friends Storm Thorgerson, Allister Logue and Matt Cogger. Most of all, endless thanks and love go to my soul mate Kris Needs, for arriving at the exact moment I was finally ready to land.

## ALSO AVAILABLE IN PRINT AND EBOOK
## EDITIONS FROM JAWBONE PRESS

STRANGE BREW: ERIC CLAPTON & THE
BRITISH BLUES BOOM CHRISTOPHER HJORT

METAL: THE DEFINITIVE GUIDE
GARRY SHARPE-YOUNG

LENNON & MCCARTNEY: TOGETHER
ALONE JOHN BLANEY

RIOT ON SUNSET STRIP: ROCK'N'ROLL'S LAST
STAND IN HOLLYWOOD DOMENIC PRIORE

MILLION DOLLAR BASH: BOB DYLAN, THE
BAND, AND THE BASEMENT TAPES SID GRIFFIN

BOWIE IN BERLIN: A NEW CAREER IN A
NEW TOWN THOMAS JEROME SEABROOK

BEATLES FOR SALE: HOW EVERYTHING THEY
TOUCHED TURNED TO GOLD JOHN BLANEY

HOT BURRITOS: THE TRUE STORY OF
THE FLYING BURRITO BROTHERS JOHN
EINARSON WITH CHRIS HILLMAN

MILLION DOLLAR LES PAUL: IN SEARCH
OF THE MOST VALUABLE GUITAR
IN THE WORLD TONY BACON

SO YOU WANT TO BE A ROCK'N'ROLL STAR:
THE BYRDS DAY-BY-DAY CHRISTOPHER HJORT

THE IMPOSSIBLE DREAM: THE STORY
OF SCOTT WALKER AND THE WALKER
BROTHERS ANTHONY REYNOLDS

TO LIVE IS TO DIE: THE LIFE AND DEATH
OF METALLICA'S CLIFF BURTON JOEL MCIVER

JACK BRUCE COMPOSING HIMSELF: THE
AUTHORISED BIOGRAPHY HARRY SHAPIRO

RETURN OF THE KING: ELVIS PRESLEY'S
GREAT COMEBACK GILLIAN G. GAAR

WHITE LIGHT/WHITE HEAT: THE VELVET
UNDERGROUND DAY-BY-DAY
RICHIE UNTERBERGER

FOREVER CHANGES: ARTHUR LEE &
THE BOOK OF LOVE JOHN EINARSON

THE 100 GREATEST METAL GUITARISTS
JOEL MCIVER

SEASONS THEY CHANGE: THE STORY OF ACID
AND PSYCHEDELIC FOLK JEANETTE LEECH

WON'T GET FOOLED AGAIN: THE WHO
FROM LIFEHOUSE TO QUADROPHENIA
RICHIE UNTERBERGER

CRAZY TRAIN: THE HIGH LIFE AND TRAGIC
DEATH OF RANDY RHOADS JOEL MCIVER

A WIZARD, A TRUE STAR: TODD RUNDGREN
IN THE STUDIO PAUL MYERS

THE RESURRECTION OF JOHNNY CASH:
HURT, REDEMPTION, AND AMERICAN
RECORDINGS GRAEME THOMSON

JUST CAN'T GET ENOUGH: THE MAKING
OF DEPECHE MODE SIMON SPENCE

THE 10 RULES OF ROCK AND
ROLL ROBERT FORSTER

GLENN HUGHES: THE AUTOBIOGRAPHY
GLENN HUGHES WITH JOEL MCIVER

ENTERTAIN US: THE RISE OF NIRVANA
GILLIAN G. GAAR

SHE BOP: THE DEFINITIVE HISTORY OF
WOMEN IN POPULAR MUSIC LUCY O'BRIEN

SOLID FOUNDATION: AN ORAL
HISTORY OF REGGAE DAVID KATZ